T0354624

Confronting Death:
College Students on the Community of Mortals

Alfred G. Killilea
Dylan D. Lynch
Editors

iUniverse LLC
Bloomington

CONFRONTING DEATH:
COLLEGE STUDENTS ON THE COMMUNITY OF MORTALS

Copyright © 2013 Alfred G. Killilea.

All rights reserved. No part of this book may be used or reproduced by any means, graphic, electronic, or mechanical, including photocopying, recording, taping or by any information storage retrieval system without the written permission of the publisher except in the case of brief quotations embodied in critical articles and reviews.

iUniverse books may be ordered through booksellers or by contacting:

iUniverse LLC
1663 Liberty Drive
Bloomington, IN 47403
www.iuniverse.com
1-800-Authors (1-800-288-4677)

Because of the dynamic nature of the Internet, any web addresses or links contained in this book may have changed since publication and may no longer be valid. The views expressed in this work are solely those of the author and do not necessarily reflect the views of the publisher, and the publisher hereby disclaims any responsibility for them.

Any people depicted in stock imagery provided by Thinkstock are models, and such images are being used for illustrative purposes only.

Certain stock imagery © Thinkstock.

ISBN: 978-1-4759-6977-1 (sc)
ISBN: 978-1-4759-6979-5 (hc)
ISBN: 978-1-4759-6978-8 (e)

Library of Congress Control Number: 2013903617

Printed in the United States of America

iUniverse rev. date: 12/26/2013

With love, to those who have helped make life so wonderful.

Dylan Lynch

For Frank, Isabel, and Addie: finis origne pendet.

Alfred Killilea

The editors gratefully acknowledge the editorial assistance of Scott Andrews, Christopher Baker, and Ilana Coenen. Professor Killilea is pleased to acknowledge his personal and intellectual debt to every URI student who has taken PSC 582 or PSC 440: The Politics of Being Mortal.

Table of Contents

Contributors

Max Cantor is a 2011 graduate of the University of Rhode Island Honors Program, where his studies concentrated on development economics, political theory, and the philosophy of the Scottish Enlightenment. He is currently a student at New York University School of Law, where he is a a Staff Editor for the NYU Journal of Law & Business.

Alexander Colantonio graduated from the University of Rhode Island with a BA in Political Science in 2011. Minoring in International Relations, he has focused his studies on human interaction through history, politics and cultural experiences. He is currently a Graduate Teaching Assistant in the Political Science Department at URI where he is expected to complete the MA program in Political Science in 2013.

Ilana Coenen is a current undergraduate student in the University of Rhode Island's class of 2013. She is a political science major with a minor in general business. In the future, Ilana hopes to pursue a career in the business sector with a focus on Event Planning, Marketing and Fundraising. Eventually, Ilana plans on going back to school after taking some time to travel and see the world.

Danielle Dirocco graduated from the University of Rhode Island in 2009 with a BA in Secondary Education and History. She is pursuing an MA in Political Science at the University of Rhode Island while serving as a Graduate Assistant and as President of *Graduate Assistants United*. She lives in Narragansett, RI with her husband, Paul Combetta, and her two lovely children, Talin and Trevor.

Margaret Frost is a South Kingstown, Rhode Island, native. Meg graduated from the University of Rhode Island in 2011 with major concentrations in Political Science and Spanish. Meg spent last year in Colombia as a Fulbright Fellow. Presently, Meg is anticipating the start of her Master's degree in Governance and Human Rights in Madrid, Spain at the start of 2013.

Liana Goff was raised in Fairfield, Connecticut and was a member of the University of Rhode Island's graduating class of 2011, with a major in Political Science and minor in Philosophy. She currently resides in New York City and plans to attend law school in the Fall of 2013.

Andrew Karanikolis is a graduate student and TA in the political science program at the University of Rhode Island. After finishing his bachelor's in 2010 he moved to Europe, where he served in the Greek army and earned dual-citizenship. During this time he also volunteered with a sea-turtle rescue shelter, engaged in the "Aganaktismenoi" protests in Athens, and traveled to other parts of Europe. Eventually he chose to return to URI and continue his studies with the tentative goal of becoming an academic.

Dylan D. Lynch graduated from the University of Rhode Island in 2010 with a BA in Political Science. While pursuing a Graduate Degree in Political Science at URI, Dylan worked as a teaching assistant. After receiving his MA, Dylan enrolled in Tulane University Law School where he is a JD candidate in the class of 2015.

Dan Magill graduated from the University of Rhode Island with a major in Political Science in 2012. He resides in Portsmouth, Rhode Island.

Tess O'Keefe graduated from the University of Rhode Island in 2011 where she majored in Political Science and minored in both Women's Studies and Asian Studies. She lived in Hawai'i, Japan, and more recently backpacked throughout China and Southeast Asia. She now resides in Boston.

Samantha Pettey is a PhD candidate at the University of North Texas focusing on American politics and research methodology. Specifically, her research interests include state and local politics, elections and women in politics with a focus on candidate emergence.

Eli Roth studied Political Science and International Development at the University of Rhode Island. He currently works with at-risk youth in Boston's nonprofit sector. Eli enjoys rowing in his spare time.

Ashley Stoehr graduated from the University of Rhode Island with a B.S. in Marine Biology and B.A. in Political Science. She is currently pursuing her doctorate, studying fish physiology, at the University of Massachusetts Dartmouth. She hopes someday to combine her keen observational senses and insatiable thirst for knowledge to participate in groundbreaking scientific research and conservation initiatives that will bridge the seemingly expanding gap between science and politics.

Shelby Sullivan-Bennis is a graduate of the University of Rhode Island where she studied Political Science and English and a current student at CUNY School of Law from which she plans to graduate and pursue a career in the Public Interest advocating for indigent, under-represented populations.

Elizabeth Toppi graduated from the University of Rhode Island as a political science major in 2010. She is a native of Smithfield, Rhode Island.

Christopher Turco is currently a law student in Boston, MA. He has earned a BA in sociology and a MA in political science from the University of Rhode Island.

Morgan Zubof graduated from The George Washington University in 2008 with a BA in International Relations with a focus on Middle East Studies and a minor in Judaic Studies. Morgan worked at the Department of Defense as an intelligence analyst for three years before moving to Rhode Island with her husband. She is currently a second year graduate student pursuing an MA in Political Science at the University of Rhode Island where she is also a graduate teaching assistant for the URI Political Science Department.

Pete Zubof is a native of Richmond, Virginia. A graduate of the University of Maryland, he currently serves as an Officer and pilot in the U.S. Navy. Pete is married to Morgan Zubof. Presently he is a graduate student at the University of Rhode Island in the department of Political Science.

Confronting Death:
College Students on the Community of Mortals

Introduction

This book about death is much more about life. At a time when our world seems to lack the moral and political will to confront enormous challenges to our planet and our very survival, confronting our common mortality may provide us with a powerful fulcrum for change. Enmities and enemies look a lot different when we are cognizant of the fact that we all will die. We all need to make sense of and find meaning in our precious lives and those of our children. All of the essays contained in this volume explore in some way this transformative power of death to change our politics and our lives.

The impetus for this book of original essays came from a co-editor who is a university teacher nearing the end of his career and a co-editor who is brimming with new ideas at the very start of his career. As the senior co-editor, I have been teaching a political theory course for a generation of students on "The Politics of Being Mortal" at the University of Rhode Island. Both undergraduates and graduate students have been very enthusiastic about the readings and discussions in the course and have reviewed it each year very positively. Curiously, while college students are often described as thinking that they will live forever, the students who have taken this course seem surprised and grateful for the opportunity to talk about death and its bearing on our most important decisions. I have been privileged for 25 years to hear and read their fresh and acutely perceptive reactions to the question of what our society would be like if the denial of death lost its sway in our culture.

Students appreciate the radical power for change that inheres in the movement to let death out of the closet. Just now when American politics suffers from deep ideological divisions that could make our nation ungovernable, our mutual mortality may be the most potent force for unifying us and helping us to find common ground. If we take seriously that we are going to die, class, race, and religious differences can shrink as identifiers as we realize that we are all in need of finding meaning and significance so that life is not mocked by death. All of these possibilities my students of all political persuasions find riveting. The only disappointment for all of us is how little current literature there is on the wider implications of a greater awareness of mortality in our culture. There are classic portrayals of the personal costs of avoiding the acknowledgment of our mortality such as Leo Tolstoy's *The Death of Ivan Ilyich*, a work my students unfailingly find engrossing. They are also enthusiastic about the striking honesty of the wildly popular *Tuesdays with Morrie* by Mitch Albom. However, these explorations of the sense of liberation and connection that come with confronting and accepting our mortality are rather lonely reminders that "in getting and spending we lay waste our powers."

After grousing for years about the dearth of published material for my course, I suddenly realized that the solution to my lament was right in front of my eyes. My students had been for years writing seminar papers on a topic of their choosing dealing with changing views on death. All of these papers were fascinating and some of them were exceptionally well written, easily as professional and polished as most of the material available from academics. These essays have the distinct added advantage of emanating from a demographic that knows well the temptation to put on airs of immortality. So these essays reveal the charged insights of independent thinkers that are as provocative as they are insightful.

There are eighteen essays in this volume, all written within the last two years. Some are directly political, such as two on terrorists on death, two on child soldiers, and two on Nazism and Fascism and death. Two essays examine suicide and one considers capital punishment. Four essays discuss death themes in classic and contemporary literature, such as in Dante, Peter Pan, Kurt Vonnegut, and Christopher Hitchens. One essay explores the Black Death, another the work of Jane Goodall, and another the threat of death on Mount Everest. Finally, one essay considers how violent street gangs deal with the proximity of death and one describes the origins of the "Grim Reaper."

Not one of the essays is morbid. They all attend to death as a way of understanding how to live. Some are serious in tone, some are lyrical. Most describe how the topic being discussed affects the author personally. Collectively these essays provide remarkable ideas about death and its power to transform people and societies, a topic both critically important and widely neglected.

Alfred G. Killilea
University of Rhode Island
Kingston, Rhode Island

I. DEATH IN CONTEMPORARY LITERATURE

CHAPTER ONE

Kurt Vonnegut on Death

Dylan Lynch

Utilizing Kurt Vonnegut's Player Piano, this chapter addresses the concepts of human mortality, its widespread denial in our everyday lives, and the subsequent difficulty human beings find in living a fulfilling life while crippled by the omnipresent fear of death. Technological society's inclination to dehumanize its population leads to an absence of human connectedness and thus to the pervasiveness of mechanical versus organic and emotional thoughts and actions. The acceptance of human mortality enables those who acknowledge it to live a life that produces a sense of immortality; the impact we have on others, our community and our society as a whole while we are alive can ensure that our actions are not lost to history.

As a nation, America has been comfortably living in a state of denial for the better part of its existence. This shadowy reliance on denial is multi-faceted, and exists to varying degrees in many aspects of daily life – from one's day job to a night on the town. In recent years, it can be seen on the national stage with the handling of enemy combatant detainees, or in the microcosm of a parent turning a blind eye to their child's obvious substance abuse problems. This state of denial has the highest demand and the widest acceptance when dealing with the inescapable and supreme end for which all human beings are destined – death.

The defiantly inspirational Hallmark-esque sayings known and adored by most people about there never being sunshine without rain nor joy without pain are rarely taken to their logical end – that we couldn't truly appreciate the beauty and wonder of life without death's resolution. Because of their overwhelming fear of death, many people live wholly unfulfilling lives. For reasons of convenience we naively force a connection between accepting our mortality and living a meaningless life, though no connection exists and this notion could not be further from reality. Social Psychologists such as Ernest Becker write – with much popularity – on seeking immortality, which he describes as an inevitable part of people's lives. Becker claims that the denial of death is both natural and unavoidable. But Becker and his like-minded followers – henceforth referred to as Denialists – fail to realize the full effect that disregard for death has on humanity.

When people fail to recognize their physical ephemerality, they are denying the foundation of their vulnerability as well as the full spectrum of emotions that come with it – all of which are essential to being human in the fullest sense of the term. To forsake these emotions is to turn away from what makes life beautiful, worthwhile, and infinitely precious. To acknowledge and exist in harmony with these emotions – including a full acceptance of mortality – is what it means to truly live. Denialists are only repudiating their own humanity, and in turn they are missing out on life.

Kurt Vonnegut – black-humorist, satirist, and a humanist with a unique worldview – recognized what could happen to a society that attempted to take human emotion completely out of a human-inhabited world. In his novel *Player Piano*, written while working at a General Electric plant in Ilium, New York, Vonnegut created an America run by managers and engineers obsessed with efficiency above all else. *Player Piano* was published in 1952, but due to his foresight and humanist leanings, Vonnegut's novel inches closer to social reality with every advance in technology. The managers and engineers brought victory to America during a great war with their industrial ability, their unfailing efficiency, and their knack for building machines capable of doing previously human tasks faster and for less money. Because of its effectiveness during the war, the system of having various machines do every human enterprise – breathing, sleeping, eating, and sex aside – was kept in place after the war. America's democratically elected government became a figurehead, a puppet mouthpiece assenting to whatever production, employment, and legislative decision the human-created machines made. The proponents of this system used as their justification the undeniable practicality of having machines work production lines instead of humans (waste and cost were both down under the new way of life), and the fact that every person who wasn't smart enough to work as an engineer was given a government supported job. Those deemed unqualified for a life of decision making were assigned to the army or the Reclamation and Reconstruction Corps, where they were conscripted to work for twenty-five years. After their twenty-five years of work, members of the R&R Corps were forced to retire to their government appointed house with their government pension, and allowed to comfortably and uneventfully wait for death. The people who oppose this way of life, whose very humanity and instincts drive them to cry out against it, are mostly those not found by the IQ machines and the job placement machines to be smart or left-brained enough to hold any kind of decision making power, including determining the course of their own lives. Once you failed the IQ test required to continue on through the undergraduate and graduate educational system, your entire life's course had been decided.

One of the main reasons for the subconscious denial of death our culture has so readily accepted is the misguided idea that once one fully recognizes death's power over life he or she will be unable to function in any useful way. That some people become completely crippled by fear is no surprise – those suffering from agoraphobia are so scared of the various avenues and events of life that they struggle to leave the confines of their home – but the fact remains that we needn't fear what we can't control. No one can control death in so far as keeping it from ever occurring. Some have taken a last-gasp at gaining some modicum of control over death by committing suicide, others try to control death through new medicines, but no one can completely overcome death's certainty. The idea of not ceding control of your life to the fear of that which is beyond your control is essential for living a fulfilling life, and it is only through accepting our own mortality that we can shake off the fear that reigns over our society.

The American citizens in *Player Piano* were so shaken by fear of death after a long war that they were willing to completely hand over control of their own lives to a Hobbesian industrialized government in order to be put at ease. What they received in return for handing over almost every aspect of what made them independent human beings was far more than they anticipated. Machines dictated every aspect of life from conveniences (televisions turned on when you entered the room, whole meals could be defrosted and cooked in minutes, your preferences marked and reviews to alert you of state-approved behaviors you are most likely to enjoy) to the more intricate jobs of crime prevention and housing development (security cameras monitored crime, cities were made up of cookie-cutter housing developments based on designs deemed most efficient). There is no room in this society for anything organic, creative, or human. The creativity that makes murals so beautiful, music so enjoyable, and life so worthwhile is cast aside because it is inefficient.

One does not have to look far in our America to see shades of the America Vonnegut created in *Player Piano*. Take for example the use of geotagging and facial recognition software in the latest iPhone, which are used to ensure that advertisements relevant to a user's tastes and location appear most frequently. The same limitations on human creativity and ingenuity seen in *Player Piano* will begin to constrict our contemporary culture.

The novel's heroes, Dr. Ed Finnerty and Dr. Paul Proteus, are two exceptions to the rule of those in power adoring the efficiency-first system. They are two men who knew early in their careers that they would advance to the highest levels of the corporate world, eventually controlling most of the decision making for every industrial plant in America. Finnerty and Proteus recognized, however, that there was something inherently wrong with the post-war American zeitgeist. Each man came to embrace the spirit expressed so succinctly by Ted Rosenthal in his poem *How Could I Not Be Among You?* – that "It's stage center for all of us," and there is no better time than now to live full, albeit imperfect lives. The Denialist idea that by ignoring death one is able to keep it at bay is ludicrous. People often relate versions of the expression "you don't know what you've got until it's gone," so it should logically follow that accepting your eventual and inevitable death – as well as that of your loved ones – will only increase the pleasure you extract from each day.

While Vonnegut's novel focuses on Proteus and Finnerty's attempt to escape the evil of an inhuman society, it also follows Dr. Ewing Halyard, a State Department civil servant whose job it is to show foreign dignitaries around the country. While touring with the diplomats, Halyard would try to convince them to hire American engineers to mechanize their less efficient states. In *Player Piano*, Halyard's charge is the Shah of Bratpuhr – the spiritual and political leader of six million people in the Kolhouri sect. During his travels with Halyard, the Shah asserts that he can't see the emperor's new clothes as he witnesses the strange concept of human beings denying their humanity and instead choosing boredom, comfort, and efficiency. As Halyard shows the Shah around Ilium, the Shah repeatedly and rather accurately refers to the Reclamation and Reconstruction Corps workers as "slaves" in his native tongue. After becoming fed up with the Shah's putative misperception of Ilium's fine citizens, Halyard decides to take him to the home of an average citizen and prove just how well each person is able to live under the efficient and practical rule of mechanized, objective decision making.

When the two arrive at the home of Edgar and Wanda Hagstrohm, Halyard and Dr. Ned Dodge – the local neighborhood manager – make a grand show of explaining the form and function of the Hagstrohm's home. Houses in this society are sold as a package that includes furniture predetermined by aggregation of extensive national surveys on furniture likes and dislikes, leaving no room for individualization. Houses also include cooking and cleaning machines and gadgets that cook meals in seconds and wash and dry clothes in minutes (even leaving them with a fresh, outdoorsy scent). As Halyard and Dodge fervently and proudly explain each machine and how it does a much better job than people ever could, the Shah – through his translator – asks what Wanda does once she assigns machines to all the household chores. Frustrated, and without a proper answer, Dodge shouts, "Live! Get a little fun out of life" (p. 164). What Halyard and Dodge fail to realize is something that the Shah, with his different paradigm, discerned immediately – there is no room in American society for people to truly live. One does not get to choose a career, those decisions are made by standardized tests. One does not get to design his or her home, that is done based on the preferences of the country as a whole. One can't take on any challenges since everything is mechanized, and can't individualize since a one-size-fits-all mentality pervades society. By trying to strip away human error, the people in *Player Piano* have gone a step further and actually limited their own humanity.

Much like our contemporary American culture, the search for immortality is not absent from *Player Piano*. Early in Proteus' transformation from elitist ally of dehumanization to a man who adores humanity for its un-machinelike qualities, a machinist named Rudy Hertz lays bare his – and his fellow citizens' – desire to live forever. Hertz first meets a young Paul Proteus when, fresh out of graduate school and looking to make a name for himself, Proteus found the fastest, most skilled assembly line worker to study. Turning Hertz's nimble fingers and unparalleled enthusiasm for work into a recorded sequence in a robot, Proteus was able effectively to replace and double the speed of Rudy Hertz with a robot version of the worker. Hertz, initially honored by being chosen as the fastest and best worker in Ilium, quickly realized what he had done to himself and his fellow workers. As more and more of the Hertz-bots were made, more and more people were laid off. Hertz was excited about the idea of a piece of him living on forever, but in seeking his immortality he sacrificed what had made his life so worthwhile on earth. He gave up something that brought him happiness and a feeling of usefulness in a vain attempt to extend his physical existence. Rudy Hertz was replaced by a snapshot of himself, and rather than achieve immortality by impacting and living on in others, he chose to live on in the form of a small recording, wasting away the rest of his days in a dive bar with barely enough drive to get out of bed in the morning.

What the people in *Player Piano* have created, and contemporary American society is in the process of creating, is an entire race of Ivan Ilyiches in whose lives the Real Thing is completely absent. With their advancement of the societal norms of absolute efficiency came an intolerance of human emotion, frailty, and character. The computers that make the people of Ilium's decisions are lauded with high praise because of their ability to reach conclusions "free of reason-muddying emotions" (p. 117). The citizens of Vonnegut's America fail to grasp the Real Thing, much like Ivan Ilyich, until it is almost too late. While

Ivan Ilyich is able to repent only on his deathbed, Paul Proteus and Ed Finnerty repent in a more useful way, revolting against the system of which they were once integral parts and waging war on the industrial society that had minimized persons' roles in their own existences. As Yeager Hudson states in his "Death and the Meaning of Life," one can only find meaning in life "as intrinsic within one's life work, his family, his own character...the promotion of an ideal, or the service of a worthy cause," (p. 93). The People of Vonnegut's America have no opportunity to find meaning in their lives because their society is entirely devoid of causes to pursue and meaningful ways to express their love and friendship. Early in the novel, Proteus expresses the thought that the world was slowly being restyled into an overall pleasant and convenient place to bide your time and await judgment day. While it is obviously desirable that the world be a pleasant place, our vibrant souls seem to demand that it be more than just convenient. To a varying extent, human beings crave to push the boundaries of their own humanity. While some conveniences have inarguably made the world a better place, for the entire planet to be nothing more than a convenient place to sweat out judgment day would negate everything enjoyable about life.

As human beings we treasure challenges, we love risks and seem to harbor a sort of infatuation with those who live fast and dangerous. Human beings want convenience when it is convenient, and otherwise strive to do that which is inconvenient to prove it can be done. Take, for example, a professional basketball player alone on a breakaway toward his opponent's basket. The average, energy-efficient and risk-averse play would be to simply lay the ball in, but nine times out of ten, the player will leap into the air and execute an acrobatic and powerful slam dunk. The dunk isn't worth any more points than the layup, but it has other qualities that elevate it above a layup in the eyes of many players and fans.

Conflicts and challenges are difficult to get through, and at times we wish they had never been brought upon us at all, but human beings tend to come out of a challenge with a lesson learned – feeling themselves stronger and a better person because of it. The experience can't be duplicated. Many trials and tribulations can (and should) be avoided, but an equal number prove to be important in one's development as a complete person. As Ted Rosenthal stated in *How Can I Not Be Among You?*, "get glass in your feet if you must, but take off the shoes." Another place in which Dr. Paul Proteus has found intolerable stagnation and even less tolerable convenience is his marriage to his wife Anita. Proteus even states, "Anita had the mechanics of marriage down pat," (p. 17). The reason that Proteus is not happy – but not at all miserable – with his marriage is that he and his wife have taken something that is wholly organic and human – love – and done their best to mechanize it. Their marriage follows a blueprint of what previous generations have decided a marriage should be, and despite the fact that they both seem to want to break out of the mold into which society has pushed them, both Anita and Paul march along to the beat of an anonymous and disinterested drum. This is the ultimate denial that takes place in Vonnegut's novel and our society, a shunning of one of the most essential human experiences – love.

While the growing mechanization of human existence may bring about a longer life expectancy, the quality and meaning of the living in those years has been diminished to the point that one must ask what purpose there is in existing at all. Yeager Hudson rightly states that "the most intensely satisfying experiences are those which come as the result of effort or striving," which does not at all imply that the result will be pleasing. Hudson makes the claim that "the happy person is not just the person to whom nice things happen; rather he is the person who actively strives and takes satisfaction in his striving," (p. 96). As the trite-but-true saying goes – happiness is a journey, not a destination. By turning a blind eye to our physical ephemerality, Denialists are undercutting their own motivation to live fully and enjoy the journey. This has already happened in *Player Piano*, where the American citizens lack the motivation to pursue any cause in life and so they see death as a welcome alternative to their drab, eventless day-to-day routine. This mentality is embodied in the extreme spike in suicide rates after the mechanization. Hudson succinctly illustrates that just as artwork requires a frame, life needs death in order to put it in its proper context. This eloquent truism finds its starkest contrast in *Player Piano* in the form of a cooking machine that bakes bread without crust, which had been deemed useless and impractical even though to many it is the most delicious part of the loaf.

Because of the deliberate shunning of humanity's most personal and creative qualities, citizens who find fault with the zeitgeist in Vonnegut's America form the Ghost Shirt Society – a group of saboteurs that seeks to overthrow the system in place and return a sense of humanness to America. At the head of the Ghost Shirt Society are Proteus and Finnerty. When the police finally discover the Ghost Shirt's meeting place they are able to arrest Proteus and interview him in the hope that he'll turn informant. Proteus learns that the powers-that-be have decided not to inform the public of the existence of the Ghost Shirt Society, an ignore-and-deny response that mirrors the way our society deflects and buries the tough, important questions about our own mortality. The government in *Player Piano* ignores the problem until a complete war between those displaced by the current system and those who benefit from it ensues. In many ways, this is an extrapolation and exaggeration of the way our societal norms have pushed Americans to ignore and deny our humanity and mortality until a crisis is reached within each of our own psyches. Instead of recognizing our mortality and using it to drive us towards a more meaningful life, we ignore it until it is too late to do anything worthwhile. We push recognition of death to the margins until it completely consumes us and demands our full attention, when – like Ivan Ilyich on his deathbed – we realize the error of our ways. Death can – and should – be used as a motivator to get more out of life and appreciate all of its myriad pleasures, big and small.

In the creed of the Ghost Shirt Society is the affirmation of finding virtue in imperfections, frailties, brilliance, and stupidity. This love of humanness is directly addressed in chapter four of Alfred Killilea's *The Politics of Being Mortal*. Killilea recognizes that some of the most important parts of a human existence are the challenges, trials, tribulations, and all the emotions that come with them. When a person invests him- or herself in something – be it a relationship, a career, or a mission to improve their community – they go through a whirlwind of emotions that couldn't possibly be experienced any other way. Success is not the only measure of meaning, because participating and truly committing oneself to something can be its own reward.

Vonnegut is alternately funny, scary, and brilliant – more often than not he is all three at once – but he is also an extremely humanistic author. He recognized and satirized human stupidity in amazing ways, but that is only because of his ability to glorify humanity itself –brilliance and stupidity included. Vonnegut presents Ed Finnerty as a sort of anti-hero we all wish we could be, at least to a certain extent. He quit his job because he realized that there was something horribly wrong with the direction it was taking the world, and he refused to shun his humanity any longer. Finnerty never fit well into the system that was thrust upon him (and who among us does?), but instead of just tolerating it, he decided to proactively meet the problem head on. This is perfectly analogous to our current societal problem with facing death. None of us are entirely happy with pushing death to the margins, but few of us ever truly realize what Ted Rosenthal said, that it is "stage center for all of us." Finnerty did what few have the constitution to do – stand up against an obviously backwards but overwhelmingly powerful social norm, and one has to admire that. Finnerty is such a hero figure in *Player Piano* not because of any one heroic act, but because of his intensely human persona. Who can't relate to feeling like one ant among millions charging along on a course you didn't design and wanting nothing more than to step out of line?

While we all understand that we are mortal (a few deranged cult leaders aside), the few people who dare to talk about death and dying are viewed as strange, as pessimistic fatalists whose sole mission is to depress the rest of us and devalue our lives. In reality, these philosophers – such as Yeager Hudson and Alfred Killilea – don't aim to use death to incite hysteria, scare us to the point that we can't function, or make life seem pointless. These extremely human thinkers see death for what it is: an unavoidable end to the only way of life we have ever known. They do not see death as the absolute end of the entirety of our existence, nor do they see death as something to shun. We live on in the impact we have, the impressions we make, and the causes we promote. Because death is entirely unavoidable, we should use it as a motivator to live the fullest lives possible – we should laugh, cry, scream, smile, and sigh at every opportunity. We should not waste a breath on seeking immortality, nor should we take a single moment for granted. As Hudson put it, death gives life meaning the same way a frame defines a picture and the same way darkness defines light – life is the blank canvas within the frame across which bountiful creativity begs to be spread. To have life without death would be absurd and completely debase the entire concept of the former. By taking a more candid and proactive approach to dealing with our own mortality, we can avoid the soul-crushing society Vonnegut designed in *Player Piano* and find deeper significance in our lives.

Politically, an increasingly larger number of Americans think of themselves as Independents believing in a moderately sized and efficient yet effective government. There are, however, certain social programs that are absolutely essential for a government to maintain its efficacy. A government loses its legitimacy if it fails to look out for the best interest of its citizens, so for some people to preach that religion should have a prominent place in public policy – something to which the Founding Fathers were wholly opposed – while driving to cut programs like social security and education shows a ludicrous and self-contradictory prioritization. There exists a wall of separation between Church and State for the benefit of both, so the idea that biblical teaching espoused by social conservatives should become public policy can, and should, be dismissed outright. In America, this staunch social conservatism is often couched in a brand of fiscal conservatism obsessed with ensuring the most efficient outcome for those at the top of the economic totem pole. This is as absurd in America today as it was in the America created by Vonnegut in *Player Piano*, where the reader was meant to find that paradigm backwards and contradictory to everything we embody as human beings. In our society, the determination to keep wages as low as possible is always pushed upon us by those at the top who reap immense benefits from their position in the relationship between elite and worker. Any attempt to place taxes on the abundantly wealthy is met with allegations of anti-Americanism, but if one stops to think for a moment the opposite becomes obvious. The truth about effectively and conscientiously exploiting efficiency is that, for those in a position to aid others through tax payments, a refusal to do so is wholly un-American. This country is built around many things, but one of the cornerstones is the idea of sacrifice for your neighbor and your nation – by avoiding the patriotic challenge placed before them and using social conservatism to draw attention away from their anti-Christian views, many conservatives in America have proven unable or unwilling to recognize the common humanity we all share.

On page 51 of *Player Piano*, Paul Proteus gives a speech about the ability of machines to do America's work far better than Americans ever could. Here, Vonnegut again shows his foresight as he lays out the effects of modern-day outsourcing, which creates a grotesque race to the bottom based on the belief that cheaper work is better work. This does not take into account the immeasurable human toll these decisions have on the lives of American citizens every day.

The society that exists in *Player Piano* allows for (and actively pursues) a rise of total mechanized production, which brings with it a sharp rise in drug addiction, alcoholism, suicide, divorce, organized vice, and juvenile delinquency. Finnerty astutely makes this point when he is among Ilium's top brass – men who have all benefitted immensely from the system they helped create – as they attempt to disillusion themselves and create separation between the decline in human usefulness and the rise of negative social traits. One of the more powerful members of the Northeast Industrial Bureau makes the claim that there isn't enough of a connection between the two for them to be worried about it – again ignoring a reality – to which Finnerty replies, "or enough imagination or honesty," (p. 54). That is what this society is missing – real honesty about our shared humanity. We create a disconnect between ourselves and the ones we negatively impact overseas and especially those with whom we are so intricately intertwined here in America. We unpatriotically look to expand profit margins at the expense of our fellow Americans. As Killilea states, we are also not honest with ourselves when it comes to death as we constantly seek to separate ourselves from those we see in the obituary pages. The people in Vonnegut's post-war America have pushed citizens to a literal death through suicide, but have handed them a sort of soul-death by stripping away their value as human beings and limiting their ability to work as full exerters of their capacities. People had become replaceable cogs in the machine, a mere means to an end that could be used up and cast aside when it was no longer as practical or efficient as it once was. This was a basic and deliberate devaluation of human life.

The difficulty in trying to conquer a problem like society's denial of death is that one cannot quantify the physical and emotional toll this disconnect has on society. Since it can't be quantified, it is seen as having no place in the cost-benefit analysis equations that push some people to strive for practicality and huge profit margins over personality and people. Since all of our time here on earth is truly limited, we should feel a common brotherhood and recognize the damage that can be done when that which makes us human is replaced with something cold, calculating, emotionless, and devoid of human considerations. Human beings, try as they might to behave like machines, are the exact opposite – we are organic and loving, and take a myriad of factors into consideration beyond just practicality in any given situation.

The more we avoid our own humanity, including a complete acceptance of our mortality, the less we will get out of life. A true acceptance of our ephemerality will lead us to take a little more time to connect with those around us and enjoy all the glories of the world. Basically – it will push us to care. What we have instead is an insistence on occupying our minds with absurd practicality – like Wanda and Edgar Hagstrohm – so that we can move as swiftly as possible from one thing to the next and leave no time to truly *live*. Only in recognizing the ultimate end that we'll all face can we ever be alive in the richest sense of the term.

CHAPTER TWO

Christopher Hitchens and Death

Danielle Dirocco

The prospect of our eventual and inevitable death is a reality that many would rather avoid confronting until we have no choice but to do so. As death approaches, many turn to believing in a god who will provide them with eternal life in heaven. Others refuse to subscribe to religion, believing instead that this life is the only life we lead, and when it is over, it is over. Enter Christopher Hitchens, one of the most prolific authors of the New Atheism movement, who was diagnosed with terminal esophageal cancer in 2010. Rather than converting, Hitchens remained a staunch Atheist to the very end, writing extensively and honestly about his thoughts on mortality and morality as he slowly succumbed to cancer. This essay focuses on the development of Hitchens' perspective on mortality as his health declined.

Christopher Hitchens gives me, a fellow non-believer, comfort and peace with my own mortality by reminding me that it is not necessary to cling to supernatural beliefs to find confidence in the face of my own mortality. I must instead look within myself and to my loved ones for genuine peace in the short time I am on this earth.

Rest in Peace, Hitch. (April 13, 1949-December 15, 2011)

Postscript—On September 4, 2012 a collection of Christopher Hitchens' writings, appropriately titled <u>Mortality</u>, was published and is available at booksellers worldwide.

As human beings, we desperately crave solace in the face of the chaotic nature of life. We long to be comforted, to be protected, to be delivered from pain and suffering, and to soothe our anguish and sorrow. This innate need is particularly acute when we are faced with the stark reality that our lives are finite. In an effort to find a sense of comfort in the face of death, many turn to the concept of a higher being, a god or something larger than ourselves, to find consolation in the face of our own death or the death of a loved one. The idea of a god that exists to console you when you feel you cannot handle anymore suffering can have a powerful impact on a person's ability to deal with death. The belief in the existence of a personal god acts as a salve for loneliness and anxiety, offering believers a sense of purpose greater than that of their short existence on this earth. When questioned about the usefulness of a personal God, it is common to hear the believer inquire, "What is the point of life, if there isn't a God?" It's as if our entire existence is rendered utterly meaningless without the promise of a life that extends beyond this mortal coil.

Where is one to turn, then, in the absence of a belief in a higher power? How does one face death with dignity in the absence of hope for an afterlife? It brings to mind the adage, "There are no Atheists in foxholes". Enter Christopher Hitchens, a devout and outspoken Atheist, who flies in the face of this common misconception. Hitchens is currently battling stage four metastasized esophageal cancer. Hitchens, 62, is an outspoken nonbeliever known for cutting criticisms of religion and the faithful masses. At the point in life where many turn to religion for comfort, Hitchens continues to rebuke the role of religion in modern society. He has poignantly rejected the traditional arguments for religion, most especially those associated with an afterlife. Thus, Hitchens is a particularly fascinating individual to consider when discussing the perspectives of those of us who do not believe in a higher power or an afterlife.

Hitchens is highly admired by his fellow freethinkers, and was awarded the Richard Dawkins Freethinker of the Year award in September of 2011. Dawkins, a evolutionary biologist and well known freethinker, introduced Hitchens at the Texas Free Thought Convention this October with great respect:

His very character has become an outstanding and unmistakable symbol of the honesty and dignity of Atheism, as well as of the worth and dignity of the human being when not debased by the infantile babblings of religion.[1]

In addition to Hitchens' reputation as an Atheist, he is also a prolific author and a skilled debater. His irreverent, often outwardly hostile position against religion and the belief in a higher power has a tendency to ruffle the feathers of the faithful. He holds back absolutely nothing in relegating religious beliefs to the refuse of history, labeling it as mythology and nothing more:

> ... If you believe in religion as a reinforcement for other people's *morality*, then why not Mormonism? Or snake-handling? Or Mithras or Dagon or Zeus, or any of the thousands of defunct deities...? True believers always balk at this point, murmuring feebly on occasion that one has to believe in *something*. Satanism does very well by this argument.[2]

It should come as no surprise, then, that Hitchens has, at least outwardly, faced his own potential demise with the same level of brutal honesty and intellectualism that we have come to expect of him.

Early Encounters with Death

In attempting to analyze Hitchens' perspective on mortality before and after his diagnosis, it is necessary to look back into Hitchens' life to consider his past, particularly any experiences with death that predate his diagnosis that he may have had. His first encounter with death came from the tragic suicide of his mother, Yvonne, when he was 24. She had been involved in an affair with a lover in Athens, whom Hitchens met and was fond of. Their forbidden love and his mother's fear that the relationship would be discovered by her husband led her and her lover into a suicide pact involving an excessive amount of sleeping pills and alcohol. Her lover also overdosed on sleeping pills, but also went so far as to slit his own wrists in a warm bath in an adjacent hotel room. Hitchens took on the solitary responsibility of recovering his mother's body from Athens, which involved having to identify her body and to view pictures revealing the state in which his mother's body was discovered.[3] Hitchens later examined the telephone records from the hotel only to find out that in the hours before she took her life, his mother had attempted to place numerous calls to him. The operator failed to successfully connect the calls. Hitchens reflects upon this fact when discussing his observations of the hotel room where she died:

> Who knows what might have changed if Yvonne could have heard my voice even in her extremity? I might have said something to cheer or even tease her: something to set against her despair and perhaps give her a momentary purchase against the death wish.[4]

He goes on to discuss further details worth noting in regards to his sense of closure and his regrets surrounding the circumstances of his mother's death:

> Whenever I hear the dull word "closure," I am made to realize that I, at least, will never achieve it. This is because the Athens police made me look at a photograph of Yvonne as she had been discovered... the bedside telephone had been dislodged from its cradle... I shall always have to wonder if she... regretted her choice, and tried at the very last to stay alive.[5]

While his father's death was far less dramatic, it is nonetheless ironically related to Hitchens' diagnosis. His father died precipitously of the very same cancer that Hitchens himself is currently battling, though he did so at a much later point in life. Hitchens' father was 79 years old when he succumbed to esophageal cancer.

Endeavors into "Cancertown"

On a somewhat lighter note, Hitchens has experienced his untimely demise, at least in a tangential sense, at the hands of a macabre editorial error. Hitchens was oddly pronounced dead in 2009 by an author of

Face to Face, a Fine Arts periodical from London. Hitchens responded to this strange event in his traditionally straightforward fashion:

> So there it is in cold print, the plain unadorned phrase
> that will one day become unarguably true."[6]

And true it eventually did become. Hitchens was diagnosed with stage four metastatic esophageal cancer in the summer of 2010. He has a tumor in his esophagus that has spread to his lymph nodes. The gravity of this diagnosis was stated best by Hitchens in an interview with CSPAN in January of 2011: "The important thing to remember about stage four cancer is that there is no stage 5."[7]

Hitchens has been interviewed numerous times and written a handful of powerful articles since his diagnosis directly addressing his experience with cancer and facing death. He has approached cancer in a particularly pragmatic fashion. He has made it a point to try every possible route to find a cure, including the more traditional route of chemotherapy as well as less traditional routes, such as having his genome sequenced and participating in experimental medicine. He certainly isn't taking his cancer diagnosis sitting down.

> I personally want to 'do' death in the active and not
> the passive, and to be there to look it in the eye and
> be doing something when it comes for me.[8]

He has written extensively and intimately about the trials and tribulations associated with chemotherapy, once again speaking so frankly that it almost hurts the reader to see what he is going through, both physically and emotionally. In an especially candid article written for Vanity Fair in September of 2010, Hitchens goes to great lengths to describe his inner struggles with facing his own mortality.

> I have been taunting the Reaper into taking a free
> scythe in my direction and have now succumbed
> to something so predictable and banal that it bores
> even me. I am badly oppressed by a gnawing sense
> of waste. I had real plans for my next decade and felt
> I'd worked hard enough to earn it. Will I really not

live to see my children married? To watch the World
Trade Center rise again?[9]

It is well known that Hitchens has spent most of his adult life
as an avid smoker and drinker, but this admission cannot possibly
measure up to the reality check that terminal cancer could have to an
individual's sense of themselves and their personal choices. As human
beings, we often fail to recognize the direct connection between our
individual choices and their inevitable consequences until they are
upon us in an undeniably real sense.

Still, Hitchens approaches his own mortality with great reverence
for rationality, objectivity, and intellectual inquiry. He recognizes
that death is one of the few things humanity universally experiences,
and once again states this fact most eloquently in his introduction
to his most recent memoir: "Everyone has to do this at one point or
another- either survive or die of something like this. It is one thing
one is certainly born to do."[10]

Perhaps the most intimate detail Hitchens has shared with us
about his battle with cancer has involved the loss of his "voice", both
literally and metaphorically. As an author and orator, Hitchens has
depended on his ability to communicate in the public sphere. He was
alarmed when the day arrived when his voice failed him, which he
discusses in his article Unspoken Truths, published in Vanity Fair in
June of 2011:

> At times, it threatened, and now threatens daily, to
> disappear altogether... I stood, frozen, like a silly cat
> that had abruptly lost its meow... like health itself,
> the loss of such a thing can't be imagined until it
> occurs. Deprivation of the ability to speak is more
> like an attack of impotence, or the amputation of part
> of the personality. To a great degree, in public and
> private, I 'was' my voice.[11]

His voice hasn't been completely extinguished, however.
Fortunately, Hitchens has continued to write prolifically, and when
his voice isn't failing him has managed to give a handful of public
addresses, though the toll of cancer is increasingly evident each time

he returns to the stage. Hitchens clearly struggles with maintaining hope in the face of such compromising conditions. It is difficult to imagine Hitchens, once vibrant, in such a diminished state. As he said in his last public appearance, "I am not what I once was."[12] He finds comfort through the presence of his friends, and hope if not for a cure, then for the remission of his cancer.

> My chief consolation in this year of living dyingly has been the presence of friends.. What do I want back? In the most beautiful apposition of two of the simplest words in our language: the freedom of speech.[13]

A Deathbed Conversion? Highly unlikely.

While Hitchens is an avid Atheist, even in the face of death, it is frequently supposed, particularly by those who believe in a personal god, that perhaps he will experience a deathbed conversion, bargaining with any deity that will hear his plea for a cure or at the very least forgiveness for spending his life denying a higher power. Will Hitchens hedge his bets at the last moment? Highly unlikely. Hitchens has said that the only time he will utter such bargains will be when he is no longer himself, perhaps afflicted with dementia.[14] He has made a point to forewarn us that should he utter such words, they certainly wouldn't come from the mouth of a lucid individual capable of making rational decisions.

Perspectives on Mortality Before and After Diagnosis

Hitchens has addressed mortality throughout his career, which provides us a sense of how his perspective may have changed since his diagnosis. Prior to his diagnosis, Hitchens discusses death as though it is something that will inevitably occur, but certainly not something within reach, nor something he has directly come to terms with. In an article in 2007, Hitchens generally addressed his concerns about his own eventual demise:

> I'm not afraid of death myself, because I'm not going to know I'm dead. I'm awed a bit by the idea, but I'm perfectly reconciled to it. Certainly I am, as everyone is,

reconciled to everyone else's death but their own. They
think an exception can be made in their own case.[15]

Once confronted with his diagnosis, Hitchens addressed mortality
in a far more "real" sense, alluding to personal fears and concerns
about his role in a world that would continue on without him. I've
mentioned many of these previously in the paper, though there are a
handful of additional quotes I would like to share. Hitchens begins to
discuss, in a vague sense, his fear of death in his memoir. He states:

> I do not especially *like* the idea that one day I shall
> be tapped on the shoulder and informed not that
> the party is over but that it is most assuredly going
> on- only henceforth in my absence... Much more
> horrible, though, would be the announcement that
> the party was continuing forever, and that I was
> forbidden to leave."[16]

Still, Hitchens has his moments of anxiety and concern over his
prognosis. While he typically prefers to view his experience as though
he is living with cancer rather than dying from it, he has certainly had
many moments where the reality of the challenge he is facing has
overwhelmed him.

> . . . As often as I am encouraged to 'battle' my own
> tumor, I can't shake the feeling that it is the cancer
> that is making war on me.[17]

It seems abundantly clear that Hitchens' perspective on life and
death has changed as his prognosis has worsened. One can practically
track his progression through Kübler-Ross' five stages of coping with
death through his writing. He has made his way past denial ("In
one way, I suppose, I have been in denial for some time, knowingly
burning the candle at both ends and finding that it often gives a lovely
light")[18], though he rejects the phase of anger, saying he recognizes it
as non-thinking and purely an exercise in self-pity.[19] His attempts to
assault his cancer with aggressive treatment in hopes of remission or a

cure constitute a sense of bargaining with the disease itself. In fact, he specifically refers to his experience with chemotherapy as a bargain:

> The oncology bargain is that, in return for at least the chance to… stick around for a bit, but in return we are going to need a few things from you. These things may include your taste buds, your ability to concentrate, your ability to digest, and the hair on your head. This certainly appears to be a reasonable trade.[20]

Though Hitchens says he rejects the anger phase as far too sentimental, the quote above surely stands as evidence that he is at the very least upset at what he has had to give up in his ultimate bargain to save his own life.

Certainly, he has progressed through the stage of depression, and likely remains there at this point. In his most recent public appearance, Hitchens shared his feelings regarding it being his "time" to die:

> There is no point in arguing about the actual date or time because I'd like to think there would be no good time. There will always be something I always feel I have left to do or say… I'm not going to quit until I absolutely have to.[21]

I have yet to find evidence that Hitchens has progressed to accepting the fact that he is going to die. He strikes me as the sort of man who will fight until his last breath on earth, and I can't help but admire that sense of perseverance, despite the fact that it may stand in the way of his coming to terms with his death. As Hitchens' health continues to unfortunately decline, I anticipate his writing to continue on the path of further intimate disclosures and unfiltered glimpses into his personal world of "Cancertown".

Politics: Will Hitchens Return to his Socialist Roots?

While I hesitate to delve too deeply into Hitchens and his politics, I'd like to briefly address the evolution of Hitchens' political beliefs. Hitchens' first endeavors into the political realm came as a self-proclaimed

Socialist and Marxist. He has since shed the label of Socialism and fully embraced Capitalism as the best model of social order.[22]

I cannot say that Hitchens and I relate, politically speaking, as of late. I do not identify myself as a Socialist, but I certainly have significant reservations regarding the machinations of Capitalism. I am particularly drawn to the issue of the unprecedented growth of wealth disparity in the United States, and am an avid supporter of the Occupy Wall Street movement. Hitchens himself states that he has benefitted from capitalism far more than he expected to in the prologue of Hitch-22. Perhaps Hitchens has come to his newfound fondness of Capitalism because it has benefitted him personally? Thus the narcissistic nature of Capitalism rears its head, leading us to proclaim our affection for a system that, in its current state in the United States, clearly benefits the wealthiest echelons of our society while leaving the rest of America behind. Regardless, it will be interesting to see if Hitchens changes his tune, politically speaking, as his condition progresses. Could facing death have a direct impact upon a person's politics? Mortality is the one quality that we all share, regardless of the rung on the social ladder that we stand upon in our lives. Perhaps a brush with mortality could lead a person towards a humanistic world view that rejects the egocentric viewpoint that Capitalism embraces. I can only hope this is the case for Hitchens.

Personal Reflections

> *"I always knew I was born into a losing struggle, but I now 'know' this in a more objective and more subjective way."*

While we are all dying given that we are alive and will eventually, regardless of who we are, what we do, or who we love, succumb to our inevitable demise, I question whether or not I can I honestly relate to the phrase above. I feel this notion is one that can only be uttered by those who have personally encountered their own demise in a real way. I refer not to the general notions of death ("Someday, I and everyone I know will die"), nor to perceived near-encounters with death ("Had I not missed my flight that morning, I would've been killed in a terrorist attack"). I refer specifically to the experience of those who have come to know their death is quite literally within arm's reach.

I am drawn to Hitchens for a number of reasons. I see Hitchens as a great thinker, a philosopher, and a personal mentor. As a fellow Atheist, I greatly appreciate articulate, outspoken free thinkers who are willing to publicly discuss their beliefs and go head to head with those who have differing points of view. I have learned more than I could possibly account for from Hitchens and others like him, such as Richard Dawkins, Sam Harris, Bertrand Russell, and even the hilarious yet poignant Douglas Adams. I find that I look up to Hitchens, and turn to his writings to help articulate my own thoughts clearly and precisely. I often find Hitchens is able to say what I couldn't have said nearly as well myself.

Hitchens has handled his illness with remarkable bravery and clear-mindedness that I can only hope to be able to muster when it is my time. I must admit that up until very recently, I have, like so many others, viewed death as though it were some far off specter that I am better off ignoring rather than confronting. Through Hitchens and other authors, I find myself inspired to muster up the courage necessary to look my own mortality in the eye.

I have been told by many well-meaning individuals that I will renounce my firm lack of faith in a higher power once I am confronted with my own demise or that of my children. I can easily summon the voice of my grandmother who on one summer day years ago questioned my sanity in my rejection of a personal God. "Where will you turn when you die? What good does it do you to turn your back on the possibility of heaven? What if you're wrong, and you spend the rest of your life in hell? What do you have to lose, believing in God?" It was as though my grandmother had channeled Pascal himself, urging me to accept God if only to hedge my bet on the nature of my existence. While she sincerely believed that I had nothing to lose and everything to gain in betting in favor of God, I felt then and still feel to this day that to put my faith in a personal God "just in case" flies in the face of my personal devotion to a life based on truth and honesty rather than self-deluded fantasy. Furthermore, believing in god simply because it could save me from an eternity in hell calls into question the integrity of a deity that would accept me into the gates of heaven simply because I was too afraid of the consequences of utilizing my "god-given gifts" of logic and deduction.

Hitchens is a well-educated and intelligent man who concisely denounces the false comforts offered by religion. Through Hitchens, I have found a sense of confirmation in my beliefs and my views regarding an afterlife. He has provided me with an example of how to maintain my devotion to logic and rationality that so many others have insisted I will inevitably shed when my life is threatened.

It is refreshing to encounter a fellow Atheist who is able to provide such a clear-headed perspective on mortality. I've often felt a sense of comfort in the idea that my life is finite, despite my fears associated with the actual act of death. While many are threatened by the idea that we are merely a speck for barely a moment in time in the vastness of the universe, I find this fact to be awe-inspiring. I am proud that I am but one tiny element that makes up this amazing universe. I am practically inconsequential on the grand scale, but what does that matter? This doesn't account for just how important an individual can be in the lives of those they touch. I am naturally highly significant to my family, most especially to my children. How can that be inconsequential? I don't need to have a higher purpose or be loved and cared for by someone or something that is intangible. I have all of the love and comfort I could possibly need through the very real people who make my life worth every moment I am here, no matter how few those moments may be. Hitchens, too, will live on in the minds of those he has inspired, remembered as one who, even in the face of death, continued to uphold the value of reason and science against superstition.

In closing, I would like to share one final quote that, in my opinion, truly conveys the power of speech that Hitchens wields, the sincerity of his convictions, and his timeless inspiration to freethinkers everywhere. The words I am about to share were the closing comments made by Hitchens at the Texas Free Thought Convention last month. They immediately followed a quote I shared earlier that ended with "I'm not going to quit until I absolutely have to." He continued:

> But in the meantime, we have the same job we've always had as thinking people and as human beings. There are no final solutions. No absolute truth. No

supreme leader. No totalitarian solution that says if you will just give up your freedom of inquiry and abandon your critical faculties, a world of idiotic bliss could be yours. You may completely lose your faculties, and you may never know as a result, that the idiotic bliss is even more idiotic than it looks. We have no need of any of this.[23]

Works Cited

Anker, C. a. (1999). *The Lost Explorer.* New York: Simon and Schuster.

BBC News. (1999 йил November). *Mount Everest Reaches New Heights.* London, UK: BBC News.

Beah, I. (2007). *A Long Way Gone.* New York: Sarah Crichton Books.

Berezin, M. (1997). *Making the Fascist Self: The Political Culture of Interwar Italy.* Ithaca: Cornell University Press.

Berlet, C. (1992 йил September). *Fascism!* Retrieved 2010 йил March from http://www.hartford-hwp.com/archives/45/051.html

Coalition to Stop the Use of Child Soldiers. (2006). *Child soldiers and Disarmament, Demobilization, Rehabilitation and Reintegration in West Africa.*

Dawkins, R. (2011, October 8). Texas Free Thought Convention. Texas.

Dawkins, R. (2006). *The God Delusion.* New York: Bantam Press.

Faulkner, F. (2001). Kindergarten Killers: Morality, Murder and the Child Soldier Problem. *Third World Quarterly, Vol. 22, No. 4* .

Federal Aviation Administration. (2003). *Operations of Aircraft at Altitudes above 25,000 Feet.* Washington D.C.: Department of Transportation.

Firth, P. (2008). Mortality on Mount Everest, 1921-2006. *British Medical Journal* .

Gray, M. (2010, September 20). *Hitchens Won't Be Attending Hitchens Prayer Day.* Retrieved October 2011, from http://newsfeed.time.com/2010/09/20/hitchens-wont-be-attending-hitchens-prayer-day/

Gregor, A. J. (1979). *Young Mussolini and the Intellectual Origins of Fascism.* Berkeley: University of California Press.

Heil, N. (2008). *Dark Summit.* New York: Henry Holt and Co.

Hitchens, C. (2007). *God is not Great.* New York: Twelve.

Hitchens, C. (2010). *Hitch-22: A Memoir.* New York: Twelve.

Hitchens, C. (2010, December). Miss Manners and the Big C. *Vanity Fair* .

Hitchens, C. (2011, January 14). Q & A with Christopher Hitchens. (B. Lamb, Interviewer)

Hitchens, C. (1982, July). The Lord and the Intellectuals. *Harper's* .

Hitchens, C. (2011). *The Quotable Hitchens: From Alcohol to Zionism.* Philadelphia: De Capo Press.

Hitchens, C. (2010, September). Topic of Cancer. *Vanity Fair* .

Hitchens, C. (2010, November). Tumortown. *Vanity Fair* .

Hitchens, C. (2010, October). Unanswerable Prayers. *Vanity Fair* .

Hitchens, C. (2011, June). Unspoken Truths. *Vanity Fair* .

Jaffre, F. (n.d.). *The Use of Children as Soldiers in Africa: A country analysis of child recruitment and participation in armed conflict.* Retrieved 2010 йил 29-4 from Relief Web International: http://www.reliefweb.int/library/documents/chilsold.htm

JFK Presidential Library. (n.d.). *JFK Presidential Library.* Retrieved 2011 йил 02-10 from www.jfklibrary.org

Jugalski, E. (2011 йил 24-September). *Ascents-Everest.* Retrieved 2011 йил 10-

October from 8000ers.com: www.8000ers.com/everest-general-info-185. html

Killilea, A. G. (1988). *The Politics of Being Mortal.* Lexington, Kentucky: The University Press of Kentucky.

Koon, T. H. (1985). *Believe, Obey, Fight.* Chapel Hill: University of North Carolina Press.

Krakauer, J. (1997). *Into Thin Air.* New York: Anchor Books.

LaGambina, G. (2007, December). Christmas with Christopher Hitchens. *A.V. Club* .

Mallory, G. (1923 йил 18-March). Climbing Mount Everest is Work for Supermen. (N. Y. Times, Interviewer)

May, T. (2009). *Death.* Durham: Acumen.

Mazzini, G. (1981). The Duties of Man. In M. Curtis, *The Great Political Theories* (Vol. 2, pp. 234-242). New York: Avon Books.

McGrath, C. (2011, October 9). A Voice, Still Vibrant, Reflects on Mortality. *The New York Times* .

Megaro, G. (1938). *Mussolini in the Making.* Boston: Houghton Mifflin Company.

Mount Washington Observatory. (2011). *Mount Washington Observatory.org.* Retrieved 2011 йил 15-October from www.mountwashingtonobservatory.org

Mussolini, B. (1935). *Fascism: Doctrine and Institutions.* Rome: Ardita Publishers.

Mussolini, B. (1923). *Mussolini as Revealed in his Political Speeches (November 1914-August 1923).* London: Dent.

National Center for PTSD. (2011). Health Services Use in the Department of Veterans Affairs among Returning Iraq Warand Afghan War Veterans with PTSD. *PTSD Research Quarterly* , 1.

National Transportation Safety Administration. (2011). *Traffic Safety Fats.* US Census Bureau.

New York Times. (1941 йил 23-February). Speech Delivered by Premier Benito Mussolini. *The New York Times* .

Pini, G. (1939). *The Official Life of Benito Mussolini.* (L. Villari, Trans.) London: Hutchinson & Co.

Pugliese, S. G. (2004). *Fascism, Anti-Fascism, and the Resistance in Italy.* Lanham: Rowman & Littlefield Publishers, Inc.

Richards, K. P. (1998). Jeunes combattants parlant de la guerre et de la paix en Sierra Leone ("When They Say Soldiers Are Rebels, It's a Lie": Young Fighters Talk about War and Peace in Sierra Leone). *Cahiers d'Études Africaines, Vol. 38, Cahier 150/152, Disciplines et déchirures. Les formes de la violence* .

Salvemini, G. (1936). *Under the Axe of Fascism.* London: Camelot Press Ltd.

Schmidt, C. T. (1939). *The Corporate State in Action: Italy Under Fascism.* New York City: Russell & Russell.

Schoene, B. (2000 йил November). Alive on Everest. (PBS/Nova, Interviewer)

Thompson, C. B. (1999). Beyond Civil Society: Child Soldier as Citizens in Mozambique. *Review of African Political Economy, Vol. 26, No. 80* .

University of Alberta. (2006). *Children and War.* Social Sciences and Research Center of Canada.

War Child. (n.d.). *Child Soldiers.* From War Child web site.

Weathers, B. (2000). *Left For Dead: My Journey Home from Everest.* New York: Random House.

West, J. (1999). Barometric Pressures on Mt. Everst; New Daya and Physiological Significance. *Journal of Applied Physiology* , 6.

Woods, R. (2006 йил 28-May). Has the Once Heroic Sport of Climbing Been Corrupted by Big Money? *The Sunday Times* .

Endnotes

[1] (Dawkins, Texas Free Thought Convention, 2011)
[2] (Hitchens, The Lord and the Intellectuals, 1982)
[3] (Hitchens, Hitch-22: A Memoir, 2010), 55.
[4] (Hitchens, Hitch-22: A Memoir, 2010), 70.
[5] (Hitchens, Hitch-22: A Memoir, 2010), 71.
[6] (Hitchens, Hitch-22: A Memoir, 2010), 21.
[7] (Hitchens, Q & A with Christopher Hitchens, 2011)
[8] (Hitchens, Hitch-22: A Memoir, 2010), 7.
[9] (Hitchens, Topic of Cancer, 2010)
[10] (Hitchens, Hitch-22: A Memoir, 2010)
[11] (Hitchens, Unspoken Truths, 2011)
[12] (Dawkins, Texas Free Thought Convention, 2011)
[13] (Hitchens, Unspoken Truths, 2011)
[14] (Hitchens, Tumortown, 2010)
[15] (LaGambina, 2007)
[16] (Hitchens, Hitch-22: A Memoir, 2010), 337.
[17] (Hitchens, Tumortown, 2010)
[18] (Hitchens, Topic of Cancer, 2010)
[19] (Hitchens, Topic of Cancer, 2010)
[20] (Hitchens, Topic of Cancer, 2010)
[21] (Dawkins, Texas Free Thought Convention, 2011)
[22] (Hitchens, The Quotable Hitchens: From Alcohol to Zionism, 2011)
[23] (Dawkins, Texas Free Thought Convention, 2011)

II. DEATH IN CLASSIC LITERATURE

CHAPTER THREE

Politics and Death in the Divine Comedy

Andrew Karanikolis

Though his *Divine Comedy* is widely considered to be a literary masterpiece, Dante Alighieri is practically unknown in political circles. Yet for those who understand his allegories, his characters, and the historical context which informed his work, Dante offers keen insights into the timeless, human challenges to justice and political order. The paper begins with a brief biography of Dante the author, an overview of his earlier (nonfiction) work "Monarchy", and a preliminary analysis of *the Comedy's* three most important characters: Virgil, Beatrice, and Dante himself. We then follow Dante's journey through the realms of the Christian afterlife: hell, purgatory, and paradise. Finally we conclude that while Dante does not shy away from complex questions like "From where is legitimate, terrestrial authority derived?" and "What is the ideal relationship between Church and State?", the answers he provides are utterly dependent on a literal Christian theology, and are therefore anathema to the pluralistic politics of today.

Dante Alighieri's epic poem *The Divine Comedy* is considered to be one of the greatest literary works of all time. *The Comedy*, as

Dante called it, is written in the first person and chronicles Dante's journey through the three realms of the afterlife: hell, purgatory, and paradise. *The Comedy* is celebrated for its detailed descriptions and rich symbolism, as well as for standardizing the Italian language in a time when the vernacular was considered inappropriate for any serious subject matter. Dante's masterful use of the first-person perspective as well as the cornucopia of historical and contemporary references make his masterpiece seem less like poetry and more like autobiography. Yet even though on the surface *The Comedy* describes one man's personal quest for salvation, allegorically it maps the path to God for all of Christendom.

Dante Alighieri was born in Florence around 1265, when the Guelph and Ghibelline factions vied for control of the city. Dante's family was prominent in Florentine politics and held loyalties to the Guelphs. At the age of nine he met and immediately fell in love with a beautiful girl named Beatrice Portinari, however he could only admire her from afar as it he had already been contracted to marry Gemma di Manetto Donati. Dante's acquaintance with Beatrice was highly influential in his life as demonstrated by his work the *Vita Nuova* and her being a major character in *The Comedy*, serving as both his motivation throughout and guide upon reaching paradise. Dante's early studies are known to have covered Latin poetry, including that of Virgil, another extremely important character in *The Comedy*. Dante's participation in the battle of Compaldino on the side of the Guelphs fostered his interest in politics, and when the Ghibellines were defeated he joined the apothecary's guild so that he could hold public office. Once the Guelphs had secured dominance however, it wasn't long until they began fighting amongst themselves, dividing into the White and Black factions. For a time the Whites retained control of Florence, but when it appeared that Pope Boniface VIII intended to intervene on the Blacks' behalf, the Whites sent a delegation to Rome. Boniface had no interest in hearing the White's appeal, and dismissed all the delegates save one: Dante Alighieri. During this time Papal Vicar Charles de Valois and the Black Guelphs captured Florence and destroyed the White opposition, leaving Dante stunned, exiled, and disillusioned.

It was at this point that Dante formed the political philosophy he would espouse in his work *Monarchy*, and later in *The Divine Comedy*.

Dante had seen firsthand the destruction wrought by mankind's infighting and cupidity, and so he turned to his two most trusted advisors for understanding and remedy: classical and Christian philosophy. Dante began with the assertion that God created man for a purpose. Humanity is unique in its capacity to learn and pass on knowledge to future generations; therefore that is its purpose. However in order to fulfill that purpose, mankind requires peace and happiness. In Dante's experience, peace was impossible without a central authority to oversee individuals and local regimes. Enter "empire," an institution with the charge of bringing about peace and order that derives its authority from God's order of the universe. Of course Dante acknowledged that such an empire could only be justified if lead by a virtuous emperor, one that could unite mankind and steer it toward peace and prosperity. For the worldly virtues by which we should measure an emperor Dante cited the teachings of Aristotle, whom he had dubbed the Supreme Philosopher. However, to ensure peace and happiness on Earth is not enough, for what of the afterlife? This is where, in Dante's mind, the classical thinkers fall short. Man is endowed with both a mortal body and an immortal soul, therefore two guides are needed: empire and church. The Church, Dante argued, holds authority in spiritual and eternal matters only; its authority derived from Jesus Christ's giving the keys to heaven to Peter, the first pope of Catholic Church. But in order to properly guide mankind to eternal salvation, the Church cannot be burdened with and subsequently corrupted by worldly authority. Rather than sharing or competing over their respective powers, Dante firmly believed that each institution should stay strictly within its own domain, and cooperate for the good of mankind. For this reason Dante felt that The Donation of Constantine was a dire mistake that all of humanity is paying for; ironically it was later proved to be a forgery. This key concept of separation of church and state was both central to Dante's philosophy and years ahead of its time. However, medieval society had no love of revolutionary thinking. Thus, after completing *Monarchy* Dante learned the value of subtlety and parable; and he would employ these lessons in his masterpiece.

In *The Divine Comedy* Dante serves as both narrator and protagonist, but it is important to distinguish between the two. Dante the narrator has already experienced the events he is recounting, including his eventual meeting with God. Dante the narrator also speaks directly to the reader on several occasions, even asking us to search for the symbolism in his lines. At the beginning of Inferno, Dante the protagonist is portrayed as trembling in fear and totally ignorant of his predicament, but as he progresses he gets closer and closer to the total awareness of Dante the narrator. Religion was a very important part of life in medieval Europe, yet failure on the part of church and empire to ensure order and peace left many ignorant of the path to God. Dante the protagonist represents the lost, and his seven-day trek through the land of the dead represents the Christian life.

Virgil was a Roman poet who lived in the time of Augustus and wrote the epic poem the *Aeneid*. The *Aeneid* tells the tale of Aeneas, a veteran of the Trojan War who journeyed to Italy to found what would become the Roman Empire. In his travels Aeneas enters the underworld where he learns of his destiny to found a mighty nation. It is easy to see why Dante the author would choose Virgil to be his guide in *The Comedy*. Virgil, at the behest of Beatrice, guides Dante through hell and purgatory, but cannot enter heaven because he lived before the time of Jesus Christ and thus lacked the required faith. In *The Comedy* Virgil symbolizes classical virtue, which is essential for building a virtuous empire, but can only guide a person so far on the path to God. Classical virtue can help one to recognize their sins, and it can help one to find the will to overcome those impulses and properly order their loves, but to bask in the grace of God Dante needs the Beatific vision.

Beatrice Portinari died in 1290, so it is appropriate that she should watch over Dante from paradise in *The Comedy*. Beatrice learned of Dante's plight from St. Lucia of Syracuse, who heard the prayers of the infinitely compassionate Virgin Mary. This evidences that Dante's journey was pre-ordained by God with the ultimate intent of Dante relating his experience to the rest of mankind upon his return. In *The Comedy* Beatrice embodies faith, love, salvation, and her namesake: the Beatific vision.

The first book of *The Divine Comedy* is Inferno, which chronicles Dante's descent through the nine circles of Hell. Though each circle punishes a specific action, there is nuance to be found as many of the sins overlap in one way or another. Hell is divided into three broad categories: sins of incontinence, sins of brutality, and sins of fraud and malice. Three areas of hell transcend this categorization: the Vestibule, Limbo, and Heresy. Though the "crimes" punished in these parts of hell are victimless and often completely out of the individual's control, they are damned just the same. This is a testament to Dante's conviction in not just Christian values, but practices such as baptism and repentance as well.

The Inferno begins with Dante wandering through a dark forest, eventually coming to the foothills of a grand mountain bathed in sunlight. But before he can proceed to salvation his path is blocked by three ferocious beasts: a leopard, a lion, and a she-wolf. The she-wolf is particularly aggressive toward Dante, indicating that more than the other sins Dante the protagonist exhibits a lack of self-restraint. Dante is rescued from his appetites by Virgil, who informs him that he was instructed from on-high to guide him through hell. Dante and Virgil pass through the gates of Hell and reach the vestibule, which houses souls who were uncommitted to any cause, including angels who remained neutral during Lucifer's rebellion. These opportunistic souls who were loyal only to their own interests are condemned to eternally chase after a blank, elusive banner while being pursued by swarms of hornets. The indifference and inaction these individuals exhibited in life is juxtaposed with this torment of constant, pointless activity, ever the while being stung by a metaphysical representation of their own consciences. This is a powerful affirmation of the preciousness of life and the inescapable duty we have not to waste it on selfish gains, a lesson that holds true regardless of one's vision of the afterlife. The poets cross the river Acheron to the first circle of hell proper: Limbo. The souls in Limbo are not punished except to exist forever in awareness of paradise with no hope of ever reaching it. In this circle one finds some of the most controversial tenets of Christianity, such as un-baptized children being damned for all eternity. Dante and Virgil come to a dome of light within the darkness of hell, whereupon they meet virtuous pagans such as the great poets and philosophers of antiquity, Julius Caesar, and others. Here is a prime example of the overlap and inconsistency in Dante's categorization of sin. Pagans, virtuous though they may be, are heretics and technically belong in the sixth circle of hell. Conversely, there are undoubtedly a host of virtuous Epicureans and members of other "heretical" sects that lay burning in Heresy. Evidently the only things that distinguish these virtuous pagans from other potentially virtuous heretics are historical renown and Dante the author's admiration. Furthermore, Dante cast the Muslim prophets Mohammad and Ali to the eighth circle of hell for sowing discord among the Semitic religions, but what makes Islam's prophecies more false and offensive to God than other heretical beliefs? I would put forth that Islam's condemnation stems from its position as a formidable rival to Christianity in Dante's time.

The poets descend to the circles of Lust and Gluttony, which are home to the souls that were slaves to their own sensual desires. The shades Dante witnesses in Lust were all prominent figures in life whose reckless love led to the crippling of their respective civilizations. It is interesting that those punished in Lust are not guilty of sexual deviance or excess, but rather of putting their passions ahead of their station. This shows Dante the author's unwillingness to separate the motivation behind a sin from its effect on the political order. The third circle of hell is the realm of the gluttons, which punishes excess in consumption of food and drink. Here Dante meets Ciacco, a Florentine who makes the first of many political predictions in the Inferno. Next the poets come to the circle of Greed, where those who hoard wealth struggle against those who wastefully spend to push enormous weights in opposite directions. Here Dante learns of Fortune, a goddess of sorts that shifts the wealth of the world from one hand to the next and from one nation to another. The imagery evoked by these Sisyphean shades and the arbitrary bestowal of riches by a whimsical deity serve to emphasize the foolishness and futility of a life spent in the pursuit of material wealth. This belief is common to all views of mortal life, and yet today, just as in Dante's time, we find ourselves scrambling to accrue frivolous goods as if we could take them with us.

Dante and Virgil advance to the fifth circle, where the wrathful constantly tear at one another in the river Styx, and the slothful lay at the bottom of the mire. Here we arrive at the first section of Hell proper that isn't characterized by misdirected love, but rather misdirected anger and passiveness. As the poets cross the marsh Dante sees Filippo Argenti, a Black Guelph. After a bitter exchange Dante expresses his desire to see Argenti suffer, which meets Virgil's approval. Although Dante's anger may seem hypocritical, it reflects the mentality of Christian Europe at the time in regards to righteous retribution. Dante and Virgil reach the city of Dis, the antithesis to paradise and the representation of a sinful political order. Before they can enter Dis the poets are harassed by furies and fallen angels, so they pray for divine aid in order to proceed. Their prayer is soon answered when an angel descends from heaven to drive away the demons and unblock the path, symbolizing reason's insufficiency for confronting heinous sin without faith. Within the infernal city the poets come to Heresy; here in the sixth circle they converse with two Epicurean Florentine shades: Farinata and Cavalcanti. Dante informs the shades of the current state of Florence, and they in turn reveal to him the nature of perception for the damned. Those in Hell have vision of the past and future but not the present, therefore when time ends with The Second Coming of Christ they will know nothing. This interesting literary device allows Dante the author to make seemingly authoritative political predictions, as well as reinforcing the idea that sinners are blind.

The poets descend into the seventh circle of Violence, which can be done against thy neighbor, against thyself, or against God. Those who commit violence against others are submerged at various depths in the final river of hell: the Phlegethon. Here Dante sees the tyrants of history boiling in the very blood they so enthusiastically spilled, but as previously stated many Italian conquerors are mysteriously omitted from the roster. Dante's reasoning for this undoubtedly stemmed from his belief that the Roman Empire was divinely endorsed and therefore justified in its bloody efforts to unite the world. Next Dante and Virgil move on to the Wood of the Suicides, where the souls of those who have done violence against themselves sprout and grow into gnarled trees. Some have questioned why Dante chose to punish suicides so harshly, but if you study Dante's political and theological philosophy closely it is obvious why a person's choice to selfishly and casually shrug off their duties in life would offend him so. Virgil further explains that as Fortune may shift without warning, one requires fortitude to endure the humiliation of lost property and status. After leaving the grim forest the poets come to a scorched wasteland, where souls who have done "violence" against God reside. Violence against God is understood to be the violation of nature's intent in the forms of blasphemy, sodomy and usury. Though these sinners could be disputed as belonging in Heresy, Lust, or Greed, it is their actions - not their motivations - Dante argues, that earn them a place in this burning desert. Sodomites, though motivated by lust, are violating the intent of nature by engaging in sexual activity outside of holy matrimony and with no utility of progeny. Usurers, or lenders who levy interest, insult God by acquiring wealth outside the approved methods: nature's bounty and human skill. Gamblers too are punished in Violence, as it leads to the dissipation of one's property. This however begs the question: if one gambles and wins, is it still a sin? Again Dante is more concerned with impact on society than with motivation.

Fraud is the eighth circle of hell and is comprised of ten ditches that form the Malebolge. In the third Bolgia are punished the clergymen who practiced simony, including Pope Nicholas III, who predicts he will soon be joined by Boniface VIII and Clement V. In the fifth Bolgia corrupt politicians seethe in boiling pitch for the bribes they accepted and the responsibility they neglected. In addition to these, the Malebolge also houses thieves, sorcerers, flatterers, pimps, hypocrites, false advisors (including Odysseus for his Trojan horse ruse), perjurers and counterfeiters, and sowers of discord (including the Muslim prophets Mohammad and Ali for breaking off from Judaism and subsequently dividing into Sunnis and Shiites). Fraud is committed against those who trust in us, and as such it is considered a malicious sin. Dante's descent through the Malebolge is notable for its criticism of the institutional leaders who failed in their charge to promote unity and peace while seeking to profit from their station.

Finally Dante and Virgil descend into Treachery, the lowest circle of hell, where Lucifer and the infamous traitors of history lie frozen in a lake of tears. Whereas above Dante had used the promise of worldly fame as a sort of currency to buy information from shades, in Cocytus the traitorous souls long for anonymity (but of course are perfectly willing to betray each other). But whether a soul in hell prefers fame or obscurity, both are a product of concern for one's worldly reputation, a disordered love that Dante felt was owed to God rather than personal legacy. Among the giants and frozen traitors of the ninth circle, Dante meets Fra Albergio, a contemporary of Dante's who the author quite ingeniously condemns to hell by developing a literary device in which especially heinous sins cause the soul to leave the body prematurely; the soul is then replaced by a devil that inhabits the body until death. After witnessing all of the horrors of the inferno, Dante and Virgil arrive at the very center of hell, where "the emperor of the woeful kingdom was standing in the ice up to his breast" (Canto XXXIV). Lucifer sought to rule God's kingdom, and for his sin he (like all denizens of hell) is appropriately punished with the ironic task of ruling over a kingdom of woe. Once called The Morning Star, Lucifer was the fairest of all God's angels, but his rebellion and banishment transformed him into a hideous winged beast with three heads. In each of his mouths Satan consumes an infamous traitor. The first is Judas Iscariot, who betrayed Jesus Christ to the Romans for thirty silver coins. The second and third are Cassius and Brutus, who participated in the assassination of Julius Caesar. Cassius and Brutus are of particular interest, as their treachery undermined the strength and unity of the Roman Empire. Dante adamantly believed that the Roman Empire (and therefore the emperor) was chosen by God to rule the world, which he validated with their role in Christ's crucifixion (they were the only authority fit to judge of the son of God). This argument is as paradoxical as it is impossible to disprove. On the one hand the disciple who betrayed Jesus suffers one of the worst torments hell has to offer, but the political authority that condemned Jesus to death is God's chosen enforcer of his order and will? The exaltation of the Roman Empire despite its antagonistic role in the Bible can only be justified by its (in Dante's mind) destined conversion to Christianity; and speaks to why Dante would choose the pagan assassins of a pagan to accompany Judas in the maws of Satan.

The Divine Comedy (especially Inferno) is rife with references from Greek and Roman mythology, and yet Dante sentences every pagan to hell with only two exceptions. In the inferno Dante meets Charon and Phlegyas the ferrymen, crosses the river Styx, and is hindered or aided by mythological beasts such as: Cerberus, centaurs, the minotaur, the furies, Medusa, and numerous giants. Dante also learns (through Virgil) of what can only be described as minor deities: Plutus (wealth), Fortune, and Nature. Though I'm sure he conceived of these as merely an extension of the creator, it is interesting that he should go so far as to assign Fortune and Nature genders (both female) and personalities. For instance, Fortune is described as blissful, whimsical, and oblivious to the suffering her redistributing of wealth causes. One wonders why Dante would include these mythological entities in his depiction of the Christian afterlife. In order to answer this query we must first keep in mind that the Bible itself makes references to giants, dragons, and even unicorns; therefore the existence of mythological monsters may not have seemed quite so outlandish to Dante. Additionally, the ancient Greeks were the intellectual ancestors of the ancient Romans, who shared an even closer relationship with medieval Italians. Thus in order to justify the Holy Roman Church/Empire, Dante gives us the impression that the ancient poets and priests were (in terms of the afterlife) on the right track, but fell short.

After traversing the depths of hell, Virgil leads Dante down Lucifer's back until they come to a cave. Dante soon realizes that they are climbing, and asks Virgil how this is possible. Virgil explains that while they were descending they passed the Earth's center of gravity, and are now ascending the southern hemisphere. This point sheds light on the medieval theologians' conception of world geography, with hell and purgatory being physical locations on Earth, directly beneath Jerusalem, rather than spiritual planes, as many today tend to view them. The poets exit the cave and see Mount Purgatory in the distance; thus begins the repentant sinner's arduous journey to Beatrice, paradise, and God. Mount Purgatory features seven terraces, where souls repent for the sin that most characterized their lives.

As with hell, purgatory proper is preceded by the Ante-purgatory and the Valley of Rulers, where the excommunicated and late-repentant reside for a span of time equaling that of their mortal lives. Though Dante the author is quick to condemn select church officials and practices to hell, his decision to place excommunicated Christians at the lowest ward of purgatory demonstrates his enduring belief in the Church's spiritual authority. Beyond the Ante-purgatory lie the seven terraces of mortal sin: Pride, Envy, Wrath, Sloth, Avarice, Gluttony, and Lust. Each of these sins has a corresponding virtue that souls must learn through purging acts; some of these acts are laborious, some painful, but all are prime examples of poetic justice. Unlike hell however, the shades in purgatory are not petty, vengeful, or anguished, but rather hopeful and even sing hymns. Purgatory is also distinct from hell in that it is less concerned with sinful acts than it is the motivations behind them, specifically the perverted, deficient, and misdirected loves that lead to sin. Repentance allows a soul to gain entrance to purgatory, but to ascend that soul must discipline itself so that its loves are properly ordered. For instance, when a proud soul purges itself by carrying a boulder on its back, it is learning humility. The envious, who took pleasure in the pain of their enemies, now huddle together with their eyes sewn shut, thus they learn the virtue of generosity. The wrathful, blinded by rage in life, must endure the dense smoke of the third terrace so they may attain the virtue of meekness. The slothful are burdened with ceaseless activity in pursuit of the virtue of zeal. On the fifth terrace the covetous purge themselves of avarice by laying face down so as to avoid temptation and learn to be content with little. The gluttonous starve beneath fruit-bearing trees whose branches they cannot reach, thus receiving the virtue of temperance. On the seventh terrace the lustful purge themselves by jumping through a wall of flame, and in doing so they learn the virtues of chastity and fidelity. Examples of each of these virtues are depicted in reliefs on the face of the mountain, with examples of the opposing sin being given by the numerous shades Dante and Virgil encounter as they climb. It should also be noted that whereas shades in hell aspired to worldly fame, the souls in purgatory wish only for prayers, which have the power to expedite their journey up the mountain. Dante's ascent takes several days and along the way he witnesses many scenes and experiences abstract dreams, all of which have allegorical meaning. The most significant of these scenes takes place at the peak of Mount Purgatory (The Garden of Eden), and is known as the Triumphant Procession. In the splendor of the earthly paradise Dante (with the beautiful Metilda, who embodies man's natural state of innocence in Eden) observes a grand parade of men, women, and beasts. The men and beasts for the most part represent specific books or figures (such as the apostles and evangelists) from the Bible. The first three women symbolize the three theological virtues of love, hope, and faith; while the following four symbolize the four cardinal (classical) virtues: prudence, justice, temperance, and fortitude. For Dante these seven virtues epitomize what it is to be good, and the protagonist witnessing them signifies that he is ready to receive Beatrice and enter paradise. At this point, having completed his task of guiding Dante through sin and purgation, Virgil takes his leave and returns to Limbo. Virgil's departure indicates that Dante is nearing the celestial realm of God and therefore no longer needs natural reason to navigate life's trials. At long last Dante is reunited with Beatrice, who will serve as his guide through paradise. Before he proceeds to heaven however, Dante must pass through the purging rivers of Lethe and Eunoe. The river Lethe washes away all memory of past sin, while drinking from the river Eunoe refreshes memories of happiness and virtuous deeds. With this act Dante and Beatrice ascend to the heavens.

Dante's theology is wholly unsympathetic to the notion of institutionalized sin. The uneducated and impoverished are kept so by social circumstances, hence some may be forced to steal, prostitute, or even kill to survive. In his championing of meekness over wrath with the image of Saint Stephen being stoned to death, Dante is holding martyrdom over the instinct to survive. In this manner martyrdom serves as Dante's ultimate test of faith, as it makes a declaration of absolute confidence in the existence and nature of the afterlife. Of course, one shouldn't have to pay the ultimate sacrifice to live virtuously, which is why the responsibility of alleviating the social conditions that cause institutionalized sin falls on the church and empire.

Paradise is the third book of *The Divine Comedy*, and like the first two is comprised of thirty-three cantos (except inferno which has thirty-four, adding up to one-hundred in total). Similarly to hell and purgatory, heaven is divided into nine celestial spheres, with each sphere housing spirits that exhibited or were deficient in specific virtues. The nine spheres are as follows: The Moon, Mercury, Venus, The Sun, Mars, Jupiter, Saturn, The Fixed Stars, and the Primum Mobile, with God residing in the Empyrean beyond physical existence. Even in paradise souls are assorted by their degree of virtuousness, but unlike hell and purgatory, spirits in heaven are totally content to dwell in whichever heavenly court God wills for them. In fact, Dante implies that God created every soul to fulfill a specific role in life; therefore every soul is destined for a specific heaven.

The first sphere of paradise is The Moon, which is populated by spirits who were inconstant in their virtue, particularly lacking fortitude. Here Beatrice is the first of many in Paradise to denounce the current state of the church, especially the Donation of Constantine, and predicts that the empire will rise once again. Mercury is the second sphere, where virtuous spirits who were deficient in justice dwell. Here Dante meets Emperor Justinian I, who was a noble ruler but was also driven by ambitions of fame. In his portrayal of Justinian as a skillful orator Dante is acknowledging that aspirations of glory are compatible with heaven when they compel one to act in accordance with the will of God. Ambition can however limit divine illumination, hence the emperor's place in the second sphere. The third sphere of paradise is Venus, the realm of the virtuous lovers who lacked temperance. This raises an interesting question: how could a portion of heaven dedicated to temperance, which by definition could not exist with the concept of excess, predate the introduction of sin? Paradise certainly existed before God cast Lucifer from it, and Lucifer's rebellion was the first sin; so then how could it be virtuous to practice self-control before there was any need for self control?

Dante and Beatrice ascend to the fourth heaven, the Sun. At this point the spheres of heaven cease to be categorized by deficiency of virtue, but rather stations in Christian life. Here as with the prior spheres, the wise (Thomas Aquinas, King Soloman, Peter Lombard, etc.) rebuke the self-indulgent practices of the clergy, juxtaposing their extravagance with the lifestyle of poverty lead by the saints. Next Dante and Beatrice rise to the sphere of the warrior-saints, Mars. Here they meet Cacciaguida, a veteran of the second crusade, who prophesizes Dante's exile from Florence (which had not yet occurred to Dante the protagonist). In addition to this crusader, Dante sees Charlemagne, William of Orange, Duke Godfrey, and many other "holy" warriors. This is perhaps the greatest contradiction of *The Comedy*: God punishes all forms of unrepentant violence in the seventh circle of hell and Jesus Christ taught his followers to "love your enemies, bless them that curse you, do good to them that hate you..." and yet the crusades and a host of other bloody campaigns are not only tolerated, but romanticized by God. Holy land or not, there is a serious break in the reasoning behind this position. Following their discussions with the thinker-saints and warrior-saints, Dante and Beatrice come to Jupiter, the sphere of just rulers. Despite his infamous donation, Emperor Constantine I resides in this sixth heaven, as do the pagans Trajan and Ripheus, a Roman emperor and Trojan veteran who by all rights should be damned to hell, but by the grace of God (Dante) they were spared.

Dante and Beatrice next pass through the sphere of Saturn, home to the contemplative souls such as Peter Damian and Benedict, who pronounce the virtue of the monastic life. Beyond the seventh heaven lie the Fixed Stars where Dante meets Peter, James, John, and Adam. St. Peter tests Dante's faith by asking him how one can know that the Bible is the word of God; when Dante responds correctly (that its wide-spread circulation despite modest beginnings is nothing short of a miracle) Peter approves and gives a harsh castigation of Pope Boniface VIII and the state of the church. St. John and St. James test Dante on the remaining theological virtues of love and hope, which Dante has in abundance. Dante then takes the opportunity to ask Adam, the first human being, his age, his language and about his stay in the Garden of Eden. From the span of his life coupled with the time he spent in Limbo and Paradise, Dante ascertains that Adam is 6,498 years old. Adam demonstrates the malleability of language when he reveals that his tongue was already extinct when Nimrod built the tower of Babel. Finally, in a testament to Dante's conviction in the sinful nature of man, Adam tells that his time in the Garden of Eden was no more than seven hours. From the heavens Dante looks down to Earth and is humbled (and somewhat detached). By all reckoning the trivial goings-on of that tiny blue planet should mean little to these celestial beings, and yet every soul Dante has encountered has expressed concern for the welfare of the living and resentment toward institutional corruption.

The Primum Mobile, the final sphere of the physical universe, is where the angels dwell. From here Dante can see God as a brilliant light surrounded by nine rings of angels. The Primum Mobile is constantly rotating with such force that the lower heavens rotate with it. This envisioning of the solar system, despite its ignorance of gravitation, is quite elegant and certainly paints a beautiful picture of the afterlife. Many secularists tend to view belief in the afterlife as a crutch for those unwilling or unable to accept their mortality. This may be true, but from reading Dante's eloquent descriptions of the heavenly spheres I sense that what prompted his faith was not fear, but rather wonder and reverence of nature. At last Dante and Beatrice ascend to the Empyrean heaven, a plane of pure light where God himself makes his abode. Dante has become enveloped in pure light so that he (as a living man) may look upon God, and see's before him an enormous white rose of light. On the petals of this rose (symbolizing divine love) sit the blessed of heaven, including the spirits of those who dwell in the lower heavens. Among the blessed are figures from both the Hebrew Bible and New Testament. The Virgin Mary oversees the women on one half of the rose, with John the Baptist leading the men on the other. At this point Beatrice (made all the more beautiful by God's presence) returns to her place among the blessed women of paradise, and St. Bernard takes the role of Dante's guide. St. Bernard discusses the nature of predestination, but as a mortal man Dante is unequipped to comprehend it, a reflection of Dante the author's belief in the limits of man's intellect. Finally, Dante comes to three radiant circles that seem to occupy the same space. This is the holy trinity: the Father, the Son, and the Holy Spirit. Within the second divine circle Dante perceives the silhouette of a man, Jesus Christ. As Dante struggles to comprehend the simultaneous humanity and divinity of Christ, he is all at once struck with the Beatific vision and is, for a moment, fully attuned to the love and will of God. Unfortunately for the reader the words to describe this moment of clarity escape Dante, fading like a dream upon awakening.

Dante professed that love is the primary impetus of all human action; but without proper guidance (from empire and church) man's love can be misdirected on secondary goods. Losing sight of the supreme goodness of God leads to sin. Sin is self-perpetuating and oppressive in life, and thus without repentance it is eternally punished by infinite oppression in hell. But repentance isn't just asking forgiveness prior to death; allegorically speaking purgatory is the conscious choice and determination of will to reform one's ways in life. This can be achieved through embracing both the classical and theological virtues. The responsibility to demonstrate and diffuse these virtues once again falls on God's institutions of empire and church.

In what may be the greatest allegory ever written, Dante clearly illustrates the relationship between sin and virtue. He also makes a solid argument for the necessity of independent, cooperative institutions of church and empire to inhibit man's inherited inclination toward sin. Nevertheless both of these ideas are built on the foundation of Christian theology, or "the whole" as Dante called it. This term is quite befitting, as it is impossible to separate one feature of Dante's philosophy from the whole so as to use it another context. We may seek to apply the classical virtues of Dante's ideal emperor to contemporary political theory, only to be foiled by our secularist (ironic considering his innovation of separation of church and state) tendency to shun absolute authority. Questioning authority leads to the emergence of rivals, this leads to power-consolidating measures, resulting in irreverence if not revolution (both of which incline one to sin). Though *the Divine Comedy* describes an immortal afterlife, its powerful allegory concerns a mortal, moral life. And while Dante's religious and political views may not be in sync with modern thinking, the timeless truth of man's quest for morality and meaning will always be relevant. *The Divine Comedy* is a superbly written tale of self-discovery, and will endure as a literary triumph long after the religion that inspired it is but another mythology.

CHAPTER FOUR

Peter Pan: Aging, Death and Immortality

Samantha Pettey

Peter Pan by J.M Barrie has captured the hearts of children and adults all over the world. The novel's most memorable legacy is Disney's animated adaptation. Although the movie reflects the basic attributes of the main characters and follows the basic story line, the novel is vastly different and arguably much darker. The book provides deeper analysis and understanding of the complexities of each character and how each plays an important role in the overall themes of the book. I reread the story for the first time since I was a child and analyzed the themes of aging, dying and immortality; three themes I initially never imagined Peter Pan to be about. All in all, children believe Peter lives an enviously, desirable life. Yet the story delves much deeper than a child's pretend world of pirates and mermaids. *Peter Pan* reflects a lesson of death and how an acceptance of death is not only good for living a fulfilling life but that death is natural.

Introduction

Peter Pan by J.M Barrie has captured the hearts of children and adults all over the world. The novel's most memorable legacy is

Disney's animated adaptation. Although the movie reflects the basic attributes of the main characters and follows the basic story line, the novel is vastly different and arguably much darker. The book provides deeper analysis and understanding of the complexities of each character and how each plays an important role in the overall themes of the book. I reread the story for the first time since I was a child and analyzed the themes of aging, dying and immortality; three themes I initially never imagined Peter Pan were about. My first reading as a child left me with a story about a boy, who can fly, crow and fight pirates. All in all, Peter to a child lives an enviously, desirable life. Yet the story delves much deeper than a child's pretend world of pirates and mermaids. *Peter Pan* reflects a lesson of death and how an acceptance of death is not only good for living a fulfilling life but that death is natural.

The Story

Peter Pan opens with Mr. and Mrs. Darling's background story. Many young men were fond of Mrs. Darling and they all wished to propose marriage to her. Mr. Darling was clever though, and took a cab to her house so that he would arrive before any others could by foot. There is an instant portrayal of Mr. Darling as being somewhat pompous and having concerns with more than his family could offer. He wanted respect as well as love and he claimed to receive this by being a man who knew the stock market. Soon after their marriage, they had a daughter named Wendy. A week or two after she was born, Mr. Darling considered 'getting rid of her' because a baby was a financial burden on the family. Mr. Darling was fond of his first child Wendy, seemingly for upholding a societal image, so he sat down and calculated how much extra Wendy would cost; everything down to how much being sick would cost them financially. The calculations fell in Wendy's favor so she was kept, and the same process was taken before her brothers John and Michael were able to stay as well.

The story quickly progresses and introduces the protagonist, Peter Pan. Mrs. Darling finds her children's drawings and notes that all talk about a boy named Peter whom Mrs. Darling had never met. She then recalls her childhood memories also involving a boy named Peter Pan. She remembers him being a boy who lived with fairies that helped children when they die so they would not be frightened of death. Mrs. Darling believes it must be someone different but Wendy reassures her mother that she must have just forgotten because Peter Pan never grows older. Later on, Mrs. Darling encounters Peter in the children's nursery and screams with fright. Nana, the Darlings' nurse dog, quickly comes and attacks Peter but only manages to catch his shadow. Peter jumps out of the window before he could be caught. Mrs. Darling puts the shadow away in a drawer and never mentions it to anyone in the family.[1]

Peter and Tinker Bell, a fairy who is friends with Peter, go back to the Darling's nursery when the children are sleeping in search of Peter's shadow. Mr. and Mrs. Darling are away at a dinner party so are not home for anything that is about to happen. Tinker Bell finds the shadow in a drawer and Peter immediately takes it back and tries to reattach it. Peter originally thought the shadow would just reattach itself but after it appeared not to, Peter uses soap to stick it on. Soon after, Peter realizes the soap is not a sufficient means to attach his shadow and he begins to cry, which in turn wakes up Wendy. Peter and Wendy begin talking about Neverland and Peter tells Wendy he has no mother. Peter did not care he had no mother and in fact, he believes they are over-rated but Wendy immediately feels sorry for Peter. Wendy did not know at the time but Peter left his mother and father long ago. He once tried to go back to them but they had another child and did not seem to care about their missing son Peter.

Peter quickly realizes how much he enjoys Wendy's company and starts using his charm and manipulation skills to convince Wendy she should travel to Neverland to meet the Lost Boys and be their mother. The Lost Boys have no mother either, so Peter convinces Wendy she is needed to do motherly tasks for them. Peter places an idea into Wendy's head that the Lost Boys, and himself, need a mother to tuck them in, tell stories, and many other 'motherly' things. He also entrances her with the idea of seeing mermaids and being able to fly. With this idea planted, Wendy becomes very excited and wakes up her younger brothers John and Michael; they were all to fly to Neverland. To fly, one must "think lovely wonderful thoughts, and they lift you up in the air" (Barrie, 764)[2] and have fairy dust sprinkled on you. They were all flying around the room when Peter convinces the children one more time to fly to Neverland with him. He easily convinces the boys they will see and fight pirates, so off to Neverland they went.

Neverland is the "second [star] to the right, and straight on till morning" (Barrie, 807). Really though, Peter knew these directions were nonsense and just said whatever popped into his head. The flight to Neverland is exciting for the children but they soon forget how long they were actually flying. Michael dozed off a few times and nearly hit water and drowned before Peter flew down to save him. During the flight, the children realize how much Peter enjoys showing off and they think about going back home. The problem was that they have no clue where home is, or how to stop themselves from flying. They placed tremendous faith and trust in Peter who often sped up in front of them and left them alone. Peter always came back for them though so they never turned around or tried to go back to the nursery. Eventually they were excited to see Neverland ahead of them.

Neverland looked just as the children imagined it at first glance with a beautiful lagoon, trees and even a pirate ship. But, the children quickly realize Neverland is becoming dark, and eerie and Tinker Bell told them the pirates had seen them flying and are now preparing to open fire. Neverland is real now. There is no going back and to be out of harms' way because the danger is not pretend and games anymore. The pirates are real and they soon start to open fire on the children and Peter. Wendy and Tinker Bell are cast upwards from the wind of the fired cannonball and Wendy loses sight of all the others except for Tinker Bell. Tink is extremely jealous of Wendy because Peter really likes Wendy but Tink is much more fond of Peter than he ever knew. Tinker Bell convinces Wendy to follow her to safety. Then she leads Wendy towards the Lost Boys. Tinker Bell flies much faster than Wendy so she speeds ahead and convinces the Lost Boys that Wendy is a large white bird that Peter wants them to kill. Wendy is quickly shot with an arrow by Tootles because he really wants to impress Peter. Wendy survives but Peter is angry at Tinker Bell for her jealous actions and Peter vows to ignore Tinker Bell for a week. To please Wendy, Peter builds a house to all of Wendy's desires around her while she recovers from the arrow.

After recovery, Wendy, John and Michael live just like the Lost Boys and Peter. Wendy came to Neverland to be their mother so she quickly starts to pretend the Lost Boys are her children. Wendy and the boys love this game because Wendy wants to be a mother and the boys want to hear the great stories mothers usually tell their children.

The relationship becomes mutually beneficial for all. Peter also takes part in their pretend game and plays along as their father. The pretend game is fun for all but soon the boys start to forget Wendy and Peter are not their real parents. The boys forget their own mothers' and fathers' and this worries Wendy. She frequently gives them quizzes and tests to help them remember that Neverland is not their real life. For Wendy is the only one who remembers their real life and knows Neverland is just pretend and games.

A turning point for Wendy, Peter and all the children happens at Mermaid Lagoon. Wendy, Peter and the Lost Boys regularly visited the mermaids and played games with them. One day though, a thick darkness swept over the lagoon and two pirates came in a rowboat with Princess Tiger Lily of the Redskins. The pirates planned to tie her to a rock and let the tide rise so that she would drown. Seeing the pirates, the Lost Boys all scatter away but stay close enough by to see Tiger Lily and what the pirates will do. Peter pretends from a distance to be Captain Hook and tells the pirates to set her free. The pirates listen to the voice and untie Tiger Lily but the real Captain Hook soon comes and realizes an imposter is among them. He tricks Peter into revealing himself and a fight pursues between the two.

Hook wins the fight. Peter becomes injured and unable to fly or swim and is left on the same rock Tiger Lily was to drown on. Wendy is near him on the rock and both are slowly realizing they are going to drown. Then a kite flies by and Peter tells Wendy to tie herself to it and float back to safety. Both knew the kite could support at least one of them but Peter insists that Wendy, being a female, should be saved. Peter is saved though by a bird he had befriended long ago. The bird lends Peter her nest which has two un-hatched eggs inside. Peter is surprisingly unselfish and thoughtful enough to place the eggs in his own hat and let them float to the shore for the bird to save. The nest is supportive enough for Peter to float to shore and recuperate there.

After the long day at the lagoon, the Redskins become Peter and the Lost Boys' allies for saving their princess Tiger Lily. The Redskins watch over the tree house, which is actually underground, to make sure the pirates will not attack. Unfortunately for all, the pirates do attack and defeat the Redskins. All the while, the children are in the tree house and hear the battle ensuing above. They could tell the battle ended but are not aware of who won the battle. Captain Hook plays the Redskins' drum, a sign of a Redskin victory, to trick the Lost Boys into thinking they are safe. At this point, the Lost Boys begin discussions about leaving Neverland with the Darlings. All decide they want to have real parents and not pretend ones anymore. Peter does not object to any of them wanting to leave but refuses to see them off. Peter hides his true sorrow that Wendy would be leaving him but he does not show this side to Wendy or any of the boys. The Lost Boys and Wendy leave with Peter's consent and are immediately captured by Captain Hook and the pirates; Peter has no idea.

Soon after, Peter falls asleep and Captain Hook sneaks into the tree house. Here he finds Peter sleeping but Hook knows it would be bad form to slay him while he is sleeping. So, in a questionable manner of good form, Hook puts poison in Peter's medicine and leaves to his ship, the *Jolly Roger,* to deal with the Lost Boys. Tinker Bell immediately wakes Peter up and tells him of the Lost Boys and poison. Peter does not believe her and in his 'matter of fact way' goes to drink the medicine but not before Tinker Bell drinks it for him first. Her light begins to flicker out and Peter knows she is dying. Yet, Peter also knows that if children believe in fairies they can bring Tink back to life. Peter speaks to all the children sleeping and dreaming of Neverland and convinces them all to clap their hands to bring Tinker Bell back to life. The children dreaming bring Tinker Bell back to life and her and Peter rush to the Pirate ship to save Wendy and the boys.

On the *Jolly Roger* Captain Hook tries to convince the boys to become pirates and join his crew. Each boy refuses to become a pirate and so, will be forced to walk the plank. At this moment, the ticking noise of the crocodile's clock reaches Hook's ears and he becomes very frightened that the crocodile will finally eat him and end his persistent chase once and for all. The ticking noise though, is emitting from Peter's mouth, and it allowed him to sneak on board and save Wendy and the Lost Boys. Peter and Hook pursue each other in another fight but this time each knows the fight is to the finish.

Little did anyone know, during the commotion, the crocodile was patiently awaiting Hook. Peter has the upper hand in the fight because Hook is tired and losing hope but Hook will not die before Peter shows him bad form. Hook asks Peter who he is and Peter says, "I'm youth, I'm joy" (Barrie, 2613). Hook is now convinced that Peter actually exemplifies good form but then Peter kicks Hook overboard when he is near the edge. The crocodile is patiently waiting and happily takes Hook. Before his end though, Hook realizes Peter shows bad form and so, Hook dies happy. Captain Jas Hook was defeated once and for all.

Peter and the Lost Boys take over the ship and sail back to the Darling's nursery. All the Lost Boys decide to leave Neverland in hopes of being adopted by the Darlings. Luckily, the Darlings welcome them all with open arms. Peter is with them at this point but refuses to be adopted because he will have to grow up, and eventually become a man. Peter is still very fond of Wendy and enjoys her company so he promises to visit her every spring so she can fly with him to do 'spring cleaning'. Peter visits Wendy the first year but forgets the second year. He goes one more time the year after but then not again until Wendy is considerably older and has a child of her own. At this point, Peter fears Wendy because she is grown up. Luckily for Peter though, Wendy has a daughter Jane and Wendy allows Jane to fly away with Peter for spring-cleaning.

The story concludes with the idea that there will always be children to fly with Peter. Eventually the children grow up and have their own children but Peter will always come back for someone. Peter is the only boy who can never grow up.

Aging

"All children, except one, grow up" (Barrie, 212) is the very first line of Peter Pan. J.M Barrie has a very unique approach in explaining aging. He uses an exchange between Wendy and Mrs. Darling to show that humans realize they age at the young age of two. Wendy, at the age of two, plucked a flower from her garden and gave it to her mother and her mother's response, "Oh, why can't you remain like this forever! (Barrie, 216)". This was all Wendy needed to hear to understand that she was constantly growing older.

J.M Barrie tells the beginning tales of Peter in *The Little White Bird*. This story is a precursor for *Peter Pan* and introduces Peter Pan, the boy who never grows up. Peter left his parents when he was only a week old. He heard them discussing what he was to be when he grew up and was frightened. After he leaves, he lives in Kensington Gardens with birds and fairies. From this point on, Peter would never age and Barrie describes Peter as being only 'half-human'. This of course referring to the fact that humans age but Peter never would. This sets the stage for all of <u>Peter Pan</u> because Peter's constant fear of aging and becoming a man is seen throughout the book. The Lost Boys are children who also had a fear of growing old and ran away. Yet there are differences between Peter and the Lost Boys because the Lost Boys still show an attachment and desire to have mothers. They often try to recall their mother and father but realize they have forgotten everything about them. They do realize though that they truly long to have a mother and father again. The Lost Boys are not allowed to stay with Peter in Neverland though if they grow up. Peter despises growing old and adults so sends them away if they age.

Peter lives in a pretend world and often they even pretended to eat. Pretending is significant to aging in the story when Peter and Wendy are in the tree house and are pretending to be the Lost Boys' father and mother. Peter enjoys bossing them around and being the captain but after a while he fears that it is not pretend anymore. He asks Wendy if they are just pretending for reassurance that he is not growing older because being a father means you are old.

Another portrayal of the fear of aging is at the end of the book when Peter revisits Wendy for 'spring cleaning' and realizes Wendy is old and has a child of her own. Peter has no idea how much time has truly passed and expected Wendy to fly away with him. Wendy told Peter she was old and Peter was actually afraid to see her. Peter would not embrace Wendy when she went to hug him and Peter went away and cried. His fear of aging is seen perfectly at this point of the book. Throughout there is the sense that he hates grown-ups but this interaction shows he is literally fearful of aging. The concept is a common theme in *The Politics of Being Mortal* where Lasch says that we have an intense fear of old age. Lasch also attributes this to a narcissistic personality, which is one of Peter's main attributes throughout the story.

Immortality

Naturally since Peter never ages the book is also about immortality. There are similarities between May's[3] view on immortality as well as Killilea's[4] views. May argues that immortality does not give lives more meaning because when there is time for everything, nothing matters. Barrie quite often portrays this through characteristics and attributes of not only Peter but the stars as well. Barrie alludes to immortality of the stars in this section:

> "Stars are beautiful, but they may not take an active part in anything, they must just look on forever. It is a punishment put on them for something they did so long ago that no star now knows what it was. So the older ones have become glassy-eyes and seldom speak, but the little ones still wonder (Barrie, 526)."

Stars are essentially immortal compared to the span of human life. Barrie alludes to the alien nature of being immortal by talking about the stars. The stars in <u>Peter Pan</u> take an active role and are not inanimate objects as we see them. Peter regularly talks to the stars and tells Wendy, John and Michael that the stars tell funny jokes. Yet the interaction as the quote says is not active and they can only 'look on forever'. Not only can they not engage actively but also the old stars have been around so long that they do not even care to talk. This idea fits well with negative impressions on immortality and how undesirable living forever truly is. Barrie also says how the stars are being punished which also points to the undesirability of being immortal. The difference between the old and young stars is also interesting. The older stars have been around longer and cannot find meaning yet the younger stars are still hopefull and interested in their surroundings. This reflects May's idea that if you are aware you are immortal it is different than if you are not aware.

Peter is also a representation of a person who is immortal without further age progression. Barrie represents Peter in a similar light to May's argument that since a person has time for everything nothing really matters. Peter often forgot people and his adventures because he has no concept of time and nothing in particular matters to him in profound ways. May also argues that virtues are undermined because there is a lack to care about what others impressions of you are. Peter is described as narcissistic, conceited, and cocky often throughout the book. He lacks and undermines virtues, such as respect for others, even to those whom he has a seemingly strong relationship with. Peter shows the most respect for Wendy because she is a girl but he soon forgets her and busies himself with other adventures.

May also argues that immortality will weaken personal relationships. Personal relationships are inhibited because there is a lack of meaning in life, which translates into a lack of meaning in relationships. Immortals will be less willing to work at relationships so they will be less serious, spurious and less sacrifices will occur for the relationships to last. Again, Peter fits this negative description perfectly. While flying to Neverland, the children often fell asleep over water and Peter would wait until the last moment to save them. Barrie describes Peter's actions as merely taken to impress the others and to show-off; rather than being done to save a human's life. During the flight to Neverland, Peter often asked the children who they were because he had already forgotten. Peter did not care for human relationships and friendships. Even the Lost Boys and Darling children in Neverland forgot previous relationships. The Darling children could only scarcely remember their own parents without Wendy prodding them to remember and recollect their names and images from home. Since immortals live forever there is no connection to time and a sense of urgency to connect with others and make worthwhile relationships with family and friends.

Relationships

Alluded to in the previous section, relationships in Peter Pan are fairly weak and do not last long. The Lost Boys forgot about their parents. The only remnant of even having parents is by one Lost Boy who says he can remember his mother wanting a checkbook. Again, in Neverland there is a disconnect between real relationships and pretend ones. Two of the Lost Boys are twins and neither of them recall their parents. Peter does not understand the genetic bond the twins have with each other and refuses to acknowledge they are brothers and share a common history. Neverland is not about family and relationships.

Captain Jas Hook also reflects the theme that relationships matter. Killilea's core idea is that life is significant because humans have the power to give life to others. No one in Neverland had children (Peter and Wendy only pretended the Lost Boys were their children). Captain Hook realizes that no children love him. As a pirate, children fear him, but after capturing Wendy and the Lost Boys he dwells on this fact for a short while. Captain Hook has no children of his own and he knew he would someday die. Hook had never previously thought of the fact that no children loved him made him upset. But being close to the end and in constant fear that the crocodile would soon catch him, Hook began to find sadness in this seemingly simple fact. Perhaps, Barrie would agree with Killilea that having children love you gives life meaning.

Relationships between Peter and others are quite strange. As discussed earlier, he often forgot the Lost Boys names and even to visit Wendy once a year for 'spring cleaning'. Yet the most critical point of Peter's lack of bond between others comes at the very end of the book when Wendy is grown up and recollecting adventures with Peter. Wendy asks how Tinker Bell is and Peter cannot seem to remember her at all. He not only forgot how close their relationship was but he did not care that he had forgotten her. Peter says there are plenty of other fairies and they always come and go. Peter also forgets Captain Hook. The two were mortal enemies for a long time and in killing Hook Peter saved Wendy and the Lost Boys. Peter not only forgot but he carelessly states "I forget them after I kill them" (Barrie, 2895). This shows the utter lack of compassion Peter has towards anyone because he is disconnected from the human race. Peter does not put the importance of relationships in his mind like mortal humans.

Dying

Death is one of the main themes throughout the entire book. Although some of the discussions of death are trivial and only mentioned here and there, the undertone of the book is one of death and dying. The crocodile perfectly represents this undercurrent theme. The crocodile swallowed a clock that constantly ticks and is chasing after Captain Hook. This clock represents the imminence of death to Captain Hook both figuratively and literally. Hook is very fearful of the crocodile, which makes Hook a good representation of the average mortal man. The interesting part about Hook and the clock is that towards the end of Hook's life, in a fight with Peter, the ticking stops before Hook is killed to spare him the knowledge. Even without the knowledge of his death being so near, Hook "went quite content to the crocodile"(Barrie, 2637). An acceptance of death and being happy with the life you have lived makes death easier to cope with. The line shows that despite the fact that Hook was afraid of dying throughout the entire book, in the end he was perfectly happy in dying. This shows us that we should not concern ourselves with worrying about our own deaths our entire life. We know we will eventually die, and dying happy is the key thing to worry about. For Hook, dying by upholding his good form seemed good enough for him.

Another more general theme of death in the book is how unfair it is. Barrie introduces a theme of unfairness that all people encounter in their lives. Peter encounters this in Mermaid lagoon when fighting Hook and is stabbed by him in a duel. The feeling made Peter feel helpless. Barrie says that the most difficult task is getting over your first unfairness. A person is never the same after they encounter it but they do live on. Peter frequently encountered unfairness but he often forgot about it, which allows his innocence, or perhaps ignorance, of the important things in life to continue. In this particular instance though, Peter 'grows up' before he forgets the unfairness. He realizes that he may die on the rock from the rising tide and states "to die would be an awfully big adventure" (Barrie, 1736). Again through this line Barrie shows that death is not the final obstacle in our lives and we should not fear it. Captain Hook died content and Peter was also ready to die happy. Barrie also shows that unfairness is a fact of life that will shape and mold us as humans but we should not solely dwell on them but rather, 'grow up' and become stronger.

Despite Peter having the previously mentioned epiphany about death and dying, he is essentially immortal so forgets. Therefore Peter does not really care about killing other humans. In fact, he becomes angry when Wendy and the Lost Boys leave and starts to breathe heavily; In Neverland, as legend has it, every time you breathe a grown-up dies. Peter was scornful and purposefully breathing as hard and fast as he could. Peter's unnatural tendencies come through often when dealing with others dying. He generally does not care for others, only himself.

Character Analysis and What's Important in Life

Smee, Captain Hook's first mate, is quite possibly the only character that has a concept of death. Neverland has a never-ending circle of feuds and fights between the Lost Boys, pirates, Redskins and animals. Barrie talks about the cyclic nature of the society when first describing Neverland. Death on Neverland is very trivialized, especially by Peter.

Yet Barrie introduces a character with a genuine connect to human life, Smee. Upon first being introduced to the character, Smee is described as wiping his glasses after he kills someone, rather than wiping the blood from his sword. All the other pirates have no care for human life and take human lives' with ease and a lack of moral concern. Even the Lost Boys see killing as a game, or adventure rather than something that is wrong.

The fact that Smee recognizes the preciousness of life allows him to recognize his own mortality. He exchanges thoughts on death with Captain Hook and says "some day, the clock will run down" (Barrie, 1131). Of course Smee is talking to Hook about the crocodile but there is still the sense that Smee is Barrie's way of alluding to the metaphor that everyone's life is a ticking clock that will soon run out.

Mr. Darling is very similar to Ivan Ilyich and his encounter with death and figuring out what is important in life. Mr. Darling had no real sense of the importance in life. He concerned himself with stocks, his job, and making sure other respected him. As previously discussed, the birth of his children became more of a financial obstacle than a personal enjoyment. Mr. Darling was very concerned with trivial, materialistic things at the onset of the book. He even got Nana the dog to be a nanny because all the other neighbors had nannies. Yet Mr. Darling was fearful of what his neighbors thought about a dog being their nanny because he was concerned with his image and position in society. Ivan was very similar in these aspects. He was constantly pushing himself away from familial relationships and obsessing over his status at work and in the community.

Both characters had a turning point though which came towards the end of the books. Of course Ivan was faced with his own death and realized the importance of living a life for the happiness oneself and not society (Tolstoy 1886). Mr. Darling was not faced with death, but rather the disappearance of his children. He was sad that his children were gone but not as much as Mrs. Darling. Mr. Darling did not discover how much his children truly meant to him until his children returned. Wendy told the Lost Boys they might be adopted by the Darlings. When Wendy asked, Mr. Darling took them all in. He did not concern himself over how much each extra child would cost and he actually broke down in tears of happiness to see all the love and compassion he was surrounded by. This is a stark difference from the Mr. Darling the reader was introduced to in the beginning and shows that relationships are important when accepting death and living life to the fullest.

The Lost Boys have a moment as well where they realize what is truly important in life. They are happy pretending in Neverland but ultimately make the decision to leave with Wendy, John and Michael. The decision to grow-up and have a relationship with real parents was an important moment for the Lost Boys. The decision to grow-up is also the point where the boys accept they will age, and ultimately die; something Peter could never accept or do which is why he chose to stay in Neverland.

Other characters have a moment of accepting death and discovering the meaning of life as well. Peter and Wendy pretend they are husband and wife and have children. Despite their interactions being more of a game, their feelings towards the situation are quite real. Peter tells Wendy that coming home and listening to her stories with the children near the fire is the best part of his day. Wendy too enjoys this and loves motherhood. Although Peter tends to forget occurrences quickly, this is another moment where Peter realizes relationships are important in life and add worthwhile meaning to life's mundane obligations.

Wendy is a character that consistently understood throughout the story that relationships are important. The reason she left her parents was because she cared for boys she had never met who were without mothers. Wendy reminds the boys constantly that Neverland is just pretend and that they have mothers and fathers who love them. Ultimately, the book ends with Wendy having her own child. Motherhood and the formation of family bonds is important to Wendy and most people as well.

Tinker Bell shows the importance of caring relationships too. She is extremely devoted to Peter throughout the story. She was willing to sacrifice herself to save Peter in the end. Dying to save someone else is the ultimate sacrifice a mortal human (or fairy) can make. Peter also made this sacrifice for Wendy in Mermaid Lagoon. The kite was only able to carry one of them to safety and Peter did not think twice. He felt that Wendy should be saved over him. Ultimately, the bird would sacrifice her eggs and nest to save Peter. Again, there is a constant theme of sacrifice and caring for others in Peter Pan, which shows the importance in life.

The relationship between Peter Pan and Captain Hook is extremely interesting. The two reflect a classic protagonist/antagonist relationship; each represents each other's fears. Peter is afraid of growing up and aging and Hook is grown up and Peter sees him as evil. On the flip side, Hook fears dying an unlived proper life and is envious of Peter's youth. Before Hook dies though, he realizes Peter is not someone to envy. Peter does not know his true self because he always pretends and lies to impress himself and others. Hook was concerned with living a proper life of 'good form' and when he realizes Peter has and never will lead such a life he dies a happy man. Hook accepts his fate and in the end Barrie shows that Hook is really the character to envy; "Misguided man though he was, we may be glad,...that in the end he was true to the traditions of his race" (Barrie, 2626).

This theme of accepting we will die and living life anyway was common in our course as well as Peter Pan. Barrie showed throughout the story that relationships are important to living a good fulfilling life. Reading the book and looking for deeper meaning helped me work through these themes that were constantly appearing throughout the semester. Peter Pan is not just a story about a boy who can fly that every child wishes to be. Peter Pan is really the story of accepting that aging and dying are natural. With this knowledge, we should seek meaningful relationships with others to make our short lives complete.

References

Barrie, J.M. (1911). *Peter Pan*. The Modern Library New York; Kindle Edition

Barrie, J.M.(1902) *The Little White Bird*. Kindle Edition.

Killilea, Alfred (1988). *The Politics of Being Mortal*. The University Press of Kentucky

May, Todd (2009) *Death (The Art of Living)*. Acumen Publishing

Tolstoy, Leo (1886). *The Death of Ivan Ilyich*. Penguin Red Classic edition, 2006

Albom, Mitch (1997) *Tuesdays With Morrie*. Broadway Books

Endnotes

[1] She would later tell Mr. Darling that she saw the boy and had the shadow but this is only after the pair realize their children are missing.

[2] The citations represent location numbers in Kindle.

[3] May, Todd *Death*

[4] Killilea, Al *Politics of Being Mortal*

III. TERRORISM AND THE CALL TO DIE

CHAPTER FIVE

The Duty of Death

Elizabeth Toppi

This essay focuses on one specific type of terrorist: the Islamic jihadist. This paper asserts that religion predetermines the individual's view concerning life and death and this idea, in the case of the Muslim jihadist, has proved to be overwhelmingly destructive. This chapter investigates the Muslim understanding of life and death through the dictation of Islam. The distinction between the Muslim and the Muslim jihadist are explored along with the jihadist's beliefs on afterlife. Lastly, the paper explains how one can place one's faith in humanity as opposed to a religion and how this perspective conflicts with the most basic assumptions of Islam.

It was July 7, 2005, a day just like any other at King's Cross subway station in London. In the midst of the usual hustle and bustle there were four young men carrying backpacks who would later be identified as the suicide bombers that killed themselves and 52 others.

Born in England and raised by his Pakistani Muslim immigrant parents, school teacher Mohammed Sidique Khan was one of the four bombers. Al Jazeera, an international news network originally located on the Arabian Peninsula, ran a chilling tape of Khan in September of the year prior. The subway bomber declared, "We are at war, and I am a soldier... Our words are dead until we give them life with our blood" (CQ Researcher, 7). The "war" he speaks of is the global *jihad*.

A jihad is a holy war fought by Islamic extremists. There has been a steady stream of hundreds of assaults on Americans and their allies as a result of the jihadists' efforts to cleanse the world of "evil." London's subway bombing is only one incident among many attacks and attempted attacks of terrorism after September 11th, 2001 and the collapse of the World Trade Centers. There have been over 100 major post 9/11 terrorist incidents in Pakistan, Afghanistan, Iraq, Israel, Turkey, Indonesia, Spain, Great Britain, Morocco, Kenya, Chechnya, and Russia. The attacks of jihadists are considered as terrorism.

"Terrorism is violence or the threat of violence conducted by private individuals and non-state organizations against the combatant civilian population for the explicit purpose of the targeted population" (Turner, 17). The goals of a terrorist can vary from simply seeking revenge to more strategic efforts to use fear as a catalyst to destabilize a government. In this paper, I will focus on one specific group of terrorists: the Islamic jihadist. I will thoroughly confer how Muslims understand the concepts of life and death through the dictation of Islam. I will discuss the distinction between the Muslim and jihadist and provide a detailed explanation of the terrorists' view on death and the afterlife. This paper asserts that religion predetermines the individual's beliefs concerning life and death. In the case of the jihadist, this idea has proved to be overwhelmingly destructive. My current perspective on the issues conflicts with the most basic assumptions of Islam, and therefore I place my faith in humanity above everything else.

An Islamic jihadist's fundamental claim is that he is fighting the ungodly in the name of God, basing himself on the holy word of God as written in the Koran (CQ Researcher, 8). If a Muslim is "godly" and that Muslim is fighting the "ungodly," one might assume the "ungodly" are non-Muslims. This may be true today, but the origins of jihad began with a conflict among the different classes of Muslims; the conflict originated between Muslims themselves, not between Muslims and non-Muslims.

Supplementary to the Koran, jihadists look to Ibn Taymiyyah, their spiritual forefather. Ibn Taymiyyah was a religious scholar, born in the mid 13th century of what is today Iraq. He advocated for rebelling against the invading Mongols even though the Mongols had converted to Islam, on the grounds that they were not true Muslims. Taymiyyah's treatment of the Mongols illustrates what contemporary scholars believe to be the key to the jihadist worldview: not all Muslims are true Muslims.

Taymiyyah was writing at a time when Islam had already been around 600 years. Islam had sprung rapidly throughout the Middle East when the Prophet Mohammed was born in the city of Mecca (in today's Saudi Arabia) in approximately A.D. 570. Mohammed was visited by the angel Gabriel and started to preach shortly thereafter. Mohammed overcame opposition from other tribal leaders and established the new religion of *Islam*, translating to "submission to God" (CQ Researcher, 9).

When Mohammed died the powerful ruling class (called the Umayyad) and Mohammed's cousin, Ali ibn Abi Talib, disputed over who should be in power. After the assassination of his Umayyad predecessor, Ali finally became *Caliph*, leader of religion and state. These events intensified the conflict and civil war ensued. Ali's followers were known as his "Shiah" who are the ancestors of today's Shiites. They were the minority. The Umayyads were the ancestors of today's Sunnis and were the majority, returning to power when Ali was assassinated in A.D. 661. The Shiites status as an oppressed minority and the Sunnis power as the majority date back to these 7th century events, marking the origins of jihad.

Jihadists do not recognize that Sunnis and Shiites are both Muslim; they are not recognized as equal. Jihadists do not maintain the respect for Jews, Christians, Zoroastrians, and Hindus (collectively known as the "People of the Book") like the Sunnis and Shiites do as commanded by traditional Islam; therefore they are not recognized as equal. Being the strangers to equality that they are, Jihadists detest everything the Western world stands for: liberty, freedom, and justice for all. The reason Islamic jihadists attack the West is because, in their culture and their minds, we are the epitome of "ungodly."

There are a multitude of distinctions between the jihadist and civilian of the western world. Equality is only one example of these differences. The role of religion in our lives and the value we assign to life are also prominent differences. Perhaps most perplexing is the disparity in perspectives on the subject of death.

The Muslim religion of Islam is not a new religion. For a fifth of the world's population, Islam is both a religion and a complete way of life. Muslims follow a religion of peace, mercy, and forgiveness and the majority of believers have nothing to do with the extremely grave events which have come to be associated with their faith. Though all Muslims share these beliefs on life and death, not all Muslims are terrorists. It is imperative to understand this distinction between the jihadist and the Muslim: although all jihadists are Muslims not all Muslims are jihadists.

All Muslims believe that their present life on earth is merely a trial in preparation for the next realm of existence. They lay so much emphasis on the belief in life after death that even a slight doubt in it renders the denial of God. The Koran very clearly says that the disbelievers have no sound basis for their denial of life after death.

And they say, "There is not but our worldly life; we die and live [i.e. some people die and others live, replacing them] *and nothing destroys us except time." And they have of that no knowledge; they are only assuming. And when Our verses are recited to them as clear evidences, their argument is only that they say, "Bring [back] our forefathers, if you should be truthful." Say, "God causes you to live, then causes you to die; then He will assemble you for the Day of Resurrection, about which there is no doubt," but most of the people do not know.* (Koran, 45:24-26)

They believe God has His own plan. There will be a day when the world ends and all the believers will be resurrected to stand before God. That day will be the beginning of a life that will never end; that day is when every person will be rewarded by God according to the individual's life on earth. The Day of Resurrection will be the day when God's attributes of justice and mercy will be in full manifestation. Those who suffered in their life on earth for the sake of God will be replenished in their afterlife and will live in eternal bliss. But those who shunned God in their lives on earth, caring nothing for the life to come, will be in the most miserable state for all of eternity. Drawing a comparison between them, the Koran states:

Then is he whom We have promised a good promise which he will meet [i.e. obtain] *like he for whom We provided enjoyment of worldly life* [but] *then he is, on the Day of Resurrection, among those presented for punishment in Hell.* (Koran, 28:61)

The Koran also states that this worldly life is a preparatory step for the eternal life after death. According to this holy book, some unfortunate people become slaves of their passions and desires, and mock virtuous and God-conscious persons. These poor souls are the ones who realize their mistake at the time of their death, and by then it is too late. They wish to be given another chance to be more "godly" but are denied. If they had fully believed in life after death the way the Koran prescribed then they would have been guaranteed an entrance to eternal bliss and would have contributed in the effort to make the world full of peace and happiness.

Muslims believe that the present life is only a trial preparation for the next realm of existence. When a Muslim dies, he or she is washed, usually by a family member, wrapped in a clean white cloth, and buried with a simple prayer. Muslims consider this one of the final services they can do for their relatives, and an opportunity to remember their own brief existence here on earth. The Prophet Mohammed taught that three things can continue to help a person even after death; charity which he had given, knowledge which he had taught and prayers on their behalf by a righteous child.

Muslims always have religion on their minds, and make no division between secular and sacred. They believe that the Divine Law, the *Shari's,* should be taken very seriously. This is opposed to some parts of the Western world, where religion does not dominate everyday life. The most significant difference between a Muslim and an extremist, or jihadist, is how they react to those who do not believe in their faith. The Islamic jihadist believes it is his duty to act violently against the non-believers to prove his love and devotion to *Allah,* the God of Islam.

Like the school teacher Khan, Mohammed Atta was another man who only in retrospect, after the attack on the World Trade Center, looked suspicious. There was a letter to the hijackers found in Atta's luggage that was left in a car at Logan Airport. Religious theorists and political scientists who translated the letter from Arabic described the letter as a collection of rituals. "The purpose of the letter and mandated rituals...was to transform a young Muslim into a warrior, instilling spiritual motives that create inner peace, fearlessness, obeisance, and lack of feeling during the killing" (Stein, 7). Rather than the letter expressing a message of raging hate to induce adrenaline, it was more like an instruction manual written by a wise father guiding his sons in the steps they are to take on a mission of great importance (Stein, 7). It reminded the men how the task laying before them demanded their attentiveness and most importantly their devoted adherence to God.

The tone of the letter was beyond hatred. "Absurdly and perversely, it is about love," says Stein (Stein, 8). The letter reads to the men: *Everywhere you go say that prayer and smile and be calm, for God is with the believers. And the angels protect you without you feeling anything...you should feel complete tranquility, because the time between you and your marriage [in heaven] is very short.* The "marriage" the letter speaks of is in reference to the relationship between God and his sons; the men will kill for their love of God.

The jihadist is programmed to believe there is a smooth passage from life to death, either by loss of self of by "well-intentioned" killing, a "marriage" of love and murder. Because the terrorists have adopted such a state of mind, the perception of the lines of love and murder are blurred. What Americans and the Western world generally views as horrible, hateful actions are pure acts of devotion to the terrorist. "What we have here is martyrdom that is murderous; military that is sacralized; a symbiotic, simultaneous killing and dying, where approaching intimacy with God the father requires being one with one's victims, 'marrying' them in death and destruction" (Stein, 25). The language of the letter points the terrorist to a transcendent mystical experience that advances him closer to his goal: the afterlife (Stein, 25).

Sheikh Ahmed Yassin, the Hamas leader who inspired the suicide bombers' attack in the state of Israel, exclaimed, "Love of martyrdom is something deep inside the heart. But these rewards are no in themselves the goal of the martyr. The only aim is to win Allah's satisfaction. That can be done in the simplest and speediest manner by dying in the cause of Allah" (Stein, 30). Yassin's words illustrate how terrorists are immersed in a state of total alienation. The outer world is just a "thing" and the letter instructs: *Completely forget something called "this world"* [or "this life"] (Stein, 31).

Death to a terrorist fighting in the name of Islam is much different from the death the majority of Westerners are familiar with. Death, to us, is the irreversible end to one's life. We attach dark and ominous images to the thought of dying. Whether or not individuals in our society believe in an afterlife they still attach some weight of significance to their own deaths - just as they do their lives. A terrorist does not; he makes no distinction between his life on earth and his death. He assigns them the same value (or lack there of) and assumes they are merely two obstacles he will face before "real" life. This "real" life is immortal life.

"The words that describe this transition into the 'real (immortal) life' in God's paradisiacal lap convey the heady, intoxicating taste of omnipotence" (Stein, 31). Assuring the terrorists that it is only a matter of a few more moments and actions that remain to be done, the letter insists: *The time to play is over and the serious time is upon us* (Stein, 32). This excerpt from the letter indicates that real existence is yet to come and the group has almost reached it. The terrorists visualize the approaching future and await their rebirth: *...Because the time between you and your marriage* [in heaven] *is very short. Afterwards begins the happy life, where God is satisfied with you, and external bliss* (Stein, 33).

These terrorists view life on earth as inferior and wasteful and the passage to the desired "real" life as nearly painless. The letter states: *And be sure that it is a matter of moments, which will then pass, God be willing, so blessed are those who win the great reward of God* (Stein, 33). Along with the passage between the two lives being painless, it is fearless as well: *...For the believers will not fear such things as their* [the enemy's] *equipment and gates and technology* (Stein, 34). It is only "the others" who experience pain and fear.

This is why the suicide bomber driving the truck which devastated the American Embassy in October 1983 smiled at the Marine Guard of the Embassy Gate on his way into the compound. He had no pain and no fear; his smile was the *bassamat-al-farah*: the "smile of joy." The *bassamat-al-farah* is worn by martyrs at the time of martyrdom because of Allah's promise of merit to come.

Being a product of Western culture, my beliefs concerning life and death have evolved by the countless contributions of other people. Currently, what I believe about life and death is in opposition to the beliefs of a Muslim and of a jihadist. However, what I *want* to (and used to) believe is similar to the most basic beliefs of a Muslim, yet conflicting to the jihadist. I was raised in a traditional Italian-American,

Roman Catholic atmosphere with Catholicism playing a huge role in my family's life. My religious views have swayed back and forth, most recently due to the captivating discussion we have in this class. I would only be pretending if I said I knew exactly where I stand on the issues of religion, life and death.

Upon entering high school, I went to church every weekend with my parents and sister, sometimes even my grandparents, aunts, and cousins. I said a prayer when I woke up in the morning and before I went to bed at night. I believed without question that Jesus was the Son of God and one day I would meet him in heaven where I would spend all of eternity in happiness.

In order to meet Jesus in heaven, I would first have to make it to heaven. This meant that I would have to live my life on earth as a follower of God. If I wanted to go to heaven I needed to abide by the Ten Commandments and thus live my life as "godly" as I could. This belief is similar to that of a Muslim's because we both essentially agree that there is a God and there is an afterlife. We both agree that the afterlife is where we will find eternal happiness.

Although Christianity and Islam are practiced mainly in separate areas of the world, they are not as different as one might assume. Their origins are identical; they begin with the same understanding of Abraham and Moses. Along with Judaism, Christianity and Islam are the first *monotheistic* religions. *Monotheism* is derived from the Greek *monos*, meaning "alone" and "only." It means to believe in one and only one God. This is opposed to *polytheism*; the belief in many gods. The word *Koran* itself is derived from the Arabic root word *Qurrah* which means to collect, implying that the Prophet Mohammad collected the content of the Koran from other sources, such as the Old Testament of the Jews and the New Testament of the Christians.

According to these religions, our chief task on earth is to be transformed into persons capable to accept and requite God's love while doing God's will. If the individual succeeds, he will be raised up into everlasting life at the moment of his death. In order to succeed, the Christian follows the Bible and the teachings of Jesus and the Muslim follows the Koran and the Five Pillars of Islam.

Because of the history of the religions, it makes it easy to understand why my Catholic views on life and death are aligned with a Muslim's view. The Catholic standpoint I had prior to high school are the views I *want* to believe. I say this because, due to many events since then, I no longer believe in all that I once did. I do not disagree with everything, but I dissent from the majority of what the Catholic Church professes. I consider myself a Christian whose faith rests in humanity.

The intricate details of my views are not stable; they are apt to change even after the most negligible occurrences in my life. Keeping my oscillating opinions and stagnant indecision in mind, I currently believe there is no afterlife. I do not believe in "God the Father, the Almighty, maker of heaven and earth, of all that is seen and unseen," as stated in the Apostles Creed that I had memorized by the age of 7. I almost feel guilty announcing it, but: I need more proof; I need hard evidence. A major factor that impacted my dissatisfaction with Catholicism was my "loss of innocence." As I got older, I began to realize just how unsettling the world really was and while it was comforting to believe in a higher power and look forward to an afterlife promising eternal bliss, I began to realize that is all it was: comforting. "Comfort" was at best the only aspect of "believing" that was definite. These views I currently support completely contradict the views of the Muslim and the jihadist.

While I *want* to believe what the core principles of Catholicism and Islam preach, an honest self-assessment insists I cannot. I predict my beliefs about life and death will continue to evolve for quite some time, but I must point out that one idea has not changed. Since I can remember I have always believed that harming others was wrong. I have consistently held the position that regardless of an individual's beliefs on life and death and anything else, it is not your right to harm them because of your differences. Whether I still believe whole heartedly in the Catholic faith or choose to dismiss it altogether, this belief will remain.

The jihadist believed in the traditional teachings of Islam but interprets them in a slightly different way than the majority of practicing Muslims. They cannot dismiss "evil" when they see it, so they must fight. Backing down or ignoring it is not an option. So, in the name of Allah, they pursue mass murder plots against innocent populations in every corner of the planet. Islamic terrorists also credit their motivation and success to their religion, as exemplified by the following quote from Osama bin Laden in May, 1998:

> *I am one of the servants of Allah. We do our duty of fighting for the sake of the religion of Allah. It is also our duty to send a call to all the people of the world to enjoy this great light and to embrace Islam and experience the happiness in Islam. Our primary mission is nothing but the furthering of this religion.*

The terrorist does not care about the wellbeing of anyone else but himself. He masks this selfishness by claiming he is acting out of his love for God. In the following quote from Abu Musab al-Zarquawi, a Sunni terrorist known for cutting his captives' throats, depicts a clear image of how atrocious a terrorist's behavior really is:

> *There is no doubt that Allah commanded us to strike the Kuffar (unbelievers), kill them, and fight them by all means necessary to achieve the goal. The servants of Allah who perform Jihad to elevate the word (laws) of Allah, are permitted to use any and all means necessary to strike the active unbeliever combatants for the purpose of killing them, snatch their souls from their body, cleanse the earth from their abomination, and lift their trial and persecution of the servants of Allah. The goal must be pursued even if the means to accomplish it affect both the intended active fighters and unintended passive ones such as women, children and any other passive category specified by our jurisprudence.*

To a society that is troubled by just the acknowledgement of death, the most disturbing thing about a terrorist is his love for death. The terrorist message after the Madrid railway bombing of 2004 exclaimed, "We will prevail because you fear death and we love death" (Killilea, 31). This concept of an assassin embracing death is not new; Machiavelli wrote of it in *The Prince* five hundred years ago. Machiavelli warned against taking property away from civilians because this would instill hatred among the people. Subsequently, this hatred would leave people willing to put aside their own self-interest. If they were willing to set aside their own personal self-interest then they would put aside survival in attempt to conspire against their ruler (Killilea, 32). Machiavelli warned the Prince could not survive a conspiracy against an assassin with no interest in plotting an escape. In modern times, the West is the Prince and the Islamic extremist is the assassin - and this is terrifying.

Jihadists belittle death, perceiving it as merely the final obstacle to a glorious afterlife full of rewards and pleasures for those who die in martyrdom. This is not accepting death but is rather a new form of denying death (Killilea, 34). Similar to fascism, jihadists are molded into an "illusion of immortality and power over death by delivering death to other people" (Killilea, 34). They try to live a perpetual life through the continuous existence of their people. This is true for any group of people who believe in some kind of life after death, including peoples of the Jewish, Catholic, and Buddhist faiths. All Muslims believe in an eternal afterlife, but terrorists do not take death seriously and portray both life and death as cheap and inconsequential.

This idea can be further illustrated by its direct correlation to the popularity of the name "Mohammed" among male Muslims. The Prophet Mohammad made himself immortal and omnipresent among the Muslims by making it obligatory for all his followers have his name as part of their name too. So today we find names like Mohammad Atta, Mohammad Bin Laden, Mohammad Khatami, Mohammad Ali and so on. It is for this reason, that his followers have been termed "Mohammadeans" – the followers of Mohammad, although they do not like this appellation.

My stomach turns just thinking about the devastation Islamic extremists have caused all over the world. I often ponder what a world without religion would be like. I think it would be a better world. Taking the stance of the Liberalist John Locke, I believe people are born with a blank slate. As opposed to Thomas Hobbes, I do not think all humans are naturally evil. Because we are not naturally evil we do not necessarily need religion to point us in the direction of morality. The individuals of a society know what is right and wrong, just and unjust, simply because of common sense and reasonableness. Thanks to religion, one may more commonly associate this principle to what is known as the "Golden Rule:" treat others as you want to be treated. There is no correlation between the effects of that rule and the existence of religion; individuals would still instinctually act towards others the way they wish to be treated. Without religion, the "Golden Rule" is called "reasonableness."

We are all humans and therefore we are all mortal. The common factor of mortality among all humans is what bonds us together as humanity. Yet, this common factor means different things to different groups and this is due to religion. If there were no religion, people would have a better chance to perceive death for what it really is - "really" in regards to unbiased, objective, open-minded personal interpretation. I am not suggesting there is one answer to what death "really" is. Rather I am suggesting that death has been digested and spit out in an incessant cycle of religious interpretation and people have lost the ability to find its meaning within them. Death should be defined by the individual and only the individual; death should be shaped by the individual's interpersonal and intrapersonal experiences, actions, decisions, and thoughts. This is impossible because we do not live in a world absent from religion.

If I could explain what "death" would mean to me in a society free of religion, I would. I obviously cannot do that, for the seeds of religion have spread way before my time and soiled the grounds of my ancestors. I am just as unfamiliar with this fictional, religion-free society as the contemporary self-proclaimed atheist. An atheist does not identify what he or she believes in; rather they specify what they do not believe in. They do not believe in a religion or God. In a world without religion, "religion" and 'God" would not exist and those words would not be in any dictionary. Therefore, "Atheism" would also not exist. I do not believe a modern atheist has the ability to give a personal explanation of what death "really" is because their definition is tainted with the inevitable residue of religion. The atheist's soul is just as fastened to religion as the next person's.

In a world where religion was not invented, there would still be different colors, shapes, and sizes of people; there would still be distinct societies of people. But there would also be a unique aspect: the individual would not be affected by possibilities introduced through preachers, prophets, and popes. This would cut out a critical factor regularly associated to the cause of war. I am not saying this religion-free world would be conflict free; there most assuredly would be problems. However, no society or group of people would be able to justify death under their devotion to "God" to reach their precious eternal afterlife. This would be a world free from jihad, thus free from Islamic terrorists.

The terrorists familiar to our Western world would not be; they would not exist. This is because terrorists are defined by their view on death and the preconceived notions of life and death interpreted through the religion of Islam. There would be no way to read the Koran as an instruction manual for murdering the "ungodly" because this holy book would never have been compiled. No man or women would find justification to harm others to satisfy God. This strife to please God, what we've come to know as *jihad,* would have no base ground because there would be no God promising an afterlife of everlasting paradise.

I am not condemning the religion of Islam, nor am I asserting all the blame for the world's problems on religion. I am expressing how I believe, at best, the only guarantee religion has to offer is comfort. Religion dictates the lives of so many people and consequently has yielded countless positive results. Unfortunately, religion has also produced incalculable atrocities, such as the Islamic extremist.

The Islamic extremist is taught an interpretation of the Koran that orders him to kill anyone who does not believe the same. He must carry out this violence in the name of Allah or else he will not be rewarded in the afterlife. The Islamic extremist is controlled by his desire for the eternal life after death promised by Allah. These jihadists are so adamant about the afterlife that they belittle the lives of those who they believe to be inferior. Those who do not believe in Allah and do not follow the Koran are infidels, and if you are a true Muslim you accept your duty to rid the world of these non-believers. Otherwise, acceptance to the afterlife will not be granted.

I have enough faith in humanity to insist that religion is not to be credited for our ability to be moral, peaceful and happy. We instinctually are civil to one another because reasonableness is embedded in our human nature. In agreement to John Stewart Mills, I believe it shouldn't matter what an individual's stance on life and death is; they should be able to live how they want to live as long as they are not harming others. Certain beliefs concerning life and death do not allow for people to "live and let live," most especially those of the jihadist. Their perspective on death dictates every action they make in their lives and consequently the lives of individuals on the other side of the world. The jihadist's perseverance for reaching eternal life is actually a form of denying death. They do not accept mortality for what it is; rather, they see death as the start of "real" life. If the individual can see death for what it really is then they are able to see life for what it really is. Islamic extremists deny their own mortality, thus alienating them from others. Our mortality cannot be denied if our goal is world peace, for it is only our mortality that fuses all the individuals in the world and creates one humanity.

Bibliography:

Global Issues. Washington, D.C.: CQ, 2007. Print.

Kill ilea, Alfred G. "The Political Impact of Death: A Reappraisal." *Midwest Quarterly* 48 (2006): 29-36. Print.

Quod.lib.umich.edu/k/koran. Tahrike Tarsile Qur'an Inc., 1983. Web. 19 Mar. 2010.

Stein, Ruth. *For the Love of the Father: A Pschoanalytical Study of Religious Terrorism.* Stanford: Stanford UP, 2010. Print.

Taylor, Maxwell. *The Terrorist.* London: Brassey's Defence, 1988. Print.

Thereligionofpeace.com. Yukon Group, 2002-2010. Web. 20 Mar. 2010.

CHAPTER SIX

Palestinian Suicide Bombers

Christopher Turco

Political and religious tensions between Palestine and Israel continue to be a complicated obstacle to peace in the Middle East, as both states have a history of attacking the other. Perhaps most puzzling to observers in the West is Palestinian suicide bombers' willingness to blow themselves up as a means of attacking Israeli soldiers and/or civilians. The following chapter sheds light on this topic by exploring how Palestinian suicide bombers view martyrdom as preferable to life due to their social condition, political position, and Muslim faith. A cinematic representation of Palestinian suicide bombers coupled with interviews of them reveals their social condition to comport with Durkheim's formulation of anomic and altruistic suicide. In conjunction, the high level of Islamic religiosity in Palestine encourages suicide bombers by presenting martyrdom as not just an honorable means of combating Israel, but also as a sure route to heaven.

Imagine the following scenario: A young Palestinian man removes his shirt and straps thirty pounds of crudely designed explosives to his chest, says a prayer, and crosses the border into the neighboring town. He walks into the city and boards a bus filled with women, children, and other civilians going about their daily activities. The young man takes a seat on the crowded bus, trying his best to blend in and not expose the horror pressed firmly against his chest, poised to explode. He closes his eyes with the detonator firmly pressed against his sweaty palm; his heart pounding in his chest is only outpaced by the thoughts racing through his mind. He thinks of his love for his people, Allah, promises of paradise his upcoming death will now fulfill, and the hollow life he has led up until this point- a desperate, blunted existence without any direction or hope for the future, but plenty of perceived humiliation and oppression from Israel. Now however, is his chance to end all of this, to give his life meaning, to help his people, and earn a trip away from the troubles of life to paradise with Allah... Moments later, his depresses the detonator and kills a busload of innocent cilivians. Israelis in town mourn at the sight of such destruction, but right over the boarder the event is jeered in Palestine by those who regard it as another justified retaliation against the enemy.

This type of killing, commonly referred to as terror attacks, is not out of the ordinary in terms of the Israeli and Palestinian conflict. Terrorist attacks in all forms pose a serious threat the civilized world. This text will examine terrorist attacks committed by Palestinians, which is a complex issue involving socio-economic and religious factors. A less frequently analyzed factor underlying this issue is Palestinian suicide bombers' views on death, an issue that needs further consideration.

The central thesis of this text is that Palestinian suicide bombers view death as preferable to life, because of the doctrines of Islam, conflict with Isreal, and the forces of 'amomie" and 'altruism' in Palestininian society. My argument will unfold by first introducing Hany Abu-Assad's film, *Paradise Now*, as an accurate dramatization of the primary factors included in my thesis. This film's factual basis will be bolstered by the work of Professor Jessica Stern, whose book, *Terror in the Name of God*, highlights many insights into the world of Palestinian suicide bombers she discovered in her experiences researching them. Included within this discussion will be quotes from the Koran and terrorist leaders, as they function to support and expand upon what Stern has discovered and the Abu-Assad's film depicts. The work of Emile Durkheim will function as theoretical lens for viewing how peoples' tendency to commit suicide- the absolute acceptance of death- is created and reinforced within a society. Alfred Killilea's book, *The Politics of Being Mortal*, will be drawn upon to explain how the acceptance of mortality can carry with it different implications depending on the context of its acceptance. Lastly, yet most importantly, will be a discussion of how suicide bombers' views on death threaten the security of the civilized world. On this topic, the work of renowned 'Antithiest' Christopher Hitchens will help explain how the founding documents of Islam and the leaders charged with upholding them remain a constant inspiration for terror attacks and a treat to the civilized world.

Hany Abu-Assad is a Dutch-Palestinian film director/writer whose 2005 film *Paradise Now* tells the story of two young Palestinian men- Said and Khaled- who become involved in a terrorist plot to blow up an Israeli bus in Tel Aviv. The film has won a Golden Globe and National Board of Review Award for best foreign language film, and was nominated for an Oscar in the same category. When asked by the American-Arab Anti-Discrimination Committee how he researched the issues and characters to be presented in Paradise Now Abu-Assad said, "I spoke to people who have known suicide bombers, I read researches about suicide bombings from both the Palestinian and the Israeli sides, but the most valuable information I used was from a lawyer, who represents people who 'failed in their mission' and are now in jail" (ADC.org, 2012).

The film's two main characters- Said and Khaled- both have a hard time finding employment, and spend most of their free time sitting around smoking hookah. Neither are interested in sports, reading, or watching films at the local cinema, and at one-point Said laments that his favorite film genre is 'boring', like his life. There is a constant Israeli military presence in their community, complete with the regular sound of bombs exploding and tanks controlling passage in and out of town. The Palestinian people here have relatively no military means to fight what they perceive as an Israeli occupation, and are thus forced to live under its thumb. The quality of life here leaves much to be desired: expensive water filters are necessary to make the water safe to drink, buildings are either crumbling from age or torn apart from violence, and compared to neighboring Tel

Aviv, Israel it looks more like a polluted war zone than a town. People within this community are Muslims with high degree of religiosity, as praise of Allah is present in almost all aspects of life. Said and Khaled, along with the people in their community, view Israel as an oppressive occupier. Those who become martyrs by killing Israelis are treated as fallen heroes. In fact, the video store in town sells and rents videos of martyrs saying their final goodbyes, like the ones eventually made by Khaled and Said (Abu-Assad 2005).

Said's hate for Israel is apparent when he talks about how he and a crowd of demonstrators burned down a cinema to protest Israel's refusal to hire any workers from the West Bank. In this spirit of rejecting inequality, Said concludes, "a life without dignity is worthless." Khaled's hate for Israel is made apparent when he describes why it is his father walks with a limp. He explains that when he was younger, Israeli soldiers broke into his house and asked his father which leg he would like to keep, and subsequently broke the other leg. Khaled later concludes that, "If we(Israelis and Palestinians) cannot live as equals at least we'll die as equals... Let us be equal in death. At least we have Paradise... In this life, we're dead anyway" (Abu-Assad 2005).

The film's plot begins when Said is approached by his long time friend and local teacher Jamal, who informs Said that he is planning to blow up a bus tomorrow in Tel Aviv, Israel, in retaliation for the assassination of a couple of people within his terror group. More importantly, Jamal tells Said that he and Khaled have been chosen to carry out the upcoming terror attack, as they had previously requested. Said says that he is ready if "It's God will." Very pleased to hear of Said's continued commitment, Jamal gives him some words of encouragement from a martyr he knew who used to say: "If you fear death, you're already dead. If you don't, you'll have a sudden and painless death" (Abu-Assad 2005).

In preparation for the upcoming attack in Tel Aviv, Said and Khaled make a farewell video explaining their reasons for what they are about to do. The following is Khaled's explanation:

> In the name of God the Merciful... In his holy book, God says: If you receive a wound, the people have received a similar one. Times like these come to pass so that God can recognize the believers and

choose martyrs. God does not love the unjust'. God speaks the truth. As an answer to the injustice, the occupation(Israel) and its crimes and in order to further the resistance, I have decided to carry out a martyr operation... Israel views partnership with, and equality for the Palestinians, under the same democratic system, as suicide for the Jewish state. Nor will they accept a two-state compromise even though it is not fair to the Palestinians. We are either to accept the occupation forever or disappear.... Israel continues to build settlements, confiscate land, 'judaize' Jerusalem, and carry out ethnic cleansing... Israel [forces] us to accept their solution: that we either accept inferiority, or we will be killed. As a martyr, I am not afraid of death. This is how I will overcome their(Israel) threats and emerge victorious, and over their military and political force. Let me die as a martyr. This is my testimony: There is only one God, and Mohammed is his prophet. God speaks the truth" (Abu-Assad 2005).

While getting ready for the trip to Tel Aviv, Jamal explains to Said that Palestinian people are forced to suffer injustice, and that "Death is better than inferiority," and his actions (terror attacks) will 'change things'. Another man involved in the terror plot, one of Jamal's superiors, explains to Said and Khaled that after they ascend into heaven, everything will be taken care of here on earth, especially the commemoration of their 'heroic act'; they will be the pride and joy of the Palestinian community, and have been chosen because of their courage. Shortly thereafter, Said and Khaled strap a large amount of explosives to their chest, put on clothes that will allow them to blend in, do a lot of praying to Allah, and take a car ride across the border into Tel Aviv (Abu-Assad 2005).

During the car ride into Israel, Said and Khaled are instructed by Jamal to kill as many police and soldiers as possible, and reminds them to "Never forget, the soldier who discovers you is a dead man. He has nothing to gain, because he's afraid of death. If you're not afraid of death, you're in control of life. If he insists on checking you, let him do so at the gates of Paradise." Jamal goes on to tell Said and Khaled that after they blow themselves up, they will be picked up by two angels. At this moment, Said turn to Khlaed and asks if they are doing the right thing, to which Khaled replies, "Of course, in one hour we will be heroes with God in heaven." Jamal tells them to read the Koran and pray if they begin to feel week (Abu-Assad 2005).

After a few complications along the road to Tel Aviv, Said and Khaled finally arrive in what appears to be a different world, in that Israel is clearly a much more prosperous and happier place to live. Once there, Khaled gets cold feet, changes his mind, and calls for a ride back home. Said goes on without him and boards a Tel Aviv bus filled with Israeli soldiers and civilians, where he then blows himself up- along with everyone else (Abu-Assad 2005).

Jessica Stern, a professor at the Kennedy School of Government at Harvard University, has spent time with terrorist groups in the Middle East. Based on her findings, she wrote a book entitled *Terror in the Name of God*, which will function to highlight the factual basis of the film *Paradise Now*.

During one of her interviews with Palestinian authorities, Stern was given a profile of the typical Palestinian suicide bomber, the bulk of which includes the following traits: young man who is mentally immature, he is frustrated by an inability to find work, he has little opportunities for personal betterment and no social safety nets to fall back on, he lacks the personal connections to get into the army, lacks a girlfriend or fiancé, he has no money to spend at the disco to meet girls, has little means of enjoying life so it feels meaningless and boring, marriage and raising a family is too expensive, he has an overwhelming sense of loss, the only refuge he finds from life is in Islam, he frequently attends the local mosque up to five times a day, gradually he is recruited by members of terror groups who notice his plight and devotion to Islam, he is told about the paradise that awaits him in the afterlife if he becomes a suicide bomber, and lastly he is told his family will receive money and fame after he becomes a martyr (Stern, 50-51). Not surprisingly then, scholars have found that the expected benefits of death such as paradise in afterlife and the social status for family for the surviving family members, are some of the primary motivations for suicide bombers (Moghadam, 52).

In this same vein, one Hamas leader named Sheik Younis al-Astal claims that poverty and hardship bring people closer to their religion, and that Islam has been a source of solidarity within the Palestinian community. Moreover, Islam – in its more fundamental form – is an omnipresent aspect of life, and those in power strive to reinforce this (Hedges, 2010). About this, Stern rightfully points out that, "hopelessness, deprivation, envy, and humiliation" certainly make death and subsequently paradise that much more appealing (Stern, 38). Furthermore, suicide bombers in Gaza are canonized as local heroes, with the names of martyrs appearing in some pop song lyrics. In fact, children will often play pretend-suicide-bomber like American kids play cops and robbers (Stern, 53).

Journalist Philip Jacobson has traveled to the Jenin region of the West Bank, where he encountered a refugee camp, in which "about a third of the 40,000 population live in wretched, sweltering squalor". Thus, it does not come as much of a shock to learn the Jenin region is known as the 'capital of Palestinian martyrdom' for its many past suicide attacks against Israel. While at a refugee camp in Jenin, a Palestinian man told Jacobson that, "Every good Muslim understands that it's better to die fighting Israel than live without hope" (Jacobson 2001).

Ironically, the Koran forbids suicide among Muslims, but it does encourage them to become martyrs. About this it says: "Think not of those who are slain in the cause of God as dead. Nay, they are alive in the presence of the Lord and are granted gifts from him" (3:169) (Stern, 52). Stern contrasts this perspective with that of more conventional soldiers, and concludes that conventional soldiers go into battle hoping to avoid death, whereas Palestinian suicide bombers are trying to die. Thus, one can infer that such a person has made a "cost-benefit analysis about the value of his life versus the value of his death," and finds greater value in death (Stern, 52).

The author and neuroscientist Sam Harris has compiled a list of some of the Koran's most provocative quotes on the matter of a violent death being preferable to life. He asserts that, "Anyone who can read passages like those quoted [below] and still not see a link between Muslim faith and Muslim violence should probably consult a neurologist" (Harris, 2011). The following selected quotes by Harris are most relevant to this discussion: "God is the enemy of the unbelievers" (2:98); "Do not say that those slain in the cause of God are dead. They are alive, but you are not aware of them"(2:154); "Those that suffered persecution for My sake and fought and were slain: I shall forgive them their sins and admit them to gardens watered by running streams, as a reward from God; God holds the richest recompense. Do not be deceived by the fortunes of the unbelievers in the land. Their prosperity is brief. Hell shall be their home, a dismal resting place"(3:195-196); (Harris 2011).

These quotes from the Koran present a theme of being rewarded in death for dying in the name of God; a theme that is reflected in Osama bin Laden's fatwa, or declaration of war, published in August of 1996 by a London based newspaper named *Al Quds Al Arabi*. The fatwa's title depicts its messages clearly: "Declaration of War against the Americans Occupying the Land of the Two Holy Places" (PBS, 1996). Although Osama bin Laden *was* not technically a Palestinian suicide bomber, the ideology expressed in his fatwa parallels that of Palestinian suicide bombers and relies on verses from the Koran for justifying violence. The following excerpts from said fatwa sum up quite well bin Laden's message.

About the youths willing to fight Jihad against non-Muslims, bin Laden says "These youths love death as you love life... Our youths believe in paradise after death...[They know that] if is one is to be killed one will die (anyway) and the most honorable death is to be killed in the way of Allah"; "If death is a predetermined must, then it is shame to die cowardly." He goes to great lengths to motivate potential martyrs by pointing out that Allah has said the following about martyrs: "He will guide them and improve their condition [and] cause them to enter the garden-paradise... The best martyrs are those who do not turn their faces away from battle till they are killed. They are in the high level of Janna (paradise)... A martyr will not feel the pain of death except like how you feel when you are pinched". This attempt at temptation goes on to include promises of seventy-two women and large jewel. Lastly, he says, "our women encourage Jihad", in that they recognize that "death is better than life in humiliation!" (PBS, 1996).

Bin Laden asks Muslims around the world to help support other Muslims being 'oppressed in their faith'. Specifically he says, "Your brothers in Palestine...are calling upon your help and asking you to take part in fighting against the enemy...the Americans and Israelis.

They are asking you to do whatever you can, with one owns means and ability to expel the enemy, humiliated and defeated, out of the sanctities of Islam" (PBS, 1996).

Some political scientists view terrorist attacks as simply a political issue, which is to say Jessica Stern's book, *Terror in the Name of God*, erroneously implicates religion as a motivating factor for terrorists. Such a criticism may argue that it is political tension between Israel and Palestine, and not Islam, which inspires acts of terror. Yet even if the ultimate ends of a terror attack are political, religion - in this region of the world being Islam - is still the necessary means of motivating people to commit such acts. The idea of religion being a necessary catalyst for otherwise unspeakable acts is captured in Steven Weinberg's quote that "for good people to do evil, that takes religion" (Weinburg). To attack religion for facilitating violence for political ends, is the same as attacking religion for facilitating dishonesty for greedy ends- 'put a dolla' in da' box. In both examples, religion is being used by one group of people to motivate another group of people to do something illogical, immoral, and/or evil they would not otherwise do, by creating the illusion that what is evil is really justified and rewarded by a higher, unquestionable authority.

Such a criticism of the utility of religion is impervious to the argument that the evils of a small minority of a religion do not negate the good of the majority, because my criticism of religion does not posit it cannot be enacted in a peaceful way by many, but rather that it provides ample opportunity and justification for those interested in committing evil acts in its name. The doctrines of Islam are the object of my criticism, not every group of Muslims, since the actual enactment of the religion does vary greatly amongst Muslims, with some rightfully rejecting, a fundamental interpretation of Islam's doctrines.

When I presented an earlier draft of this paper, my audience tended to fall back on the all too familiar idea that a religion is whatever the interpreter makes of it, whereby Islam is only bad when bad people make it that way. Thus, it's the otherwise good teachings of religion being corrupted by bad people; not otherwise good people being corrupted by the bad teachings of religion.

I disagree with this assumption, and agree with Christopher Hitchens that one can criticize Islam based solely on the violence and barbarism in its founding documents and the actions of those charged with upholding them. Doing so does not discriminate against Islam, because clearly the Bible and Pope have a lot to answer to under this perspective. Rather this perspective is to treats religion as what it is, a written ideology formed during the more primitive, barbaric, and cruel existence of our species- a mindset that embraces faith in the supernatural at the expense of logic and scientific doubt. Religion puts unquestionable authority and justification behind otherwise inhumane acts, and for this reason is something we as a species should outgrow (DanielBerlinTV, 2011). Surely, people can interpret and practice religion in a peaceful and humane manner, yet under certain social conditions like those found in Palestine, the cruel aspects of religion come into full bloom and serve as the sufficient catalyst for violence. Perhaps this point would have come through clearer in my presentation if I had included the following quote from Christopher Hitchens:

> It is to excuse the filthy, vicious forces of Islamic Jihad, to offer any other explanation than it is their[Palestinian suicide bombers'] own evil preaching, their own vile religion, their own racism, their own apocalyptic ideology that makes them think they have the right to kill everyone in this room and go to paradise as a reward (Gregsto, 2011).

Admittedly, this quote does make some error in overlooking the social and political forces *also* motivating Palestinian suicide bombers. To sum up this discussion of Islam's doctrines is a criticism of Islam couched in Marxian criticism of religion: My criticism of Islam has plucked absolute faith in its violent doctrines from the acceptable, so that Palestinian society will reject such doctrines and cultivate a society emancipated from them. Such a society would render the 'sigh of the oppressed creature' no longer violent in its political applications.

Cleary the discussion thus far has shown that Palestinian suicide bombers live in a society in which death is often regarded as preferable to perceived oppression from Israel, and martyrdom is embraced by the numerous Muslim faithful. But, what other factors may motivate a person to commit suicide- the ultimate acceptance of death? The question of why Palestinian Muslims choose to blow themselves up more frequently than the many more peaceful Muslim groups will be examined from the theoretical perspective of Emile Durkheim.

One of Emile Durkheim's greatest contributions to the study of sociology is "the fundamental proposition that social facts are objective," and that 'collective tendencies' have as real an impact on individuals as do 'cosmic forces'. In this way, he treats social facts, or the tendencies of the collective, as having their own distinguishable existence and effect(s) (Durkheim, 343). His theoretical perspective will be used to explain how peoples' tendencies to commit suicide are created and reinforces within a society. Those insights will then be applied to the life of the typical Palestinian suicide bomber.

Durkheim asserts that social forces are "a totality of energies that determine us from outside how to act, in the same way as do the physico-chemical energies that operate on us"(Durkheim, 343). In this way, his writing examines the causes of suicide created by society, rather than focusing simply on the individual; thus generating a novel approach to examining the causes of suicide based societal factors. While we usually view the decision to commit suicide as a private one, irrespective of society's collective tendency to commit such an act, Durkheim's work provides a lens for viewing how a society's collective tendencies towards suicide can influence a person's decision to commit the act. Viewed from the perspective, a person's suicide can be connected to the ethos of his or her society.

In the book, *On Suicide*, Emile Durkheim examines how the rate of suicide varies from year to year within societies. Although he is more interested in explaining fluctuations in the rate of suicide, his conclusions are revelatory in that they turn our attention away from the personal nature of individuals who choose to commit suicide, and redirect our thinking to examine how collective tendencies in a society influence one to commit suicide. In doing so, Durkheim dismisses the relationship of suicide to physical and biological facts as "dubious and ambiguous" (Durkheim, 331).

His analysis finds that each nation or social group has its own unique collective tendency towards suicide, "from which individual tendencies derive," instead of collective tendencies being derived from individual tendencies (Durkheim, 332). A social group's collective tendency is comprised of "the currents of egoism, altruism, and anomie, which operate within the society in question," (Durkheim, 332). These currents are the cause of feelings of 'melancholy', 'renunciation', and/ or 'lassitude' within a society. Thus, a persons' decision to commit suicide results from the tendencies of the collective group (Durkheim, 332).

Unpleasant happenings in one's life, which are often the blame for a suicide, can be inconclusive. This is because the degree to which an unpleasant happening makes someone feel suicidal is set the by the "moral state of society"(Durkheim, 332). Thus, the sadness one may feel after a sad event does come from outside, but not from the event itself, but rather how the event is regarded in one's own social group (Durkheim, 332). "[Suicides then] which at first glance seem to express only personal temperament - are in reality the outcome and extension of a social state to which they give external form" (Durkheim, 331).

Arguably then, the number of suicides in a society will remain constant so long as the social conditions and 'impersonal forces' that produce an inclination to suicide remains the same, not because the number of individuals with a mind prone to suicide remains the same. In short, "the social conditions on which the number of suicides depends are the only ones according to which it can vary" (Durkheim, 357).

Of most importance to this text however, is Durkheim's interest in how a society's level of regulation or knowing how to go on, and its level of integration or sense belonging, can cause its 'normal' rate of suicide to fluctuate. As such, Durkheim lays out four different explanations of why one might commit suicide that are based on a society's levels of regulation and integration. The first explanation of suicide is *Anomic* suicide, which exists on the low end of the regulation spectrum; here, individuals feel as though their lives are directionless and find it hard to know how to go on. On the other end of the regulation spectrum is *Fatalistic* suicide; here, individuals kills themselves because life is unbearably scripted and constraining with little to no opportunity for choice. The third type is *Egoistic* suicide, which exists on the low end of the integration spectrum; here, individuals feel very estranged from their community and have little connection of consequence to society. Lastly, on the high end of the integration spectrum is *Altruistic* suicide; here, individuals almost lose themselves by being overwhelmed with societies beliefs and goals- one lives by the likes of the group and is often encouraged to take one for the team (Durkheim 2006).

These criteria for types of suicide are useful in revealing how the levels of regulation and integration in a society can influence people to commit suicide. For our purposes, Durkheim's *anomic* and *altruistic* concepts of suicide are consistent with Jessica Stern's findings, and the social facts surrounding Said and Khaled.

The social circumstances of these two characters exemplify the traits of a typical Palestinian suicide bomber detailed by Jessica Stern, and are consistent with Durkheim's *anomic* and *altruistic* suicides. Said and Khaled live in a society that is under the thumb of the Israeli military force, and lead lives without much direction. Both men have a hard time finding steady work, are unsure of their future, are plagued by boredom, and feel as though smoking hookah is the highlight of their days. Furthermore, they acknowledge that because their people lack an adequate military force there isn't much they can do to beat back the far superior Israeli army. In short, Said and Khaled feel lost about what to do with their lives and have very little going on in general. Yet, both men are highly integrated into their relatively small society, and believe they must do what it takes to revitalize their home.

In this type of *altruistic* society, Palestinian suicide bombers feel very connected to their community and aspire to do what it takes to achieve the goals of the collective via personal sacrifice. Killing oneself for the betterment of the whole is viewed collectively in such societies as a way to give one's life meaning and some direction, however briefly. Thus, people like Said and Khaled find martyrdom to be preferable to life.

One could argue that it is not *anomie* and *altruism* in Palestinian society that leads to such a high rate of suicide bombings, but rather *fatalism*. Arguably, since Palestine has a far weaker military capability than Israel, their citizens are scripted to assume suicide bombings are their own choice. For example, Said thought blowing himself up was his only line of offense, or he might call it defense, and in fact he says the unevenness between his people's military and the Israelis' will only be balanced when "my life becomes a weapon" (Abu-Assad 2005).

However, I do not think Durkheim would categorize Palestinian suicide bombers as *fatalistic*. Rather, I think he would refute this assertion by arguing that these individuals live in a society that is so low on the spectrum of regulation (*anomie*) that they are almost beginning to come full circle, and literally in turn, are pointing towards *fatalism*. This is to say, these individuals live in a society in which meaning, direction, and purpose are so low that suicide bombings have become a popular means of creating meaning, direction and purpose (avoiding anomie). It is not because the moral constitution of their society leaves them no other choice but to blow themselves up (Khaled felt as though he had other options), but rather their lives are so *anomic* that committing a suicide bombing is a way of pushing back against what is perceived to be the source of their *anomie*. For example, if Said and others like him feel as they are "dead already", then they might as well become actually dead by blowing themselves up; here at least society will find in the narrative of their life some meaning and purpose. Combine this collective tendency with a highly integrated society (*altruism*), in which suicide bombings are encouraged as a noble act of taking one for the team, and it's easier to understand why people like Said strap on some explosives.

Lastly, the high level of regulation needed for *fatalistic* suicide is not present in the lives of the typical Palestinian suicide bomber described by Stern and *Paradise Now*. Both portray lives that lack many things, which by way of social forces regulate one's life: steady employment, wife, children, allegiance to a military, dismal police force, and day-to-day obligations in general.

On another note, if the world is going to transform these societies with high rates of suicide bombings then loads of tanks and bombs are not going to do the trick. Powerful nations like the United State need not flex their military might, but rather their economic strength. If opportunities for jobs, education, and general prosperity were injected into these societies then perhaps they would be less *anomic*, and their people would feel like though their lives had goals and direction. Acts of terror may then be discouraged in such a society not just because young men lose their lives, but also because they dampen present and future economic growth opportunities with other nations. Furthermore, the impressive *altruism* such societies exhibit could be utilized for national growth rather than encouraging acts of terror.

Getting back to the central theme, which is suicide bombers' views on death, it is now clear that how society treats death and the implications thereof, depends on the nature of religion of the society in question. For instance within American culture, a greater acceptance and expanded dialogue about death would most likely be consistent with Alfred Killilea's writing on the subject. He posits: "Rather than threatening to deprive of life all meaning, death deepens an appreciation of life and the capacity of every person to give life to others" (Killilea, 148). Also, "More open attitudes toward death in our society can serve as a catalyst for a wider acceptance of the social values of equality and community" (Killilea, 13). However, the acceptance of death within the current Palestinian society seems to inspire violence instead solidarity, solidify religious tensions instead of erode them, and lessen the meaning of life rather than increase it.

Said, and all of the countless number of people his life represents, is an example of how a greater acceptance of death can be destructive rather than constructive. His anomic and altruistic society, draped in Muslim faith, positions death to be a relief from the humiliation, depression, and meaninglessness he experiences on a daily basis. Death in Palestinian society is believed to be a ticket from the struggles on earth to eternal salvation in the after-life, if one is willing to become a martyr, of course. Thus, a greater acceptance of death, or rather an increase in the pre-existing willingness to commit suicide in Palestinian society would lead to more violence against civilians and increased tensions between Israel and Palestine. Yet, increased martyrdom, and the increased acceptance of death this necessitates, could function as a means of greater solidarity within the Palestinian community.

One may argue that Palestinian suicide bombers do not truly accept death, by looking past all of its implications, ie the suffering of grieving loved ones. However, this is not the case. Palestinian suicide bombers spend a great amount of energy contemplating the implications of their death, which is why notions of rewards in the after-life, fame within their community, and videos left behind for loved ones are common to almost all of these martyrs. The idea that Palestinian suicide bombers are not actually facing the real implications of death and simply looking past them at something else is an argument one cannot falsify. Considering the implications of death within a society are culturally dependent and the implications for the individual rest on personal beliefs, any account of the *true* implications of death will be inherently ethnocentric and personally biased by one's cultural values and personal convictions, thus there is no concrete rubric for the *true* implications of death. If someone truly believes that death via a suicide bomb will deliver him to paradise in the after-life, then to this person those are the *true* implications of death- a conviction that, although lamentable, cannot be disproved.

One could argue that the belief in the after-life negates an acceptance of death, because such a belief implies a continuation of life in some way. So then, what does it mean to die, and to accept one's death? I think it is fine to assume dying means leaving one's earthy body. Surely, the idea of an after-life presupposes that one must first die. Furthermore, leaving one's earthly body (the conventional concept of death) includes leaving behind all projects and relationships, forever- the very essence of death.

Also, one could argue that suicide is not a true acceptance of death because it removes the mystery of when it will happen. Yet, how is passively waiting for death more of an acceptance of it than proactively thrusting it upon one's self. Surely, living life constantly stalked by death and the mystery of its arrival is part of the human condition, but purposefully turning to embrace death is a paramount condition of acceptance reserved only for suicide.

Aside from this, what is less contentious is the imminent threat suicide bombers pose to the rest of the world, especially within the nuclear age. The combination of a population of people that view life as an opportunity for reaping the rewards of martyrdom and a supply of nuclear bombs powerful enough to blow up the world many times over remains a serious threat to us all. All it would take for a nuclear catastrophe is a small group of terrorists getting their hands on poorly guarded nuclear weapons- perhaps those in Pakistan. The best protection is to eliminate nuclear weapons from locations where people are determined to use them, and try to change the ideologies and social forces motivating such people. Views about death are an integral part of this security puzzle, and should be considered when piecing it together.

Works Cited:

American-Arab Anti-Discrimination Committee. "Interview with Hany Abu Assad, 'Paradise Now.'" *ADC*. N.p., n.d. Web. 1 Mar. 2012. <http://www. adc.org/index.php?id=2637>.

DanielBerlinTV. *Why Religion Is Immoral by Christopher Hitchens. YouTube*. N.p., 23 Jan. 2011. Web. 1 Mar. 2012. <http://www.youtube.com/watch?v=ArQ_Vc-Ev8E>

Durkheim, Emile. On Suicide: Penguin Publishing, 2006. Print.

Gregsto. *Christopher Hitchens Ends Chris Hedges Career. LiveLeak.com*. N.p., 4 Oct. 2011. Web. 1 Mar. 2012. <http://www.liveleak.com/view?i=2ec_1317718541>.

Harris, Sam. "Verses from the Koran." *truthdig*. N.p., n.d. Web. 17 Oct. 2011. <http://www.truthdig.com/images/diguploads/verses.html>.

Hedges, Chris. "Gaza Dirary." *Fast Times in Palestine*. N.p., 12 Feb. 2010. Web. 14 Oct. 2011. <http://fasttimesinpalestine.wordpress.com/2010/02/12/gaza-diary-chris-hedges/>.

Jacobson, Philip. "Home-grown martyrs of the West Bank reap deadly harvest." *The Telegraph*. N.p., 19 Aug. 2001. Web. 12 Oct. 2001. <http://www.telegraph. co.uk/news/worldnews/middleeast/1337939/Home-grown-martyrs-of-the-West-Bank-reap-deadly-harvest.html>.

Killilea, Alred G. *The Politics of Being Mortal*. Lexington: The University Press of Kentucky, 1988. Print.

Moghadam, Assaf. "Motives for Martyrdom ." *International Security* 33.3 (2008/2009): 46-48. *Harvard College and the Massachusetts Institute of Technology*. Web. 20 Oct. 2011.

Paradise Now. Dir. Hany Abu-Assad. 2005. Augustus Film. DVD

PBS. "Bin Laden's Fatwa." *PBS Newshour*. N.p., Aug. 1996. Web. 18 Oct. 2011. <http://www.pbs.org/newshour/terrorism/international/fatwa_1996. html>.

Stern, Jessica. Terror in the Name of God. New York: Harper Collins, 2003. Print. pp. 50-5

Weinberg, Steven. "A Designer Universe?" *Physics and Astronomy Online*. Physlink. org, n.d. Web. 1 Mar. 2012. <http://www.physlink.com/Education/essay_weinberg.cfm>.

IV. THE LOSS OF INNOCENCE AND OF LIFE

CHAPTER SEVEN

Sub-Saharan African Child Soldiers' Views Concerning Human Mortality

Margaret Frost

In fiction and non-fiction works alike, Western literature often oversimplifies the role of interpersonal relationships in life and death, portraying human interaction as the key to affirming life and solitary confinement as an acceptance of one's own mortality. Such treatments claim to take into consideration cultural, political, and quality-of-life factors; however, what happens when conflict situations across the globe become increasingly messy and complex, and killing becomes a necessary survival mechanism inside of societal constructs, even for children? In countries such as Sierra Leone, Uganda, and Colombia, to cite just three examples, where armed rebel groups train and utilize child soldiers, human beings are transformed into death machines before hitting puberty: eight- and ten-year-olds are forced to massacre men, women, and other children as ordered by rebel leadership; twelve year olds are thrust into blood baths so gruesome that the searing sights, sounds, and smells will never liberate their young memories.

This essay examines three accounts—one novel, one autobiography, and one autobiographical novel—of three boys from three countries with three diverse life stories, in order to answer the question: In the case of child soldiers, who from a young age are barred from forming meaningful interpersonal relationships and instead, learn to protect themselves by rejecting love, does an absence of human connection cause them to welcome death more easily than those who experience loving relationships? Or, conversely, does a lack of proper socialization fail to prepare child soldiers for the reality of the human condition, causing them to fear the unknown all the more?

Through comparing the three works, it is clear that several common threads link the three boys, regardless of space, time, politics, and familial structures: numbness becomes the standard emotional state, music becomes a creative medium and an escape, and although the boys' views on life tend to differ, their perceptions regarding eventual death are consistent. Treating their own mortality as disposable, their accounts challenge simple Western perceptions of objectivity and the morality of the most inhumane of acts and implore us to seek subjective answers to questions of life and death.

Introduction

"I was able to expel all human hope. On every form of joy, in order to strangle it, I pounced stealthily like a wild animal." Une Saison en Enfer

"Soldier soldier
Kill kill kill
That is how you live.
That is how you die." – Beasts of No Nation

Throughout the course of a lifetime, it becomes evident that our relationships with others are what render us fundamentally *human*. Put simply, one could argue that our ability to find humanity in others and an understanding that our individual actions have impacts on others' lives often facilitate acceptance of personal death. If one reads *Tuesdays with Morrie* by Mitch Albom, for example, it is entirely clear that a community of love and support might help a human come to contented grips with his or her mortality. Similarly, upon concluding Leo Tolstoy's *The Death of Ivan Ilyich*, one observes that a lack of interpersonal contact during a human's dying days might ruin every last hope of experiencing a peaceful death.

What happens, however, when humans are thrown into situations in which real, person-to-person relationships are simply not a possibility? Child soldiers serving around the globe, but in particular for this piece, in Sub-Saharan Africa, are not given an opportunity to form relationships with other people from a young age, even with those who serve with them. In this area of the world and under these living conditions, evidence shows that child soldiers will more easily accept death in the absence of interpersonal relationships: The lack of passion in those relationships that do exist and the unremitting presence of suffering throughout life reduce the act of living to a futile effort. Thus, that individual is more likely to accept that death is on the way, no matter whether sooner or later: The deficiency of human connection and love bring a human closer to realizing that the relief of death will someday become his or her final destiny.

To answer the question of whether a presence or a lack of relationships assists individuals in accepting death, particularly in the case of child soldiers, I read three different accounts of life as a child solder: *Beasts of No Nation*, a novel written by Uzodinma Iweala, a fiction writer; *War Child*, a non-fiction memoir by Sudanese musician Emmanuel Jal; and *A Long Way Gone*, a true-life autobiography of UNICEF representative Ishmael Beah.

Although there exist many differences among the three treatments, many more salient common threads link their stories. To that end, perhaps most importantly, a consistent lack of meaningful human relationships characterizes the trio, and from there, one can trace a long line of similarities that connect their views of life and death as direct extensions of their experiences. The protagonists, in each case child soldiers, tend to accept death as something that will come for everyone, and thus, they pray *toward* it based on the conditions in which they find themselves. Commonly, they do not view death as something that they are not mature enough to accept, for in all ways literal and figurative, they are surrounded by it.

Uzodinma Iweala

Background

Beasts of No Nation is a gripping novel written by Uzodinma Iweala, a man who, in the realm of reality, was never a child soldier and did not grow up amongst former child soldiers. This lack of personal exposure, one might observe, does not at all weaken Iweala's haunting stories that sear themselves into the reader's memory, nor the candid commentary that allows a first-world inhabitant to be temporarily transformed into a third-world citizen struggling to survive in the face of the most treacherous of civil conflicts.

Writing from a fictional standpoint, Iweala vividly—and in first person—paints Agu, a nine or ten year old boy from a nameless African country with a political climate that resembles that of Nigeria during the 1990s. Purportedly, the point of the book is not to know exactly where the story takes place, as the author attempts to paint a plethora of common threads that link all child soldiers, regardless of their countries of origin.

Nine- or ten-year-old Agu's simple and honest writing style comprises incorrect pluralizations, the overuse of the simple progressive tense, and improper spellings of individuals' titles. It is choppy and, at times, incoherent, as Agu rambles on for entire chapters about starvation, thoughts of suicide, and attitudes toward death. Although one might have trouble adjusting to such a style for the first two chapters, Iweala's unsophisticated use of language ultimately affects the story in a positive way, by making it all the more believable and poignant.

Throughout the course of the story, Agu reveals that he grows up in a small village as a member of a large family. One night, in response to word of an impending attack from rebel groups, his mothers and sisters flee the village with aid workers, leaving Agu and his father to defend their home. During the battle, Agu's father is shot and killed. Agu hides in an old barn and waits for the battle to end. The attacking rebel group ultimately discovers Agu in his hiding place, and they force him to become a fighter in their movement. Wishing to avoid the pain of his own death and with hopes of one day reuniting with the remaining members of his family, Agu accepts and is trained as a child soldier.

Agu's tenure with the movement is harsh and seemingly never-ending. In addition to months of rough training, Agu unintentionally finds himself involved in many harmful relationships with rebel leaders—perhaps as a direct result of his father's passing and consequent lack of male role models in his life. More often than not a favorite of the commanders and lieutenants, Agu is raped and forced to wait on older men, including the 'Luftenant' (Lieutenant) himself.

Although he seeks acceptance from those of higher rank, but clearly conveys that he appeases the leaders for his own good as a soldier, he describes days full of pain caused by physical and emotional abuse, which the leadership exercises to convince Agu that the things they do to him are not wrong. Agu sensitively shares with the reader that such activities sicken him, and that while they are taking place, he pretends that he is not alive—for he would much rather be dead.

The story is fast-paced but simultaneously monotonous; the rebel group travels from village to village, terrorizing innocent people in the same manner: verbally abusing, intimidating, physically beating, raping, murdering—and in the most disgusting of moments, violently maiming humans in 'creative' and twisted ways that haunt one who has never even in the wildest of nightmares has imagined such acts. As a result of these descriptive anecdotes, the reader nearly participates in Agu's existential transformation from a boy with no choice but to fight to satisfy a desire to kill those who murdered his father, to a blood-thirsty animal that has no real regard for human life. Agu, though very much the protagonist throughout the novel, discusses how he comes to enjoy—and even revel in—the feeling of domination over other humans. He loses himself in the act of killing.

Views on death

The quote at the beginning of this piece, "Soldier soldier, Kill kill kill, That is how you live, That is how you die" (Iweala 23), belongs to Agu. It documents his very first attempt to convince himself that he is not doing anything morally wrong—although he knows well and recognizes throughout the novel that killing other humans is objectively immoral. His voice shakes as he cautiously proclaims, "I am not a bad boy. I am soldier and soldier is not bad if he is killing. I am telling this to myself because solder is supposed to be killing, killing, killing. So if I am killing, then I am only doing what is right" (Iweala 23).

In moments of authentic clarity, Agu writes, "I am not wanting to fight today because I am not liking the gun shooting and the knife chopping and the people running. I am not liking to hear people scream or to be looking at blood. I am not liking any of these thing. So I am asking to myself, why am I fighting?" (Iweala 42).

Toward the middle of the story, in contrast, Agu breaks away from his former self; in desperation, he rejects his past, deeply internalizes his feelings of revenge, and begins to take pleasure in the act of killing. Surrounded by others who have belonged to the rebel army for longer than he, Agu becomes significantly less emotional. He becomes a killing machine, no longer cognizant of the irreversible damage he is doing unto other humans.

Eventually, Agu escapes his aggressive killer stage. As rebel resources and enthusiasm wane, and as he becomes hungrier and closer to wishing for his ultimate death, Agu becomes frightened yet aware of all of the horrible things he does, even if not originally by choice. In an act of potential self-sacrifice, he decides to run, after realizing that he can no longer behave like a violent animal. He writes:

> And then I am thinking of all the thing I am doing. If they are ordering me KILL, I am killing, SHOOT, I am shooting, ENTER WOMAN, I am entering woman and not even saying anything even if I am not liking it. I am killing everybody, mother, father, grandmother, grandfather, soldier. It is all the same. It is not mattering who it is, just that they are dying. I am thinking thinking thinking. I am thinking that I cannot be doing this anymore. – 135

The end of the story showcases Agu's most interesting and touching phase. After fleeing the rebel camp after lower-level rebel leadership stages a semi-coup, Agu travels with a small group of former soldiers along a dusty road that seemingly leads to nowhere. Completely famished, Agu's body grows weak, and he goes days without hydration of any kind.

During this time period, Agu admits that he views death as something that is coming for everyone. In rambling passages where he shares that he thinks he is dying, Agu states that a person continues living from day-to-day because it is human nature to do so: "I am thinking I am car and trying to make my feets to move like wheel that is never stopping, but I cannot. I am hungry and I want to stop and rest and eat" (Iweala 125). Toward the end of the novel, Agu increasingly fantasizes about death and what it would be like to die. He communicates that death would be better than the life he is currently leading.

Although Agu supplies the reader with a detailed epilogue describing 'heaven,' one cannot be sure that Agu actually dies. Through descriptions of healing and luxury that flow together in a dreamlike sequence, one gathers that Agu finds refuge in a hospital, although he believes that he has died.

Views on life

Throughout the novel, Agu comes to view life as something monotonous and heavy-to-carry, something through which he is forced to survive day-to-day, for he does not know what awaits if he is to die. Based on the things he witnesses, life does not mean anything to him. Agu knows no friends and no kindness. His physical and emotional suffering exacerbates feelings of a loss of family, and this creates a revenge spiral, into which anyone different-looking falls.

In the last chapter especially, Agu blurs the lines between life and death—for the life of starving and trekking and killing is a life worse than death, but human instinct drives him to live on. He writes, "I am so hungry I can even be eating my skin small by small if it is not making me bleed to death. I am so hungry that I am wanting to die, but if I am dying, then I will be dead" (Iweala 118).

Agu's account simultaneously grips and terrorizes, as his identity as a soldier—and in his case, essentially a killing machine—progresses from absolute reluctance, to uneasy withdrawal, to classic indifference, to animalistic enjoyment, ending at emotional and physical collapse. His account demonstrates, based on what one observes in his human relationships—the presence of relentless competition with other young soldiers, his lack of long-lasting friendships, and the principally sexual relations into which he is forced with other soldiers—Agu is only given a chance to affirm his voids. In other words, he is better served praying for death, as he has not a single chance for human goodness in his life.

Emmanuel Jal

Background

Emmanuel Jal's story is in many ways similar to Agu's account of pain and terror, but rather than a fictional character, Emmanuel Jal is a real person who survived his living hell to tell his tale. At the age of seven, war first touched Jal and his family. He intensely recounts his first experience with death, of seeing a mother's corpse on a sidewalk, her eye sockets replaced with holes lying a few mere feet from the dead body of her own daughter. He claims that once he saw one dead person, he could not escape death for the remainder of his life: He considers himself jinxed.

Jal tells of his happy childhood in a medium-sized village in Southern Sudan. All in all, he remembers being content with the world, until he witnesses his first rape. From that moment on, the entirety of the beginning of his story is foreshadowing of what is to come. As such, the reader grows attached to Jal's closest family members, although one knows that war will take most or all of them. Based on Jal's description of his siblings, one knows that the majority will be sold into some form of slavery, and based on his incredibly loving picture of his mother, the reader easily gathers that she is killed before Jal leaves his village.

Perhaps the most interesting relationship that Jal shares with the reader is of that with his father. A powerful man in the rebel movement, Jal's father is barely home once the movement is fully underway. He makes brief stops after Jal's family is forced to leave the village, but overall, he is the least trustworthy character in the book. Despite his inherent distrust in his father that has been fed by years of isolation juxtaposed with a sprinkling of superficial mini-visits, Jal describes his deeply rooted feelings of yearning to see his father and his perpetual desire to impress him.

His short-lived relationship with his mother is entirely opposite to the air of mistrust that surrounds his father. Jal spends chapters fondly remembering his mother's look, smell, and way of being. Her reassuring attitude and words of wisdom permeate the entire story, augmenting the profound pain Jal feels after losing her. As he reports that she was killed by 'Arabs' between sentences of sheer hatred for her killers, Jal's mother's death instills a hatred in light-skinned people, mainly 'Arabs,' that evokes a feeling of revenge in Jal. He spends the entirety of his tenure as a soldier killing light-skinned people and succumbing to his deep hatred for them. Only when Jal is safe in Kenya does he begin to fight his deep-seated prejudices.

Just weeks after Jal's mother dies and he and his siblings are forced to leave their village, Jal's father calls for him. His father's aids tell Jal that he has been chosen to attend school in Ethiopia, for his father is paying for him to go to school. Jal is ecstatic at the news; from a very young age, this has been Jal's only real dream. Now that the war has begun, Jal wishes to gain skills in a classroom setting and bring them back to stop the fighting in his country.

Countless children die on the long journey to Ethiopia. Jal is one of the lucky ones to make it to a refugee camp after their boat capsizes, leaving all travelers with no tangible resources. Finally, Jal shares with the reader that his father has sold him to a group that will train him to be a child soldier. Feeling betrayed and alone in the world, and at this point, only eight years old, Jal works as hard as he can to become a strong soldier, arguably in an effort to impress his father, his only known living relative. High command realizes that he is smart and talented; however, his mischief-making tendencies keep him back from the tougher battles at the beginning of his experience as a fighter.

Jal's story is equally as painful as Agu's, but in different ways. Jal, in contrast to Agu, escapes the rebel movement within a few years of joining, for he is rescued by an aid worker and brought to Kenya. He spends almost half of his story discussing his relationship with Emma, the aid worker from England, so his story is as much about his survival and healing process as it is about his day-to-day experiences as an active participant in war.

Emma successfully sneaks Jal out of the refugee camp where he finds himself after a battle and into Kenya, where she resides with her husband, a high-ranking commander in the rebel movement. She is incredibly patient with Jal, who by any standards, is not yet fit for life as an urban schoolboy. He tells of experiences as a victim of bullying and shares anecdotes of pain resulting from frustration with school. Students ridicule Jal for the color of his skin and shun him for being in such rudimentary levels in school, due to his appearance as such a physically mature boy. Teachers and administrators give him less of a chance to succeed, based on his poor behavioral record.

Without divulging all details of his story, it helps to know that Jal becomes a popular musical artist, after Emma is killed in a car accident during his years as a high schooler. Her death inspires him to succeed as the founder of various non-profit organizations and motivates him to try his luck at becoming a professional recording artist.

Views on death

Jal's story is unique in that he has essentially lived two different lives, one as a child soldier and the other as an individual who is given a second chance by a meaningful human relationship. As a child soldier, Jal never gives up hope, unlike Agu, but he also never falls into the trap of enjoying the feeling of killing others. Discussing war and death, Jal shares:

> *Inside I was like water—moving to flow around whatever dropped into my path because children adapt easily to change, whether good or bad. But two things I could not get used to. The first thing was waiting for war. At least when it came, you had something to run from as your heart hammered, but waiting was like having the breath slowly squeezed out of you. The other thing was death. The dead were everywhere—skeletons no one buried, people with bullet marks in them and burned bodies lying amid the ruins of a tukul...I couldn't stop the pictures in my head... - 18*

Although they fundamentally disagree on how it feels to kill, Jal shares Agu's feelings of bewilderment at how meaningless such atrocities can deem a human life. Recounting several occasions of death of people of all ages, many gruesome and unrepeatable, Jal reports coping with his own temptations toward and cravings for his own final death by remembering his mother. At times throughout the story, he admits that feelings of defeat:

> *Those who died of hunger were buried on the way to the river, but those that had been sick like this boy were taken to the forest and buried in holes dug with sticks. Soon we would say prayers to God as we put the boy in the ground, and as I looked into the dark pit, I wondered when it would be my turn to die. – 61*

Although Jal speaks of seeking revenge through his killing of 'Arabs', he never fully admits to killing someone based on the memory of his family, unlike Agu's tendency to picture his mother's face when he experiences 'trouble' with human emotion. According to Jal in the middle of his story, "I had not killed anyone to pay for [my mother's] death as Lam had for his father. I could not even picture Mamma's face properly anymore. I just knew that death had been in my heart for so long I wanted to see it face-to-face one day soon" (Jal 131).

It is entirely apparent throughout his story, abounding successes toward the end aside, that death always haunts Jal. He shares colorful dream sequences in which members of his family are killed, and he fights with feelings of suicide many times in his life, especially after Emma's death. After reuniting with his sister, perhaps he explains it best, "But I'd thought again and again of the shadows in [sister] Nyaruach's eyes every time I sat down to write [songs] after she'd arrived in Nairobi. War had scarred her, just as it had me, and we were just two among a people who all knew death by his first name" (Jal 232).

Views on life

Jal's views on life and death, due to his living two full lives, differ from those of Agu and Ishmael. His ability to find faith in Christian music, as a result of his mother's influence in both of his lives after her death and his good fortune of finding someone with whom to connect have provided him with entirely different views of life.

As a child solder, Jal describes the atrocities he witnesses and those in which he is an active participant. In many separate instances, he vividly depicts images of suffering, especially during long journeys from one place to the next, in which many people are lost from starvation and weakness. He distastefully describes the government and its indifference to the suffering of its citizens.

Jal describes music as an integral part of his life after Emma rescues him from the refugee camp. He writes lyrics and performs his works in front of audiences, which according to Jal, brings new meaning to his life on this planet. Upon realizing that he needs to do something with his life to help others like him, because he can, Jal becomes an unstoppable force—and today, seems to be quite happy and adapting to living a full life.

Jal's experience differs greatly from Agu's, for Jal has found the ability to feel an emotion that Agu never does: love. Jal, through the memories of his mother and Emma, which fill him with humanity and purpose, and music, the art that proves to him that he can profoundly touch the lives of others, is able to overcome feelings of emotional weakness; he realizes that his existence *means something* to himself and to others.

Ishmael Beah

Background

Although some prominent public dispute exists surrounding the credibility of <u>A Long Way Gone</u>, a memoir by Ishmael Beah, it can be argued that the story contributes to the extant literature an important treatment of life and death as related to the topic of child soldiers. After all, <u>Beasts of No Nation</u> is a novel, and it also sheds a unique light on crucial elements of becoming and sustaining oneself as a child soldier, as diverse child-soldier experiences exist across the globe.

The acts of becoming and sustaining oneself as a child soldier are consistent in most treatments, especially in those of survivors; perhaps naturally, Ishmael's story is closely related to Jal's, for they both ultimately survive to live second lives, so to speak, and to tell their stories to first-world audiences. After living a life of fear, brainwash, and control, these individuals wish to renew themselves as human beings and start again.

Born and raised in perpetually war-torn Sierra Leone, Ishmael Beah is forced to become a child soldier at age twelve, an age much older than Agu and Jal are when they are first recruited. War touches him much later than it does the others, as he is old enough to travel *alone* by the time his world is literally turned upside down. His story is perhaps the most painful during the period in which he is recruited, for he is old enough to remember the details of his families' facial features and the nuances of familial adventures. He has formed close relationships by the time he finds himself stuck in his child-soldier structure, which makes it harder for him to adjust to such a terrible way of life than in the experiences of Agu and Jal.

On the day of the infamous attack on his village, Ishmael and his friends travel to another village across the river to shop and have fun. Meanwhile, they hear that their village has been attacked and their relatives killed. Ishmael is unaware, for most of his story, whether or not his father, mother, grandmother, grandfather, and siblings survive. During Ishmael and friends' attempt to escape the war, an army recruits them to become young soldiers. Ishmael conveys his initial dismay and his attempted escape of listening to United States rap music to calm his nerves and profound anxiety.

Throughout the course of his story, Ishmael discusses the eventual numbness of killing when affected by drug usage. He describes how it feels to snort gun powder-like substances, smoke many types of leaves, and drink copious amounts of alcohol. This, he says, the soldiers must do to separate themselves from the atrocities they commit. Drugs and alcohol are present in the other two treatments, but I believe Ishmael does the best job describing consciousness while killing and the impacts of using substances to influence the quality of human brain activity.

Views on death

It is entirely apparent in all parts of his story that others' experiences deeply affect the very sensitive Ishmael. It hurts him more than the next person to see his fellow soldiers die, and he loathes witnessing their suffering. A close friend from the beginning of the tale, Saidu, dies of starvation and exhaustion along the way. His funeral is one of the most affecting, and it teaches Ishmael of the monotony of grieving, the dull, repeating pain of death, and the inability to maintain real friendships as a child soldier. One passage in particular, captured before Saidu's death, highlights:

> *After a few hours had gone by, Saidu spoke in a very deep voice, as if someone were speaking through him. "How many more times do we have to come to terms with death before we find safety?" he asked. 'He waited a few minutes, but the three of us didn't say anything. He continued:*

> *"Every time people come at us with the intention of killing us, I close my eyes and wait for death. Even though I am still alive, I feel like each time I accept death, a part of me dies. Very soon I will completely die and all that will be left of me is my empty body walking with you. It will be quieter than I am. -70*

Although in the other two treatments, the authors seem to resign to their deaths, Ishmael suffers for three years but debatably, does not entirely give up hope. Using as fodder for strength the vivid memories of his family members and the wise words of his father, which he remembers well from childhood, Ishmael perseveres.

Views on life

Similar to his views on death, Ishmael derives power from formerly strong family ties and the memories contained therein. In contrast to Jal's story, Ishmael's strongest relationship seems to be with his late father, whom he portrays as an incredibly wise man. Ishmael demonstrates his wish to be close to his father more than to any other member of the family. Along the journey, he inserts various phrases that his father coined, in order to continue on. He writes:

> When I was young, my father used to say, 'If you are alive, there is hope for a better day and something good to happen. If there is nothing good left in the destiny of a person, he or she will die.' I thought about these words during my journey, and they kept me moving even when I didn't know where I was going. Those words became the vehicle that drove my spirit forward and made it stay alive. -54

As with Jal, Ishmael is afforded what he considers to be two lives. He lives one life as a child soldier, unendingly miserable and always in pain, and the other, as a newfound voice for current child soldiers. One of his main messages, according to his memoir, is to live life to the fullest, for one never knows when his or her life will suddenly end. In his first life, he communicates uncertainty at when or how his life will end. In his second life, he conveys deep thankfulness for his UNICEF rescue, which reintroduced him to his mother in New York City. In his first life, or in his case, his in-between life, he is devoid of most human contact. In his second life, he finds human connection, especially with his mother in the United States. It only takes one human to truly believe in him and success abounds.

Ishmael prioritizes not ignoring what has happened to him in the past, for that, he says, would be harmful to his future and to the present situations of those suffering in this instant. Instead, "These days I live in three worlds: my dreams, and the experiences of my new life, which triggers memories from the past" (Beah 20).

Ishmael's experience, similar to Jal's, aptly proves that a human being at his or her lowest point, in the absence of positive human relationships, significance to life, and love, will strive toward nothing but relief. In the sad realities of individuals without options, this form of ultimate relief is predominately death.

Common threads

Throughout this process, I found that differences exist inside of the authors' individual histories, based on their ages, their personal experiences, and the regions where they live in Sub-Saharan Africa. Cultural nuances, although subtle in these treatments, are present; family structures and relationships slightly vary. For example, the role and closeness of siblings differs between the boys. Jal is very close to his siblings, whereas Agu tends not to mention them individually. Political climates, especially those of the Sudan and Sierra Leone, contrast based on the severity of conflict, the duration of fighting, and political regime. Although all three authors mention political situations and the indifference and corruption of powerful individuals *in passing*, the three purposely do not concentrate on leaders and governments: They are so far removed from any form of participation in political life that such discussion does not matter for their treatments.

The maturity of the three individual boys fluctuates throughout the course of each story, though at different rates and times; for example, Ishmael at age thirteen is initially more mature than Jal at age seven. Their experiences also differ based on physical size. Jal is treated as a pipsqueak for much of his story, due to his age and stature, while Agu is coveted by the leaders, both sexually and skill-wise, due to his size and physical appearance.

Concerning the authors' views of life as such views relate to death and human relationships, however, perceptions do not seem to change. Hence, there seems to be a recipe for becoming a child soldier and an equation that causes an imbalance between entrapment as a child soldier and freedom. Firstly, all three treatments highlight the importance of male relationships in the context of daily life in African cultures. All three authors have strong connections to at least the *thoughts* and *memories* of their fathers' fundamental roles in their lives, whether Jal is clinging to the memory of a man who sold him into the army, Agu is remembering his dead father whenever he shoots an enemy, or Ishmael is imagining his father by his side, quoting sayings his father coined, in order to stay alive. This particular aspect identifies that family bonds are important in all three contexts, regardless of the situations surrounding them.

Secondly, revenge for killing or wronging a family and consequent hatred of different-looking types of people always results in these stories. For example, in an Agu passage:

> *I can see the tear on the face of one enemy. He is coughing and sniffling and whispering. I think he is saying, I am not wanting to die. Please God. I am not wanting to die, but I am too far away to be hearing him. I think this is what he is saying and I am looking at him and even feeling sorry for him, but then I am remembering my father. 17*

In each story, feelings of revenge against individuals and certain one-time situations morph into long-term fundamental cultural hatred. All three boys express feeling fear and hatred toward those who do not resemble them physically; Jal hates the 'Arabs', and Ishmael and Agu hate light-skinned people. Agu communicates that he is shocked to learn that some members of the army fighting against his are dark-skinned.

Thirdly, Agu, Jal, and Ishmael all collectively express the concept of governmental rule as largely being cold. Clearly, the politics of these nations have no place in stories of their citizens. As previously conveyed, the boys all communicate being utterly disgusted and entirely removed from political life, which proves that the three countries' political leadership has little to no reach, let alone impact on the lives of citizens.

By expressing their disconnect from politicians, the three boys prove that politicians and common people are always viewed in those countries as occupying space in different realms of life. They also prove that although violence takes place on a daily basis and on a large scale, governments do not care about individual human life. Instead, their corrupt regimes opt to draft policies that satisfy those whose votes they require to retain power, rather than policies that benefit the poorest and most destitute of inhabitants.

In two of the three stories, the boys find someone who ultimately rescues them from their lives as child soldiers. In the third account, that of Agu, a lack of human connection causes him to further spiral into the hopelessness of his way of life. In all three treatments, the early absence of natural human connection forces the boys to reject it throughout the majority of their stories. More specifically, in a normal context in the life of a child soldier, the boys avoid human contact at all costs: They are used to being hurt, so they reject significant human relationships. Jal explains that it is difficult for him to feel anything for others, especially his own sister, after surviving for such an extended period of time in numbness. Ishmael is unable to form connections with his fellow soldiers, despite his natural sensitivity and curiosity in others. Agu has a friend, but upon witnessing the friendship's growth, rebel leadership ends the bond by pitting the two friends against one another.

The last major common thread between the two is music. In all three cases, the boys discuss music as a way to cope with their situations of suffering. Ishmael cites U.S. American rappers, such as P. Diddy, Nas, and Tupac as inspiration that led him out of suffering. Jal uses English and Kenyan rappers as examples of people who write about their pain; he later succeeds as a professional musical artist.

Conclusion

While I agree wholeheartedly with the notion that humans might accept death when they realize that recognizing the humanity in others leads to interconnectedness *in a Western context*—in other words, in lands largely free of child soldiers and similar kinds of human suffering and destitution—I believe that it is child soldiers' lack of human contact that allows them to more readily accept death. All three boys share that they come to the point of no longer caring about their personal lives, as a direct result of famine and physical exhaustion. Their deficiency in human connection gives them nothing onto which to hold, so they accept death more easily.

Affirmation of one's impact on others, in contrast, allows one to live a more meaningful life, and such facilitates humans' acceptance of their own morality. However, the fact that child soldiers do not have the ability to form personal connections might hide the real impacts of what they do unto others; if they do not have significant relationships, they are less likely to desire to live at all.

Impact on my views

Although I do not personally know child soldiers or freedom fighters of any kind, this project opened my mind to the negligent ways in which governments around the world treat their citizens, and the desperate ways in which citizens in strife react to conditions that their governments directly and indirectly thrust upon them, through policy and law enforcement.

Throughout this process, I learned a great deal about three boys' personal experiences and about how cruelly humans can be forced to behave through brainwash and perpetual instillation of fear. Before studying child soldiers, I had no notion that killing has an ability to cause one's mind to numb all brain function—and I underestimated the true strength of the bonds between parents and children in a wartime context.

Lastly, as Agu, Jal, and Ishmael shared a love for music that sustained them through their years of suffering during war and later brought meaning to their post-war lives, I am beginning to learn of the true importance of music in human life. Music, especially hip hop, rap, and other types of music that encourage personal expression, should not be underestimated: It has the power to transform the toughest of conditions into situations of inspiration and hope.

I fully believe that my own views regarding death have been expanded in the process; I have now ceased to believe that personal death is a collective issue—and now I believe that oftentimes, problems of life and death must be pondered subjectively. Such a realization presents a plethora of philosophical dilemmas that must be explored further: In a society in which killing is forced, inaction is fatal, and the ethical lines between violence and nonviolence become blood-stained and blurred, *even for children*, how is a Western society to judge based on age-old notions of simplistic moral objectivity? Additionally, how is one to know when his or her recognition of humanity in others and the importance of interconnectedness aid in the acceptance of personal death or simply the affirmation of the meaning and the *enrichment of the quality* of life? In the face of such dilemmas, perhaps it suffices to live each day on this earth perpetually searching for humanity and striving to positively influence others' lives. As in the case of the three child soldiers, although one never knows when his or her personal life will end, through seeking meaning in every aspect of life, one must maintain hope that there exists potential for perpetual betterment in this world.

CHAPTER EIGHT

African Child Soldiers on Life and Death

Alexander Colantonio

Severely traumatic experiences especially during the formative years of adolescence undoubtedly have far reaching consequences. Torture, drug use and violence suffered by child soldiers can create a "pillager mentality" which dictates that anything one desires can and should be taken by force These unfortunate children develop skewed views on life and death, right and wrong and the interaction of the strong with the weak as a result of their exposure to death and destruction on such grand scale at such a young age. Age-appropriate perspective regarding morality and mortality are replaced with violence as children emulate their barbaric superiors. This mentality can prove difficult but necessary to overcome if there is hope for their return to society.

When we hear the word "child" a number of mental images come to mind: Thoughts of boys and girls playing in sandboxes, opening toys on their birthdays and waiting at bus stops where they will ride to school and learn to read and write. There is a general innocence associated with and inherent to children, who have yet to create their own individual worldviews or opinions. Children remain oblivious to the harsh realities of the life because they have not yet grown and developed both socially and emotionally into adulthood. They lack the ability to survive on their own and need adult protection and guidance to grow into successful members of society. The experiences of their early life directly influence the way they view the world. Children enter the world with no preconceived notions; we are born naked of hate, malice and discontent.

Let us take another word into consideration: "soldier." This word also brings a variety of images to mind. For most, we imagine a protector, a defender, an individual willing to use frightening force to protect the things we value most. We want our soldiers to follow orders, to kill or be killed in an effort to defeat those who would harm us or our way of lives. We condition these men and women to be almost totally emotionless and to be able to end another human's life if circumstances demand it. On the other end of the spectrum, when many hear the word "soldier," especially if they or a loved one has served in combat, their mind wanders to the darker issues of violence, chaos and death. Those who have experienced battle will tell you that war is "Hell on Earth." I've had many conversations with friends serving in Iraq and Afghanistan who have told me they would not wish combat on our worst enemy from home. Their stories are horrifying, but having been woken by his screams at night solidified my views of combat's effect. In this country, we have a volunteer armed force, which exists for able bodied men and women who make a conscious decision to put their lives on the line. They are willing to kill or be killed, all in an effort to defend the society which has provided the security and safety they enjoyed as children.

If the word "child" calls images of new life, innocence and something to be nurtured, and "soldier" creates opposing thoughts of facing death with all of the horrors of combat to defend ones way of life, then the term "child soldier" must strike fear and sorrow into one's mind. To borrow *War Child's* slogan "some words just don't belong together." *War Child* is a non-governmental organization who provides services and assistance to these troubled children. They claim there are over a quarter of a million children who are currently engaged as soldiers, ammunition runners, cooks, sex slaves and various roles in both governmental and non-governmental armed forces around the world.[1] These youths are strong-armed into service, given drugs and forced to commit atrocities. Regardless of their exact role all of these entrapped youths inevitable from their experience emerge scarred for life. Their outlooks on life and death are unavoidably altered by the tragedies they have endured. Their future as functional members of society is in peril. Adults who have made the knowing decision to face battle return physically, emotionally and mentally wounded. How can such a young person who has gone through the rigors and destruction of combat, who has witnessed death all around them and has even taken life with their own hands return to a life with any degree of normalcy?

Child Soldiers' Life Experience's

The use of child soldiers in the late 20th century has become a continuing problem for much of the world. For the purpose of this paper I have looked at mainly African youth combatants but their experience is in no way exclusive to all underage soldiers. Children as young as six years old are conscripted to bolster both rebel and government forces. The advent of the use of children in battle has become a problem in modern times with the advent of "modern technology (which) has provided weapons which weigh less than seven pounds, cost about US$6, and can be stripped, reassembled, loaded and fired by an illiterate child of 10"[2]. The use of these young, impressionable boys and girls is incredibly traumatizing and seriously debilitates their return to normal society. The brutality they witness leaves lasting memories that they must struggle to overcome. Youths are used in conflicts around the globe but their largest deployment took place and continues in Africa.

Children are sought after for use by both governmental and non-governmental combat groups for a variety of reasons. Firstly, recruitment of children is considered desirable because of children's energy levels. Children will march all day without the addition of stimulants which their overlords use to push them even further. Second, they are more susceptible to propaganda and therefore, more readily obey. A child's mind is more easily molded and manipulated by malicious brainwashing. Third, their moral values are still in formation so they can, more easily than an adult, suspend moral judgments.[3] Child soldiers see what many hope to never witness. They see drugs, death, rape, destruction on a grand scale every single day.

Conscription begins with the youngest, no more than six or seven years old. The youngest are not typically used in open combat. They are used initially as porters carrying ammunition or food to the troops or as spies. People do not suspect children to be combatants making them prime candidates.[4] They also are used to collect supplies, often sent to pillage from local villages once again because they are easily overlooked. Typical recruitment follows raids. A group will take a village, slaughter the older populations and then force the children into service. Their families are often murdered before their eyes, to show that the armed force that they join is now their new family. Children are abducted, fed drugs and forced to commit atrocities such as murder and rape.

Around the age of ten they are given automatic rifles and very little training. They are often seen as "perceived to be dispensable commodities"[5] which leads to their commanders disregard for their survival. In an interview with a government child soldier from Sierra Leone, he describes how the rebels added to their numbers "They take all the items. Sometimes they take the people to carry the items. So the people, the very same people [they have captured], join them"[6]. He goes on with a further account of the brutality that children are led to become part of. He describes the torture of captured rebels:

> Sometimes we melt plastic on them, because that one is a hard punishment. Le 50.00 for plastic, we buy it at about Le 50.00. We melt it on their backs. Sometimes we cut their ears or cut their fingers, because that is the way they treat other people, our soldiers, our men. They cut some of our men's hands. So that's how we get rid of them. So first we cut one finger. If you do not talk we cut another one. When they say "I want to talk" we cut another one.[7]

He later goes on to recount his units' use of marijuana, cocaine and palm wine. By getting their men hooked on drugs, the commanders ensure their obedience. The use the drugs to dull the minds of their soldiers, to keep them going when they normally would stop. He talks about how they would use marijuana to forget about the cold, the cocaine to keep fighting and the palm wine to stave off hunger.

This boy was a member of the government forces encouraged to join willingly; within the rebel forces these practices were even more rampant.

Women and young girls are of no exception to being forcefully conscripted to serve in an armed group. Women are often taken and "young girls have suffered sustained sexual and psychological abuse, and became the 'prizes' given to top RUF commanders"[8]. Girls are taken and forced onto the men. In Mozambique "girls became personal servants, including sexual services with some remaining with one man or boy for years, later to be designated as 'wife'."[9] Even worse, sometimes women are indeed forced to fight. "Grace A. gave birth on open ground to a girl fathered by one of her [LRA] rebel abductors. Then she was forced to continue fighting. *"I picked up a gun and strapped the baby on my back."*[10] This kind of trauma is depilating to young women. Being forced to try to nurture life when surrounded by so much death has major effects on their fragile psyches.

As stated above the use of children as combatants and sex slaves is not limited to simply rebel or non-governmental resistance groups. The use of children, defined as boys and girls under the age of 18 exists throughout much of Africa. Weak, fledgling governments will overlook age requirements in order to swell their ranks. They will often conscript young men and boys to fight to defend their assets against rebel groups. Their experiences may be only slightly better. While they may not be beaten and raped they must still endure the brutality of war, for tormented by the sights, sounds and experience of their service. While here in America we have the luxury of delaying our recognition of our own mortality these children must stare death in the face on a daily basis.

Child Soldiers Views on Life and Death

Child soldiers are at risk because of the horrible acts they are forced to commit. Kids who should be playing soldier with imaginary weapons are now forced into actual combat with automatic rifles and grenades. For developing young minds this can be incredibly traumatic. Even worse, it becomes the norm and a pillager mentality arises in these children. They feel like anything they want in theirs for the taking. They honor military might as the only importance and see violence as a normal mode of behavior.

Since these boys and girls grow to adulthood (if they survive) enduring violence and destruction everywhere they go it becomes standard procedure. Their brains become hardwired for violence. They begin to equate the ability to destroy as the only real power.

These children therefore accept war as a 'normal way of life'. The power of the AK 47 assault rifle transforms them from mere children into adults with power and 'authority' to kill or not. War causes schools to close, disrupts normal activities and destroys social amenities.[11]

For these children the normal interpersonal relationships and experiences during our formative years which mold our future adult lives are vacant. When kids live and play together as children they learn from each other and their elders that more can be accomplished through cooperation and compromise. Children learn that while they can accomplish much through their own devices, greater achievements can be reached by working collaboratively with their peers. Not only are they denied quality learning experiences, through school and play, but witnessing and being part of such terrible violence further restricts social integration. They see death as tool, a means to an end, to be used as a first resort when attempting to influence others. Instead of attempting to reconcile differences and compromise, these youths fall back on the only social interaction that they have any experience with: Force.

These young boys and girls become death drones because their commanders mold them that way. They take the role of guiding advisors and respected elders. These warlords are the last role model the poor, starved youth of Africa should be growing up emulating. They witness the power and the wealth that these men simply take as their own and many see it as the only way for them to escape their poverty. Though they may initially distain their captors turned commanders many boys eventually come to look up to them.[12] Their regard for life and death is altered by their daily dealings with it. For these young men and boys the act of taking life becomes habitual; a deadly routine orchestrated by their overlords to remove any remorse or contradiction to orders.

Ishmael Beah, in *A Long Way Gone*, writes a memoir about his time as a child soldier. His firsthand account is an eye-opening tale which winds its way through his life from capture, service and release as a child soldier. Ishmael was a young man in Sierra Leone when the Revolutionary United Front, the RUF, attacked his village and forced him into service. He writes a harrowing story which highlights the struggle for survival which these youths face on a day to day basis. These groups of armed forces specifically target young males for combat and young girls for "soldier wives," basically sex slaves. Ishmael describes how "Young boys were immediately recruited, and the initials RUF were carved wherever it pleased the rebels with a hot bayonet,"[13] displaying the harsh treatment of these pre-pubescent boys. His tale highlights the specific ways that the commanders of these groups re-shape their new recruits ideological point of view in regards to life and death.

Ishmael's experience with drugs is a common thread throughout the child soldier population. Many soldiers have troubles overcoming the concept of taking life; especially children. The commanders of these units have a method to overcome these apprehensions, drugs and violence. Nearly universal to the child soldier experience is their introduction to drugs. At such an early stage, when the brain is still developing, this type of drug use can impair appropriate function. Ishmael writes about how he was given drugs to numb him from the realities of his situation. Child soldiers often report use of marijuana, amphetamines, alcohol, heroine and a mixture of cocaine and gunpowder called Brown Brown.[14] Powerful psychoactive drugs cause both the physical developmental issues from their use at a young age but also emotional and psychological damage. These drugs were used to make the kids work harder. With the addition of stimulants such as amphetamines and cocaine these youths can be forced to march for days on end. The use of drugs also distorts their views on life and death themselves. On these drugs the child soldiers ignore pain and become numb to the act of taking life. They feel both invulnerable and empowered. With their AK-47 and stimulant drugs they not only feel a sense of omnipotence but are pushed to disregard the lives of others. They kill, taking life with little thought of repercussions during their time under the influence.

Ishmael Beah maintains a very interesting view on his own life. He views his own experience as two lives. He considers his first life ending when he was a child soldier. When he finally was freed from his service as a child soldier he put that life behind him. He considers it as a separate life where he was not himself. His new life begins when he enters a UNICEF camp and begins his decommission from murder machine to human being. I found this incredibly enlightening and interesting because it shows how their actions as youth combatants are often so heinous and unforgivable that they must completely separate it from their new person. Ishmael is one of the lucky few whom; with the success of his book and travel to America he was able to overcome his past. This idea of a figurative death of his previous character is a coping tool that may prove useful to others in similar situations.

Child Soldiers Post Combat

As stated, Ishmael overcame the demons of his past by creating this concept of his previous self literally dying and a new self being reborn, free of any prior guilt. During my undergraduate studies I researched child soldiers and their return to civil society. I analyzed at both Mozambique and Sierra Leone, who used entirely different methods of reintegration. These methods are entitled Disarmament, Demobilization, Reunification and Reintegration (DDRR) processes. Sierra Leone's was based on a four phase timetable. In their first phase, 189 children were demobilized. A total of 6,845 child combatants were demobilized between September 1998 and January 2002; eight per cent were girls.[15] Around 80% were sent to one of twelve Sierra Leonean ICC's or Interim Care Centers. Here they were given I.D. cards as well as food and shelter. They were given "healthcare services, educational and recreational activities, non-food items, life-skill training, psychosocial support, career guidance and services for special needs"[16] These camps were to act as a middle ground between war and peace. Their goal was to teach the young boys and girls the necessary skills to survive in life without combat and pillage. This was the type of camp which Ishmael Beah had his rebirth. These programs were initially successful to some degree but Mozambique offered a different approach which they report to be both progressive and effective in reintegrating these traumatized youths with society.

Mozambique followed a unique approach to its DDRR. After initial western approaches failed in the early 1980's it was decided that a different method was necessary. Mozambique then pursued a community based reintegration policy. This strategy focused on ritual cleansing of the sins of the past. It made use of community involvement and especially healers called *curandeiro* to provide a way for returning soldiers to abolish the atrocities that they committed and start life anew.[17] This rebirth is viewed by all members of the community that the person who completes these rituals is in fact new person. No ties exist to the past nor any sort of retribution handed down. All is forgiven. This approach is effective because the ex-soldier is not seen as one who has some sort of stigma attached to them. They are free to become full-fledged members of society. This communal washing away of one's misgivings and previous actions, regardless of one's history, allows for a rebirth similar to Ishmael's. It differs in one key area, the aspect of its community interaction. Where Sierra Leone used camps, run by government and non-governmental organizations such as UNICEF, the Mozambique approach focuses more on the individuals' communities. By using village elders and spiritual leaders to literally wipe away the past of these child soldiers they can shed their previous views on life and death and rejoin civil society. They can cast aside their brainwashed disregard for the sanctity of life and accept a less fanatic view. By being cleansed they can reform their extremely skewed ideology of the power in dealing death and begin to rehabilitate themselves into successful members of society.

Discussion and Conclusion

Child soldiers have an extreme view of life and death. They see their ability to take life as the ultimate power. Being so young and granted control over life and death distorts their outlook. It bloats their sense of themselves and creates pillager mentality. Whatever they want they can take by force. This is thought provoking because normally when we, as Americans and even Westerners, think of death we put it off as a distant concern that we must deal with eventually. These children must face death before any of us are ready for it. They are forced to witness the worst in human behavior in extreme amounts from a young age. How can this not affect their adult lives?

Studies have placed American veterans of Iraq and Afghanistan at a 10% rate of diagnosis of Post Traumatic Stress Disorder.[18] This number reflects American service men and woman who exhibit the symptoms of PTSD.

> Defined "Posttraumatic Stress Disorder (PTSD) is an anxiety disorder that can occur following the

> experience or witnessing of a traumatic event. A
> traumatic event is a life-threatening event such as
> military combat, natural disasters, terrorist incidents,
> serious accidents, or physical or sexual assault in adult
> or childhood.[19]

If American Servicemen and women experience this at a rate of 10%, after having voluntarily signed up for this role, what must the rate of PTSD in children who cannot make that decision for themselves be? Unfortunately data for this population does not exist but one can theorize it must be extremely high. These youths are forced to take drugs and commit acts of rape and murder. How can this not damage the mind of a child?

My research for this paper did not drastically alter my view on child soldiers. From my initial understanding of their existence I could see the inherent problems with the use of children in combat scenarios. It is not a stretch for one to conceive the multitude of obstacles these youths must now face. Their experiences shape their lives, just as our own childhoods mold our adulthoods.

The use of child soldiers is appalling. To me it breaches every code of conduct I have grown to accept. Children are a sacred demographic, they are our future. In order for the future to be progressive and increase in quality of life our children must be granted safe developmental environments where they can learn the human experience. Acting in an armed conflict severely distorts their reality. Instead of seeing cooperation and compromise as the most successful method for social advancement, they see only force. They see the ability to take life as the only designation of power. These kids are taught from their most impressionable ages that there is only one way to get what you want: take it at the barrel of a gun. Their entire reward structure is rewired, replacing civil society with a pillager mentality which states that the strongest should have all and the weak are mere hindrances to their individual gains.

In Killlilea's book he writes continually about how our realization of our own mortality can act as a catalyst to a common brotherhood of man consciousness. This is denied to child soldiers. They are given drugs and forced to kill leading them to feel a sense of immortality. With the combination of the psychoactive drugs and the power to take life with the pull of a trigger these children are denied a true sense of life and death. Their commanders keep them in a state of dissolution to their own mortality. Child soldiers don't think twice about their actions; they do as they are programmed. Without truly understanding the repercussions of their actions children cannot see the chaos they are inflicting.

Africa is a poor continent plagued by the perverse use of children to fight political battles. This poverty is increasingly difficult to overcome because of the effects combat has on its youth. These children grow up lacking any sort of normal human interaction. How then, once the conflict they are involved in has ended can they be expected to become functioning members of society? They not only face lingering drug addictions but are plagued by their actions as soldiers. Some are seen as murders and are not wanted in their communities. Often their families are killed so where can these children even go after their involvement? While programs from state/non-governmental organization run camps to tribal spiritual cleansing exist these children are still in danger. The effects of their horrible experiences are not easily removed. These kids are denied a childhood, a chance to grow and develop into teens and adults with normal social interactions. For many killing and death is all they know. This proves a huge problem for African societies looking to recover from wars that plague their nations. With so much of the youth so detrimentally impacted by their tragic experiences how can Africa rebound? By destroying the lives of their youths many African nations seem to have condemned themselves to massive problems with rehabilitation and reintegration. Africa, as well as any nation, country or continent, which uses children to fight their battles, must face the reality of dealing with the scars of their service. They must work diligently to change the mindset of these children from pillaging to nation building.

References

Anker, C. a. (1999). *The Lost Explorer.* New York: Simon and Schuster.

BBC News. (1999 йил November). Mount Everest Reaches New Heights. London, UK: BBC News.

Beah, I. (2007). *A Long Way Gone.* New York: Sarah Crichton Books.

Berezin, M. (1997). *Making the Fascist Self: The Political Culture of Interwar Italy.* Ithaca: Cornell University Press.

Berlet, C. (1992 йил September). *Fascism!* Retrieved 2010 йил March from http://www.hartford-hwp.com/archives/45/051.html

Coalition to Stop the Use of Child Soldiers. (2006). *Child soldiers and Disarmament, Demobilization, Rehabilitation and Reintegration in West Africa.*

Dawkins, R. (2011, October 8). Texas Free Thought Convention. Texas.

Dawkins, R. (2006). *The God Delusion.* New York: Bantam Press.

Faulkner, F. (2001). Kindergarten Killers: Morality, Murder and the Child Soldier Problem. *Third World Quarterly, Vol. 22, No. 4* .

Federal Aviation Administration. (2003). *Operations of Aircraft at Altitudes above 25,000 Feet.* Washington D.C.: Department of Transportation.

Firth, P. (2008). Mortality on Mount Everest, 1921-2006. *British Medical Journal* .

Gray, M. (2010, September 20). *Hitchens Won't Be Attending Hitchens Prayer Day.* Retrieved October 2011, from http://newsfeed.time.com/2010/09/20/hitchens-wont-be-attending-hitchens-prayer-day/

Gregor, A. J. (1979). *Young Mussolini and the Intellectual Origins of Fascism.* Berkeley: University of California Press.

Heil, N. (2008). *Dark Summit.* New York: Henry Holt and Co.

Hitchens, C. (2007). *God is not Great.* New York: Twelve.

Hitchens, C. (2010). *Hitch-22: A Memoir.* New York: Twelve.

Hitchens, C. (2010, December). Miss Manners and the Big C. *Vanity Fair* .

Hitchens, C. (2011, January 14). Q & A with Christopher Hitchens. (B. Lamb, Interviewer)

Hitchens, C. (1982, July). The Lord and the Intellectuals. *Harper's* .

Hitchens, C. (2011). *The Quotable Hitchens: From Alcohol to Zionism.* Philadelphia: De Capo Press.

Hitchens, C. (2010, September). Topic of Cancer. *Vanity Fair* .

Hitchens, C. (2010, November). Tumortown. *Vanity Fair* .

Hitchens, C. (2010, October). Unanswerable Prayers. *Vanity Fair* .

Hitchens, C. (2011, June). Unspoken Truths. *Vanity Fair* .

Jaffre, F. (n.d.). *The Use of Children as Soldiers in Africa: A country analysis of child recruitment and participation in armed conflict.* Retrieved 2010 йил 29-4 from Relief Web International: http://www.reliefweb.int/library/documents/chilsold.htm

JFK Presidential Library. (n.d.). *JFK Presidential Library.* Retrieved 2011 йил 02-10 from www.jfklibrary.org

Jugalski, E. (2011 йил 24-September). *Ascents-Everest.* Retrieved 2011 йил 10-October from 8000ers.com: www.8000ers.com/everest-general-info-185.html

Killilea, A. G. (1988). *The Politics of Being Mortal.* Lexington, Kentucky: The University Press of Kentucky.

Koon, T. H. (1985). *Believe, Obey, Fight.* Chapel Hill: University of North Carolina Press.

Krakauer, J. (1997). *Into Thin Air.* New York: Anchor Books.

LaGambina, G. (2007, December). Christmas with Christopher Hitchens. *A.V. Club* .

Mallory, G. (1923 йил 18-March). Climbing Mount Everest is Work for Supermen. (N. Y. Times, Interviewer)

May, T. (2009). *Death*. Durham: Acumen.

Mazzini, G. (1981). The Duties of Man. In M. Curtis, *The Great Political Theories* (Vol. 2, pp. 234-242). New York: Avon Books.

McGrath, C. (2011, October 9). A Voice, Still Vibrant, Reflects on Mortality. *The New York Times* .

Megaro, G. (1938). *Mussolini in the Making*. Boston: Houghton Mifflin Company.

Mount Washington Observatory. (2011). *Mount Washington Observatory.org*. Retrieved 2011 йил 15-October from www.mountwashingtonobservatory.org

Mussolini, B. (1935). *Fascism: Doctrine and Institutions*. Rome: Ardita Publishers.

Mussolini, B. (1923). *Mussolini as Revealed in his Political Speeches (November 1914-August 1923)*. London: Dent.

National Center for PTSD. (2011). Health Services Use in the Department of Veterans Affairs among Returning Iraq War and Afghan War Veterans with PTSD. *PTSD Research Quarterly* , 1.

National Transportation Safety Administration. (2011). *Traffic Safety Fats*. US Census Bureau.

New York Times. (1941 йил 23-February). Speech Delivered by Premier Benito Mussolini. *The New York Times* .

Pini, G. (1939). *The Official Life of Benito Mussolini*. (L. Villari, Trans.) London: Hutchinson & Co.

Pugliese, S. G. (2004). *Fascism, Anti-Fascism, and the Resistance in Italy*. Lanham: Rowman & Littlefield Publishers, Inc.

Richards, K. P. (1998). Jeunes combattants parlant de la guerre et de la paix en Sierra Leone ("When They Say Soldiers Are Rebels, It's a Lie": Young Fighters Talk about War and Peace in Sierra Leone). *Cahiers d'Études Africaines, Vol. 38, Cahier 150/152, Disciplines et déchirures. Les formes de la violence* .

Salvemini, G. (1936). *Under the Axe of Fascism*. London: Camelot Press Ltd.

Schmidt, C. T. (1939). *The Corporate State in Action: Italy Under Fascism*. New York City: Russell & Russell.

Schoene, B. (2000 йил November). Alive on Everest. (PBS/Nova, Interviewer)

Thompson, C. B. (1999). Beyond Civil Society: Child Soldier as Citizens in Mozambique. *Review of African Political Economy, Vol. 26, No. 80* .

University of Alberta. (2006). *Children and War*. Social Sciences and Research Center of Canada.

War Child. (n.d.). *Child Soldiers*. From War Child web site.

Weathers, B. (2000). *Left For Dead: My Journey Home from Everest*. New York: Random House.

West, J. (1999). Barometric Pressures on Mt. Everst; New Daya and Physiological Significance. *Journal of Applied Physiology* , 6.

Woods, R. (2006 йил 28-May). Has the Once Heroic Sport of Climbing Been Corrupted by Big Money? *The Sunday Times* .

Endnotes

[1] (War Child) http://www.warchild.org.uk/issues/child-soldiers?_kk=child%20 soldiers&_kt=34d0a30a-ab2f-4c8a-9b0b-6e877056c4e3&gclid=CKfCtPPCk6w CFUZ-5QodvDPRpw

[2] Thompson Carol B. *Beyond Civil Society: Child Soldiers as Citizens in Mozambique*, Review of African Political Economy, Vol. 26, No. 80, Bringing Imperialism Back In (Jun., 1999), pg. 191

[3] Thompson Carol B. pg 193

[4] Jaffré,,Françoise, *The Use of Children as Soldiers in Africa A country analysis of child recruitment and participation in armed conflict* http://www.reliefweb.int/library/documents/chilsold.htm accessed 4-29-10

[5] Jaffré, Françoise, accessed 4-29-10

[6] Peters, Krijn and Richards, Paul, *Jeunes combattants parlant de la guerre et de la paix en Sierra Leone ("When They Say Soldiers Are Rebels, It's a Lie"): Young Fighters Talk about War and Peace in Sierra Leone)* Cahiers d'Études Africaines, Vol. 38, Cahier 150/152, Disciplines et déchirures. Les formes de la violence (1998), pg. 591

[7] Peters, Krijn and Richards, Paul, pg. 591

[8] Faulkner Frank, Kindergarten *Killers: Morality, Murder and the Child Soldier Problem.* Third World Quarterly, Vol. 22, No. 4 (Aug., 2001), pg. 499

[9] Thompson, Carol B. pg. 192

[10] Jaffré, Françoise, accessed 4-29-10

[11] University of Alberta. (2006)

[12] (University of Alberta, 2006)

[13] Ishmael Beah, A Long Way Gone, Sarah Crichton Books, New York, 2007 pg. 24

[14] Ishmael Beah, A Long Way Gone, Sarah Crichton Books, New York, 2007 pg. pg 124

[15] Peters, Krijn and Richards, Paul, pg. 577

[16] Coalition to stop the use of child soldiers, *Child soldiers and Disarmament, Demobilization, Rehabilitation and Reintegration in West Africa*, Nov. 2006, pg. 12

[17] (Coalition to Stop the Use of Child Soldiers, 2006)

[18] Awodola Bosede, *Comparative International Experience with Reintegration Programmes for Child Soldiers: The Liberian Experience*, Peace & Conflict Review Volume 4, Issue 1, pg. 4

[19] National Center for PTSD, U.S. Department of Veterans Affairs. What is posttraumatic stress disorder (PTSD)?,http://www.ncptsd.va.gov/ncmain/ncdocs/fact_shts/fs_what_is_ptsd.html.

CHAPTER NINE

Blood Out: Nihilism in Gang Culture

Ilana Coenen

Gang members have developed a nihilist view on death showing no fear of the subject and acceptance of its constant and repetitive presence in their lives. Often luring in our nation's youth, gangs desensitize them to see their own death as inevitable and around the corner. This paper argues that gang members have a full acceptance of the brutality of death and understand death as a necessity in life. Nihilism is having lived without love, hope or meaning and in the case of gang members nihilism is death. They see death as forever present, forever in their future and as nothing to hide from or fear. Having no fear for death creates a form of acceptance for mortality in life.

Gang life confronts the grim reaper's fearful face of death. Gangs show no fear and no mercy. "[To] be a gang member, youth must display a level of toughness that warrants respect, which includes the display of fearlessness."[1] Death serves as a game; once you're in the game, it is kill or be killed. With easier access to weapons and growing inner city populations, gang violence has plagued many of America's cities. While most people have heard of "the game," most of us do not know what it is like to be a participant. This so called "game" becomes a reality to many; one filled with semi-automatic guns, drugs, money and respect. Along with the glory of wealth and power comes the grave realization that death is around the corner. Gang members have developed a nihilist view on death- showing no fear of the subject and acceptance of its constant presence in their lives.

This view begins with the cold-blooded initiation, during this process the deep seed of nihilism spreads it roots inside of the gangsters. This paper will go through the various aspects of gang life including the violence and risk involved. A constant presence of death in the lives of gang members creates a certain view on death within them. This nihilist view can be found within the lifestyle, in testimonials from gang members and in rap music [which was pioneered by gang members from 1992-2000].[2] Nihilism represents a rejection of established norms and absolute destructiveness focused especially at the world at large. Gang members are desensitized at a young age allowing them to see death as a game in which only the strong survive. This desensitization and constant presence of violence makes death a matter of fact for them, one that they do not fear but rather expect to come to them.

The initiation process seeks to separate the weak in the beginning. Gang members try to attract those younger people who might be looking for a family or for someone to protect them from being victimized. Often, these young recruits come from broken homes and spend a lot of time unsupervised. "To put it another way, gang members are youth for whom everything is going wrong."[3] Living with a lack of family presence and male influence, they are attracted to the idea of brotherhood and a family. "Yeah, it was like a family. You know, at the time, that was all I had to lean on."[4] Most gang members join at a young age, between the age of 12 and 15.[5] They are also attracted to the money, and the idea of the fast and rebellious life. As Curtis Crump, a member of LMG put it, "We love having sex, we love getting money and if you fuck up it's murder."[6] What these young kids don't know, however, is the reality of what they are signing up for. It takes nothing to join, but in many cases, once you do, you can never get out.

Initiation can begin in many ways, some violent, some not. Each gang adopts a different set of codes to enforce. Some use drive-by shooting as initiation, others use "beat ins;" and in the most violent gangs, there is only one way in and one way out: blood. A "beat in" consists of five to six gang members beating you for a period of time. In some cases you have to fight your way out of the circle. Other gangs, building larger empires will let anyone join, but no one gets out. A similar initiation philosophy is blood in, blood out, which is exactly what it sounds like - you must kill someone to get in and the only way out is death. "Its blood in, never blood out. You put your life in a nation you can't get out of. You're going to die being a Blood."[7] "While anyone can join [18th Street,] no one can leave. There's only one way to get out and that's getting killed."[8] Initiation is a right of passage; it bonds the family because you all had to join the gang in the same way. The readiness to use violence shows both your commitment and potential to the gang. "Members are expected to always be ready to commit violence, to participate in violent acts, and to engage in some sort of violence in their initiation into the gang."[9] After completing this initiation, you are welcomed with warm embrace as a new brother or sister.

Though not all gang initiations are violent, in their code they emphasize territory, respect and violence from the beginning. "At the heart of street culture is the issue of respect, defined as being treated right or being granted the deference one deserves." If gangs are formed based upon bleak surroundings and the need for a family influence, then disrespecting a gang is seen to be a mockery of their existence and of their family. "When one is disrespected, violent retaliation is warranted, if not expected."[10] Respect for a gang is closely related to territory. The disrespect of gang territory is offensive and an insult of the gang itself. "My territory, my domain; I would die for it." They consider their neighborhood their holy ground; no one can disrespect them on it. It is a gangs' safezone; it is something they can hold onto, to claim and own. Territory is often the cause of threats and violence. If rival gangs are seen on your territory, there is reason to believe they are not there with good intentions. This causes rival competition often ending in violence. After each initial reaction, there is warrented retaliation in play. As inmate 019 stated in an interview, gang members will do whatever it takes to get their rivals off their territory.

> INT: If someone from another gang comes to your turf, what does your gang do?

019: First try to tell him to leave.
INT: If he don't leave?
019: He'll leave one way or another-carry him out in
a Hefty bag[11]

Gang members want no one to dishonor their territory and will protect it at all costs. They believe their actions are justified by their strong emphasis on protecting their honor, family and neighborhood. Gangs feel no emotional connection to violence, allowing them to act without hesitations or regret. One gang member recollects; "They feared me because I didn't have no problems with taking a life. I mean, you know, you disrespect me or do something wrong to me, you'll die for it."[12] This could be an explanation for the extreme forms of violence used by gangsters. The stress on materials and territory mixed with a strong value for respect leads to violence with rival gangs. "The threat of violence also "enables" gang members to engage in violent acts (especially retaliatory violence) that they might not have chosen under other circumstances."[13] Gangs are highly sensitive to any threats made toward them, making their reactions quick and extreme. "The concern that a rival gang is considering an attack often compels a peremptory strike (particularly drive-by shooting) from the gang that considers itself under threat."[14] These peremptory strikes are made to ensure they maintain their status. Gangs arrange themselves in a way to maximize their influence on their territory and maintain a hold on their organization.

Hierarchy in a gang is formed by how "bad" you are, how ruthless, how invincible. "The more bad things you do, the more crimes you commit, the more you kill, and the more you make of yourself."[15] Gang members are raised in their own sub-society, which prohibits all fear. "In a sense, gang members are not allowed to show fear. If they do show fear, then they are likely ostracized, kept on the fringe of gang activities, or pushed out of the gang completely."[16] Fear is a weakness gangs do not recognize. This allows them to disconnect death from fear. Death is an action of retaliation, of force, of territory, of life. To a gang member it's not given much thought other than the fact that it could be coming to them, at any point.

This nihilist, "come-at-me" attitude toward death might be one of the most realistic examples of accepting death. Do they accept it to find a higher meaning? No, but they do accept it as something which occurs every day, one that will meet them in the future, near or far. If accepting death means embracing it for its brutality and understanding its necessity in the circle of life, then gang members have full acceptance. They see it as a presence- forever there, forever coming, and nothing to hide from.

Violence plays an active role in how feelings about life and death are formed. People prone to join gangs come from gang run neighborhoods. A gang member recalls, "It's a pretty violent neighborhood. A lot of drug dealers, gangs. A lot of people getting killed in my neighborhood."[17] "Violence is a part of the everyday life of gang members, even when they are apart from their gang; it is in their neighborhood, their families...Violence is an expected part of their individual status and roles as gang members."[18] Thus, violence is a surrounding force in their lives making them more prone act violently. "On average, the gang members committed their first criminal offense at the age of 9."[19] People are more likely to engage in these activities when they are common to them. "The gun becomes the symbol of power and remedy for disputes."[20] Gang membership is associated with a 169% increase in the odds of weapon carrying.[21] With easy access to weapons and violence surrounding you, it is easy to become involved. This constant occurrence of violence aids in the forming of a distorted mindset toward death. These individuals see violence and death as the norm, while others see it as a rare occurance. The belief that violence and guns are the norm for daily life can change ones perception, disconnecting death from feelings allowing for their nihilist and passive view.

Having no fear for death creates a form of acceptance of mortality in life. Although they may be living in a semi-Hobbesian state where the life of man is solitary, poor, nasty, brutish and short. This nihilism, this dismissal of the norm has led gangsters to be capable of accepting death. Death is so present to them that gang members refer to it as a game- something to be played with. Death, to a gangster is a flip of a coin; it has no place for anxiety or denial. Acceptance of life means we are ready to die. It has been stated by multiple previous gang members that everybody dies. "I'm ready to die and nobody can save me."[22] There is eagerness in this statement, or it is just the fact-that some accept death and are ready for it, whenever it may come.

"Many who adopt the street code also express a lack of fear for death, a notion that dying, "ain't a big deal" as a way to express toughness. Not fearing death makes it easier to convey the message that you fear no one."[23] One gang member recalls; "There has never been fear in my heart, I knew what I was doing"[24] Kubrin finds a correlation with nihilism and "gangsta rap" music, forming three subcategories. These subcategories are their bleak hopeless surroundings, continuous violence in the ghetto and preoccupation with death. It is possible that the constant presence of death and violence allows gang members to see it more readily as a fact of life. Mortality is very present in the gang community. "It was folks dead everywhere. Dead in the garbage can. Dead in the snow. Dead standing up on the wall, just death" Wild, a member of LMG (Love Murdering Gangsters, Nashville, TN) said as he recalled living in Nashville.[25]

Not many people have such a constant reminder of death in their lives. While there is no study done to show a quantitative connection between gang members and their attitudes toward death, in their speech a connection can be formed. They speak of it as a commonality, a way of life. Wild describes when he joined LMG; "It's like an imaginary story but it's not, it's like a death trap."[26] In a gang, violence is warranted and met with retaliation. Murder is a way to spread fear, show power and control, thus death shows status and achievement in the gang world. In a gang, murder can show your commitment and credibility. This praidal for killing helps warp the attitude these members have toward death. If death is seen as a duty, an honor and a way of life, then there is no reason to walk around afraid of it daily. Therefore, there is no place for fear of death. "Cause life is hell everybody dies."[27] Upon entering a gang, you become forced to accept death. You become constantly aware of its face in mortality; you begin to see it as a simple fact of life.

Nihilism is most often associated with Fredrich Nietzche, the philosopher. The concept is based upon the idea that there is neither objective nor structure to the world except what we give it. Nihilism can be found in gangs in their ethical and existential beliefs. Gangs reject moral codes and ethical values for their own set of values, such as brotherhood, respect and territory. On an existential stage, gang members affirm that life has no real meaning. There is an element of superficial meaning with the money and the drugs but gangs show no substantial value for life itself. This, I believe, stems from the hardships they face from poverty and crime in their neighborhoods. "A key feature of these communities is the limited opportunity structure available for residents to obtain the types of social status and roles available to youth in other environments."[28] The youth in gang populated areas have almost no other options. It is easy to get drawn into the gang life when it surrounds you; it seems like a stable way of gaining power and money. The youth are reared in a perpetual spiral without hope and must live with a constant reminder of this hopelessness. "[H]ow hard it must be to live only with what one knows and what one remembers, cut off from what one hopes for!... There can be no peace without hope."[29] The lack of hope for another type of lifestyle makes joining a gang that much more compelling. Nihilism, in the case of gang members is shaped by the lifestyle they have entered willingly.

"The conditions in extremely disadvantaged communities have led scholars to cite a growing sense of nihilism in black youth culture, an outgrowth of living in an environment filled with violence and limited opportunities."[30] The youth have seen a constant, high death rate among their peers causing them to believe they don't have a chance to live past twenty-five. "One must understand that some young people bereft of hope for the future of hope for the future have made peace with their peace with death and talk about planning their own funerals."[31] I agree with Kubrin's findings that the youth in these areas have found an acceptance of death. Death becomes so prevalent in gang life that they talk about it entering their lives freely. To show fear of death makes you weak. As I noted previously, gangs seek to weed out the weak immediately.

When looking at my own view on death, it is difficult to completely relate with gang members due to variations of the environment we were raised in. I found, however, that I can connect to America's youth prone to join gangs. The lack of love, family and hope can tear a person apart; the only solution is to find a community to embrace you and accept you as one of their own. Similar to young gangsters, I was lacking some part of my family influence; often I turned to friends for support. Quickly, I realized how easy it is to get involved with people who influence you negatively. The lure and attraction of drugs, sex, money, and power is emphasized daily in America -- isn't that what we all really want? After the death of my father, I fell hard into bad habits, trouble and nihilism toward life. My relation with death, as it is with gang members, is personal, it's family -- it cuts you up and forces you to look death in the eye.

While I have never held a gun nor played the "Grim Reaper's game", I understand the notion of not fearing our mortality. Fear is a game of the weak; it will not allow for progress, growth or acceptance. When it comes to my mortality, I have questions about what it all means, but I do not feel fear. "You can't fear for your life. If you fear for your life, you ain't gonna live long."[32] Fear can act as an entrapment, suffocating you from reality. I feel open for what is "around the corner;" I feel excited to say I have lived. Although gang members share this fearlessness, my acceptance of death is not as progressed. I won't condone the actions of these gang members but this paper proposes we look at them in a different way; nihilism is found not due to a pure hatred of society but because society has left no alternative. Whether they have begun in a gang, ended in a gang or ended up dead, gang members look death right in the eye. They look at something the average person fears and simply say- this is a fact. Mortality is a fact of life and you can't beat it, so accept it until your day comes. How would our society be if we all took such a bold acceptance of mortality? Death is called the great equalizer, the equilibrium of life that maintains balance. Opinions on death vary so vastly we forget how common it is. Gang members are forced to see it as a simple common occurrence. To these gangsters, mortality truly is the equalizer, the problem solver. Death shows no mercy, and it takes no prisoners. Gang members live and act with the same attitude.

The youth in gang run communities becomes admitted into a cycle. This cycle includes their surroundings, the lack of hope in their environments and the likelihood of them to join gangs due to these conditions. Due to the admittance into gangs occurring at such a young age, gangs have the ability to shape how their members view society. They represent a brotherhood, a family that protects eachother with honor and loyalty. Without this influence, these specific youths would not share the same nihilist view toward life. This cycle influences gangsters' view and acceptance of death; it reinforces their hopelessness in society. Fear is something true and unique to them; while their peers influence them, members choose who they wish to be within the gang. Their rejection of fear comes from their peers and surroundings but it also brews from within. The acceptance of mortality could be linked to each individual's feelings toward the world. For example, a gang member can simply be in the gang or try to gain status creating a name for themselves within the gang. The gang member who does not seek to climb the ladder may not have the same acceptance of death than the gang member who has killed more and has developed a status in the gang. In the gang world, status and greed place a target on your back. Thus the members who have a growing name and reputation are more likely to become a target to competition and rival gangs. These members may have developed a higher acceptance of death given the riskier lives they live. Given all conditions of gang life, members are shaped to feel no fear for death.

It can be argued that the actions of gang members are driven by anarchy rather than nihilism.

> It is important to remember the distinction between anarchism and nihilism. Anarchism is a very joyful social view. It stems from Jean-Jacques Rousseau's philosophy of the natural man. Man in his natural state is pure good, but he is corrupted by society. Thus, anarchism's goal of destruction is to return to this natural, purely good state.[33]

While the violence and irrational behavior of gang members may appear as anarchy it appears that it is their nihilistic view on life and death that allows them to act out such behavior. Gang members join at a prepubescent age [12-15]. Detective Gerry Hyder of Metro Nashville P.D. notes that in some case these juveniles are born into the gang life. "We see 9 and 10 year old boys reach that age where they can make that decision, it's a no brainer because they are gonna emulate their role models. Their role models are the ones that are out here running and gunning and banging. Sometimes they have no alternative but to follow in those footsteps."[34] Whether they were born into the gang, or simply attracted to joining a gang, at this age, the youth does not fully understand societal pressures and alienation. After joining a gang at this young age, the nihilistic view of life is adopted. Therefore, they adopt nihilistic values before fully understanding the nature of their surroundings. While some youth know there is a gang presence in the community, they do not join gangs as a means to overthrow society to restore its natural state. They join these gangs because they want a piece of the action, because there is nothing better for them to do. This boredom or lack of alternatives slowly becomes no hope; this hopelessness grows into no meaning in life or death.

Often when we think of nihilism we think nothingness, or link it to existentialism. Nietzsche gives nihilism the rational that there is no meaning in anything at all and any action would be fruitless as it has no rationale, societal or religious meaning.[35] This is how gang members have come to feel about mortality. Anything they do has no meaning, no rationale in society or religion. They can perform any action, because we all die in the end. Life can be a cold blood bath because we all have the same fate- that fate has no meaning. "Nihilism... is far more, the lived experience of coping with a life of horrifying meaninglessness, hopelessness, and most importantly, lovelessness."[36] The lives these gang members have survived place them in such a state. No love, meaning or hope can be found for the youth in the ghetto. There is no meaning in life or death therefore; there is nothing to fear in life and this notion allows them to accept death. "Nihilism, [like alcoholism or drug addiction] is a disease of the soul. It can never be cured and there is always a possibility of relapse."[37] The societal constraints on gang members enforce feelings of personal worthlessness allowing for a collapse of meaning, resulting in nihilism. One can detach from a gang, but one cannot detach from the mentality burned into the soul after being a member of a gang. "The major enemy of black survival in America is neither oppression nor exploitation but rather the nihilistic threat- that is the loss of hope and absence of meaning."[38] Nihilism is embedded into a subculture of America. This subculture is the one often associated with gang membership. For example, many of the findings of nihilism in society involve black youth, impoverished neighborhoods, unstable family lives etc. Each characteristic is also associated with gangs. According to Cornel West, nihilism is not about a struggle with death, *it is death*.[39] "There is nothing creative or meaningful about it."[40] This statement further connects with my hypothesis that the nihilistic view of gang members has allowed them to accept death. Members see mortality in a simple way; life is death; death is just that, the end.

As I said, I have seen death but I have not seen the same amount of heartbreak those compelled to join gangs have. I have not seen that amount of hopelessness. Can there be life without hope? Hope, in hard times can act as a shield to all evil. Once you demount that shield and throw hope out the window, man acts in drastic ways. The disposal of hope in some ways can be the downfall of one's sanity. There truly cannot be peace without hope. If we do not fear death, does that mean we have accepted it? How would you see life if everyday is a constant battle? To live a life in constant violence, hatred, and battle does not allow for one to see the glass half full. If I had to wonder everyday if I would die a violent death, I too would find no meaning in life. The life common society values, is one of hope, love, good role models and a stable home. Remove all of these influences, and one's moral values can be easily shifted. It has been said by numerous authors that hope is one of the most powerful things you can give someone. Without hope, we all fail. This is the exact predicament gang members are faced with. Take away hope and the meanings of life and death begin to crumble. Take away love and mark yourself as a societal disgrace - the meaning of everything disappears. I said I do not fear death. My position is simple; I cannot fear what I don't understand. I cannot fear the inevitable path of life. I know death will come to me and I will not be afraid of that. I will not, however, wait for my death to come. In comparison, gang members do not fear that which has no meaning i.e. life and death.

Nihilism becomes a structure of thought that embeds nothingness into the lives of gang members. "Nihilism is about the expression of undaunted yearning, desperate (violently so, perhaps even to the extreme of self destruction), meaningful in its furious revolt against a world of bewildering violence and meaningless death."[41] The violent nature of gangs doesn't stem from anarchy, rather their inner nihilism. It is a battle against the meaninglessness of death. In doing so, death simply becomes more and more meaningless. Life becomes so detached from meaning there is nothing to question about our mortality.

The type of brutal, reoccurring violence used by gang members has allowed for further detachment from remorse. "[T]he one thing more prevalent in the ghetto than poverty, family disruption and limited opportunities is violence and death."[42] The type of violence used is barbarous and boorish. Violence has become more prevalent with the increase in illegal gun carrying.[43] Studies by Decker, Rosenfeld and Van Winkle reveal that gang members are more likely than other juveniles to carry guns most or all of the time.[44] Two thirds of the gang members studied had used their guns at least once.[45] The homicide problem associated with gangs "is largely a gun homicide problem."[46] "Gang violence has been exacerbated by the ready availability and use of firearms, especially more lethal guns, coupled with frequent use of automobiles in attacks on other gangs."[47] One gang member recalls the reoccurring presence of violence; "Shoot-outs mostly everyday. I mean, it was always somebody got into something with another person or some type of altercation that escalated into a shoot out... The guns are the problem solvers."[48] Violence does not stop with guns and drive-by shootings. The frequency and brutality of gang violence makes it distinct from other violent occurrences. Gang members often use overkill to send a message.[49] Jesse (name changed for safety), a member on the run from 18th Street Gang, recalls his method of killing; "I choose stabbing, anybody can shoot a gun. It takes a real person to go up to somebody and stab him or her."[50] This shows a personal connection with the killing. These individuals show no mercy and no value for human life. An example of this is found in the Los Zetas gang. Sarah Carter, a reporter for The Washington Times recalls; "They have kidnapped innocent people and their bodies have never been found. The Zetas take them out into the dessert and bury them in vats. They have put them in acid and watched their bodies disintegrate. They have fed them to wild animals."[51] Not only is there overkill, but also these gang members watch their victims suffer, further diminishing the value for humanity. This type of extreme violence is distinct to gangs. It is a mark of power used to spread fear of the gang and force people to show respect for them.

This type of killing is meant to send a message. "Sometimes torture is necessary, everything is necessary in circumstances."[52] Gang member have made justifications for their actions. They believe they are necessary in their circle of life and can set an example for rival gangs. This bloodthirsty violence reinforces their lack of fear, their value of respect and the temporariness of life.

The nature and actions of gang members are all a reflection of their view toward life. Change is not expected, they simply accept the reality in which they live. Once you are ball and chained to a fate you did not choose, there is no desire to uphold societal morals. It becomes easier to shoot, kill, steal; it becomes harder to feel remorse and apathy. When life has given you no choice, you become infused with negativity. As Ted Rosenthal said, "Once you have nothing, you can do anything." When life has given you no choice and stripped you of all dignity it becomes easier to break the rules. It becomes easier to be violent and resentful. In this case, nihilism is not simply the notion of meaninglessness. In gang life it becomes an addiction for the disadvantaged. It is a cycle that allows you to kill and be killed without any care in the world.

People always ask this question: Who is the killer, the gun or the man? In respect to gangs the man kills without fear or sorrow. Man kills and kills until he too gets killed. There is no question that gang members are affected by this lifestyle. At a certain point, there is no turning back. Upon entering a gang, you are molded to adhere to their beliefs. You become locked into a new lifestyle. You become a slave to your gun and your new family. Hope, fear and societal values fade away. Your world becomes filled with materials yet nothing is satisfying. Death becomes a reality and approaches you daily. Death is the end of the alley you have been walking down. Whether you are a major player in the gang or a simple foot soldier, death is all that awaits you. The actions you take in life have no value, no meaning, you can live as ruthlessly as you like. Death is nothing to fear so grab onto that gun and walk. Walk into the dark alley to find what awaits you. Any day could be the day you go, you aren't afraid so the game continues. Then one day, you're walking into that alley, in your neighborhood, on your turf. You hear someone closing in on you from behind. One thought will come to mind and one alone. So you think to yourself, *this is it.* As you try to grab your gun that's when you hear it. *Bang. Bang. Bang. Bang. Bang.* A flash of white enters your mind as your body hits the pavement. Man is the killer in the game of gangs. The winner of the game is the gun.

Bibliography

Camus, A. (1962). *The Plague.* New York: Time.

De Genova, N. (1995). Gangster Rap and Nihilism in Black America: Some Questions of Life and Death. *Social Text , 43*, 89-132.

Decker, S. H. (1996). Collective and Normative Features of Gang Violence. *Justice Quarterly , 13* (2), 243-264.

Decker, S. H., & Van Winkle, B. (1996). *Life in the Gang: Family, Friends and Violence.* Cambridge, UK: Cambridge UP.

Fleisher, M. S. (2010). A World of Gangs: Armed Young Men and Gangsta Culture . By John M. Hagedorn . *Social Service Review* , *84* (2), 328-332.

Green, J., & Pranis, K. (2007). Gang Wars: The Failure of Enforcement Tactics and the Need for Effective Public Safety Strategies. *Justice Policy Issue Report*, 1-101.

Hagedorn, J. (2008). *A World of Gangs: Armed Young Men and Gangsta Culture.* Minneappolis : University of Minnesota Press.

History Channel, T. (2012). Born into Gangland. *Gangland* . The History Channel.

History Channel, T. (n.d.). Gangs: Code of Violence. *Gangland* . 2012: The History Channel.

History Channel, T. (2009, March 3). Kill or Be Killed. *Gangland* . The History Channel.

History Channel, T. (2008, May 8). Murder By Numbers. *Gangland* . The History Channel.

Howell, J. C., & Decker, S. H. (1999). The Youth Gangs, Drugs and Violence Connection. *Juvenile Justice Bulletin* , 1-9.

Kubrin, C. E. (2005). I See Death Around The Corner": Nihilism In Rap Music. *Sociological Perspectives* , *48* (4), 433-459.

Melde, C., Taylor, T. J., & Esbensen, F.-A. (2009). I Got Your Back": An Examination Of The Protective Function Of Gang Membership In Adolescence. *Criminology* , *47* (2), 565--594.

Pinizzotto, A. J. (2007). Street-gang Mentality: A Mosaic of Remorseless Violence and Relentless Loyalty. *FBI Law Enforcement Bulletin* , *76* (9), 1-32.

Endnotes

[1] (Melde, Taylor, & Esbensen, 2009) p.586-587

[2] (Kubrin, 2005) p.439-440

[3] (Green & Pranis, 2007) p.45-46

[4] (Pinizzotto, 2007) p.2-4

[5] Green and Pranis, op cit., p.46

[6] "Kill or Be Killed"

[7] ibid.

[8] "Murder by Numbers"

[9] (Howell & Decker, 1999) p.5-8

[10] Kubrin, op cit., p.439-440

[11] (Decker, Collective and Normative Features of Gang Violence, 1996) p.258-259

[12] Pinizzotto, op cit., p.2-4

[13] Decker, op cit., p.246

[14] Kubrin, op cit., p.447

[15] Howell & Decker, op cit., p.5-8

[16] Melde, Taylor & Esbensen, op cit., p.586-587

[17] Pinizzotto, op cit., p.2-4

[18] Howell & Decker, op cit., p.5-8

[19] Decker, op cit., p.246

[20] Pinizzotto, op cit., p.6

[21] Melde, Taylor & Esbensen, op cit., p.369

22 Kubrin, op cit., p.451
23 Kubrin, op cit., p.441
24 "Murder By Numbers"
25 ibid.
26 ibid.
27 Kubrin, op cit., p.446
28 Kubrin, op cit., p.438
29 (Camus, 1962) p.262-263
30 ibid.
31 (Hagedorn, 2008) p.328-332
32 "Murder By Numbers"
33 Hagedorn, op cit., p.328-332
34 "Born into Gangland"
35 (Fleisher, 2010) p.216
36 (De Genova, 1995) p.92
37 De Genova, op cit., p.101-102
38 De Genova, op cit., p.92
39 ibid.
40 ibid.
41 De Genova, op cit., p.101-102
42 Kubrin, op cit., p.447
43 Howell & Decker, op cit., p.5-8
44 ibid.
45 Hagedorn, op cit., p.328-332
46 ibid.
47 Kubrin, op cit., p.444
48 Kubrin, op cit., p.446
49 "Gangs: Code of Violence"
50 Howell & Decker, op cit., p.5-8
51 "Gangs: Code of Violence"
52 ibid.

V. DEATH IN NAZISM AND FASCISM

CHAPTER TEN

Death Through the Eyes of the Nazi Schutzstaffel

Morgan Zubof

When faced with the darkest moment of history, the pain and suffering that man has proven all too willing to impose on others, we often dismiss such events as the random acts of 'monsters.' The atrocities committed by the Nazi Schutzstaffel (SS) are no different. However, such an explanation is a gross oversimplification of a complex social and political ideology that fostered an environment where such atrocities were acceptable and overlooks the moral and political lessons that still apply today. This paper argues that the Final Solution, proposed and carried out largely by the Nazi SS, was a direct result of the social and political ideology embraced by the SS with particular focus paid to the organization's views on the meaning of life, death, and the moral implications of murder.

Throughout the twentieth century there have been cases of genocide on almost every continent, however, no case is more notorious than the Holocaust. For many people, the Holocaust is a difficult time in European history to grasp. In facing the atrocities committed by the

Third Reich many rational individuals simply dismiss the systematic murder of millions of people as the actions of 'monsters'. Webster's dictionary defines a 'monster' as "an animal or plant of abnormal form or structure; an animal of strange or terrifying shape." This definition refers to the imaginary terrors that children throughout the ages have thought lived in the shadows under their beds or in their closets but it certainly has no place in describing those SS members who created and carried out the Final Solution that led to the deaths of more than ten million individuals. However, Webster's dictionary goes on to describe a 'monster' as "one who deviates from normal or acceptable behavior or character; a threatening force." This version of a monster can certainly be applied to the SS members who led millions to their deaths; however, it remains unsatisfactory. To dismiss the greatest instance of genocide in the twentieth century as the actions of 'monsters' ignores the causes that lead to the Holocaust as well as belittles the moral and political lessons that must be remembered.

The ability to commit the atrocities seen throughout the Third Reich required an individual with a particular personality and an individual with a rather unique opinion regarding death and, by extension, life. The factors that contributed to the formation of such a personality are numerous and complex and it would be a folly to suggest that any one person could explore all of them. However, it seems likely that one of the main causes was the political and social ideology embraced by the Nazi Schutzstaffel SS, particularly as it relates to the organization's views on the moral implications of murder. While Adolf Hitler was the leader of the Nazi party and the Head of State of the Third Reich, the SS became synonymous with the mass murders because of its critical role in the creation and implementation of the Final Solution.

The ideology of the SS was similar to the ideology of the larger Nazi party as established by Hitler. It was rooted in the revolutionary changes that shook traditional institutions throughout Europe in the aftermath of the First World War. Furthermore, it was strongly influenced by the radicalization of the middle and upper level classes throughout Germany as a result of Germany's defeat in World War I and the global depression of the 1920s. However, the SS ideology did possess unique components, which are captured adequately by

Michael Burleigh in his book *The Third Reich: A New History,* who stated (2000, 194):

> ...[SS ideology was a] synthetic mixture of the novel and traditional, overlain with death-fixated kitsch... The SS fused deracinated versions of traditional military virtues; attitudes derived from the war and its aftermath; and a new/old anti-Christian morality...

It was the ideological combination described by Burleigh, which made the SS ideal for carrying out much of the Third Reich's 'dirty work.'

One of the cornerstones of the SS ideology, and a belief that directly affected members' beliefs on life and death, was the superiority of the Aryan race. Like Hitler, the SS believed the Aryans, led by the Germans, were chosen as 'the master race' and were destined to dominate lesser humans. According to Hitler and SS ideology, the Aryans were limited in number but drew their strength from a collective power based in racial purity (Burleigh 2000,92). Therefore, the preservation of a pure Aryan race became the primary goal of the Third Reich. The SS believed it was imperative that the German state be re-established under a racial hierarchy where all ethnic Germans were geographically located within the boarders of the Third Reich (Shirer 1960, 82). SS ideology called for the creation of a new world order in which the Aryan race reigned supreme and non-Aryan races, especially Slavs, were relegated to the fringes of society performing degrading and humiliating tasks for their Aryan masters (88).

While the Slavic populations of Eastern Europe were considered lesser humans, the SS saw the Jewish population as the greatest threat to a purified Aryan race (Breitman 1991, 91). The Nazi party was certainly not unique in their deep hatred of European Jewry. In fact, many scholars believe that anti-Semitism in Europe can be traced back to the complex relationship between Jews and Christians and the "folkloric beliefs" about Jews propelled by the Catholic Church (Burleigh 2000,93). However, anti-Semitism rose to unprecedented levels in Germany following the First World War in large part because the Jewish population was blamed for Germany's defeat and the increasingly dire economic situation. SS ideology played off the already widely accepted vilification of German Jews by claiming that they were simply parasites who had corrupted German blood through racial intermingling (Breitman 1991, 91).

The SS was popular with veterans of World War I, especially individuals who were unable to readjust to civilian life following Germany's defeat. This was partially due to the willingness of the organization to adopt Hitler's claim that the Nazi party was the heir to the First World War's frontline soldier tradition. While the soldiers fighting on the front line during the war had represented the true Germany, Hitler argued that the true Germany was now represented by the members of the Nazi party (Buchheim 1965, 322). Veterans were also attracted to the SS because the organization adopted the concept of the 'political soldier,' which appears in a rudimentary form in the beliefs of German soldiers during World War I. Traditionally, the 'political solider' had a dual meaning. On one hand, it indicated the soldier with political conviction, an individual who knew what he was fighting for. On the other hand, it was used to describe the individual who acted in politics as he would in war (311). Within SS ideology, however, the 'political solider' was grossly perverted to stress the importance of fighting to SS members.

It is also important to note at this time that within SS ideology the traditional meaning of the word 'soldierly' was completely stripped away. The term 'soldierly' came to represent the (Buchheim 1965, 322) "general belligerent attitude" that became acceptable throughout the SS. Hans Buchheim points out in his article "Command and Compliance" that a Wehrmacht General stated (322), "...members of the Waffen-SS were not soldiers but fighters..." Buchheim goes on to argue that such a statement is significant in understanding the mentality of the SS because it highlights a critical difference between the concept of the soldier and the interpretation of the soldier by the SS. In the traditional sense, the soldier's choice is that of a profession; he learns the trade of fighting and uses that trade when necessary. The fighter's choice, on the other hand, is that of a method to approaching life; an attitude that dictates a pattern of behavior. In other words, the soldier trains for specific events in which fighting is necessary, but maintains a social presence separate from the fighting he engages in. The fighter, however, is always preparing for an inevitable conflict and accepts a worldview, which is dominated by the presence of fighting (322). It is the notion of the fighter, which better fits the SS belief that life is dominated by a constant struggle.

In embracing the fighter, SS ideology imprinted upon members of the organization a grossly perverted notion of the 'political soldier,' in which they were expected to fight for fighting sake. Within this new notion of the 'political soldier' the idea of a struggle was turned into (Buchheim 1965, 322-323) "an absolute concept and coupled it with an ideology glorifying the 'struggle for existence.'" As a result, SS members were placed in a state of constant tension, where accepted rules of behavior became abnormal and questionably moral behavior, usually tolerated only during periods of extreme stress, became the norm. Any indication of relaxation by an SS member was considered an assault on the entire organization and was therefore viewed as a sign of weakness (323).

While a true SS fighter was expected to be independent, reliant on no one but himself, freethinking was not encouraged. SS members were expected to carry out orders without question from superiors who were beyond refute. The SS believed that their cause was the only cause and therefore its virtue was absolute. As a result, the SS fighter was taught that success was the only option, failure was unacceptable and nothing was to be considered impossible (Buchheim 1965, 327; Burleigh 2000, 195 – 196).

An essential aspect of SS ideology, which was present in large part because of the adoption of the perverted notion of the 'political soldier,' was 'hardness.' Heinrich Himmler stated on 4 October 1943 (Buchheim 1965, 334):

> For the SS man there is one absolute principle; he must be honest, decent, loyal, and friendly to persons of our own blood – and to no one else.

All soldiers are taught to embrace a certain level of 'hardness' in order to survive the brutality of the battlefield; however, the emphasis that SS ideology placed on being 'hard' led to a degradation of its members' humanity. The loss of this humanity inevitably caused members to become unsympathetic, ruthless, and cruel. The complete disregard for human life was further evident within the SS through its crucial teaching, which stated that the SS fighter must never hesitate in shedding blood, either that of his own or that of his enemy (Buchheim 1965, 334).

In order to counteract the inhumane system established under SS ideology, members embraced the concept of camaraderie. The sense of 'comradeship' that developed made the 'hard' nature of the SS culture tolerable; it provided protection for those within the SS ranks from the otherwise impossible standards, degrading conditions, and unrealistic expectations that were imposed (Buchheim 1965, 343). In general, camaraderie creates a bond between members of a specific group and encourages members of that group to become a cohesive unit. In military organizations, camaraderie provides a sense of solidarity that allows the human spirit to survive moments of extreme stress and exposure to the darkest components of human nature. The SS was no exception. Within the SS, members expressed a desire to share each other's burdens and the weak were brought under the protection of stronger members (343). However, due to the perverted notion of a 'soldier' and the disproportionate emphasis placed on 'hardness' in SS ideology, camaraderie throughout the SS resulted in the dismissal of individual responsibility and the toleration of extreme personality disorders. Throughout the organization personal faults were ignored, if not completely covered up, and moral standards slipped (344). The strong sense of camaraderie that existed throughout the SS resulted in a cultish identity among its members. The organization became intolerant of resignations and personal aspects of life were brought into the folds of the organization. For example, religious weddings were outlawed and marriage vows were exchanged during a SS centric ceremony (Burleigh 2000, 194).

One key component of the SS social ideology that must be examined in order to understand how its members viewed death was their belief in a social hierarchy based on racial qualifications rather than economic status. The SS desired a society where success was no longer measured by an individual's birth but by an individual's commitment, performance, reliability, and effectiveness. While the group dismissed the importance of nobility, they strongly supported the creation of a social elite chosen on racial factors (Burleigh 2000, 193). Many SS members felt that the SS itself was the social elite of the Third Reich because of its close association with Hitler and the strict eugenic and racial qualifications used for entrance into the organization (192).

While SS ideology may not directly address the issue of human immortality, death, and the moral implications of murder, it clearly provided roots for a culture that disregarded the value of human life and tolerated unusually high levels of cruelty. The SS believed that the preservation of the Aryan race was essential to the survival of not only Germany, but all of mankind. The presence of 'sub-humans,' became an issue of national security for the Third Reich. Himmler warned that if Germany failed in uniting under a racially pure society there would be (Breitman 1991, 51) "nothing left for the Germans – no Indian-style reservation; all Germans would be starved and butchered." By creating the notion that each German was in danger as long as a Jewish presence continued in Germany the SS reduced any actions against the Jews to merely an act of self-defense. Just like any other animal, humans possess a strong sense of self-preservation and are instinctually programmed to take whatever measures are necessary to survive. It is because of this, that even civilized societies tolerate acts of violence in the case of self-defense. Within our own judicial system a homeowner is not tried for murder if he shoots an intruder. Each of us tolerates a certain level of violence against another individual when we feel our life is in danger. In a twisted view of reality, European Jewry became a personal threat to Germany and Aryan supremacy making it easier for SS members to disregard the importance of their victims lives and ignore any potential moral conflicts with killing them. Within this distorted version of reality, the death of others became an integral part of their outlook on life. Without the death of their victims, they believed their own survival was at risk.

Fear for personal survival was not the only rationalization used by members of the SS to justify the killing of millions of people. SS ideology also reinforced the notion that since Slavs and Jews were 'lesser humans' or 'sub-humans' they did not deserve the same quality of life, or even the same right to life, that members of the Aryan race did. As 'parasites' feeding off the strength of the Aryan people, these groups had to be exterminated just as any rational person would exterminate a cockroach infestation in their home. The notion that their victims were nothing more than a pest was reaffirmed by the SS's extermination method of choice. In extermination camps throughout

Eastern Europe, victims of the Third Reich were gassed using Zyclon B, a pesticide originally designed for delousing. Through terms such as 'lesser human,' 'sub-human,' and 'parasite' the victims of the SS were dehumanized, which allowed SS members to accept their deaths more readily. During the process of dehumanization, the persecutor is able to separate themselves from their victims and identify differences between themselves and their victims. When a person ceases to be a person ending their life becomes exponentially easier.

Another key aspect of SS ideology that illustrates the organization's views on death was the pressure for efficiency combined with the notion that failure was unacceptable. Many scholars of the time period argue that The Final Solution was born out of Hitler's obsession with racial purity but formulated because of the bureaucratic efficiency and seriousness with which the SS approached 'The Jewish Question' (Breitman 1991, 246). To a certain extent, this argument is probably true. The Final Solution was not formed overnight, nor did the desire to exterminate all of European Jewry. While the SS agenda entertained the idea of killing Jews as early as 1938, early SS plans dealt with German Jews only and focused on forced immigration and sterilization (246). However, as the number of Jews under Nazi control expanded earlier plans became less and less feasible.

The failure to find a moderate approach to 'the Jewish question' led SS leadership to embrace extreme measures in order to find an efficient and concrete solution. Within our own culture there are respected boundaries to pursuing one's goals; we must all balance the desire to succeed with a moral and legal code that prevents severe actions. Throughout the Republican Primaries we have seen candidates verbally attack their opponents in order to drum up support; however, no candidate would assassinate their opponent in order to win the nomination. Such a severe action would be considered repugnant, morally debase, and not to mention illegal. This balance between pursuing goals and acting morally was completely lacking within the SS. Rather, SS ideology reinforced the notion of success at all costs, regardless of the moral or legal repercussions, allowing the SS to gradually escalate from racial restrictions to mass murder.

While the disregard for moral implications in the pursuit of one's goals led the SS to extreme measures against European Jewry, it was their desire for efficiency that led to mass extermination and concentration camps. Richard Breitman lays out the connections superbly in his book *the Architect of Genocide: Himmler and The Final Solution*. According to Breitman, the idea of mass extermination in concentration camps became a logical solution because it provided a streamlined process, which was necessary given the large number of Jews that fell under the Third Reich's control by 1940 (1991, 88). Furthermore, Breitman argues that Himmer, the Commander of the SS (197), "...wanted a neater, cleaner, less upsetting way of killing large numbers of people, and poison gas was the obvious solution." Breitman is referring to the decision to move away from mass executions by shooting carried out by the Einsatzgruppen in the Soviet Union during the German invasion of 1941 to more established killing centers where gassing could be used. The SS, a bureaucracy consumed by the need for organization and efficiency, chose to gas millions of people with a pesticide because it was the fastest and most inexpensive method available. While the desire to murder someone is evidence enough of complete indifference to the value of human life, the decision by the SS to use a rather slow and painful method of execution further shows their disregard for their victims. In the United States, capital punishment is carried out via several methods; however, lethal injection has become the most common because it is believed to be the quickest, most humane method available. While it would certainly be more cost effective for the government to put a single bullet in the condemned's head, this method would be considered inhumane and therefore unacceptable. Since the SS was able to place efficiency above moral implications the organization was able to eliminate millions of people in a short time span. Their combined desire to succeed at all costs and the emphasis placed on efficiency further enforced the blatant disregard for human life.

While the obsessive desire to preserve racial purity, the inability to accept failure, and the emphasis placed on efficiency made SS members susceptible to the idea of mass extermination, it was the belligerent attitude and extreme 'hardness' embraced by the organization that allowed SS members to tolerate the gruesome tasks assigned to them. The mere sight of blood is enough to make many people's knees go weak and even those who handle blood well are touched by an uneasy stomach at scenes of absolute cruelty and mass graves. It is for this reason that the airing of disturbing pictures on news channels is limited and viewers are warned before a troubling episode of *Law and Order*. The ability to witness, let alone carry out, the atrocities committed by the SS could not have been tolerated by the average person – the brutality, the inhumanity, and the pain would have brought most people to the brink of illness.

However, evidence that SS members became ill when faced with their orders simply does not exist. In fact, there is plenty of evidence that indicates that some SS officers enjoyed their assignments. Dr. Joseph Mengele, was an SS officer and camp doctor at Auschwitz. Camp doctors were responsible for performing Ramp Selection (determining who would be gassed immediately and who would be used for hard labor); however a task that should have been split evenly between the twenty-two camp doctors fell proportionally more often on Mengele (Astor 1985, 62). Additionally, Mengele sent as many as eighty to ninety percent of new arrivals directly to their deaths when official orders stated that twenty to twenty-five percent should be saved for hard labor (61). Mengele's demeanor during the selection process was described by Arminio Wachsberger, a Roman Jew transported to Auschwitz, as (59):

> He had a gentle manner And a quite poise that almost always lay between the edges of smugness and the height of charm

Mengele's willingness to send people to their deaths has been well documented, but is perhaps best shown during the Yom Kippur Massacre of 1943. On Yom Kippur Mengele gathered 2,000 boys on a soccer field. When one of the younger boys lied about his age, Mengele had a piece of wood nailed to a goal post and required all of the boys to pass beneath it. Anyone who did not reach the height of the marker was selected. While the guards gathered up the smaller boys Mengele reportedly started laughing as they cried for their mothers. On that day, 1,000 boys were selected and gassed (Astor 1985, 67–68). It is clear that Mengele was happy with his role at Auschwitz. His eagerness to perform ramp selections indicates that he enjoyed the process and the description of his appearance suggests he was comfortable in his role. Furthermore, his willingness to spontaneously send 1,000 boys to their deaths implies that he thrived on his power over the inmates; his right to grant life or take it away. This behavior is indicative of the hardness SS members were expected to show. They were trained to harden themselves to human emotions – to the cries, the pain, the sadness, and the suffering of their victims. Compassion towards them was interpreted as a weakness and could not be tolerated. The belligerent attitude nurtured throughout SS ideology led the organization and its members to dismiss their humanity, allowing them to accept and even enjoy the pain and suffering of others.

It is impossible to fully understand the organization's views on death without exploring its views and acceptance of the death of its members. While there is virtually no information available indicating how individual members of the SS felt about their own deaths or whether they even considered their own mortality, their actions during and after World War II provide some insight into their views on their personal deaths. Since its formation, the SS, as a whole, suffered from an extremely high suicide rate. Scholars of the period indicate that this was primarily due to the continued exposure to stressful situations and the pressure to embrace a worldview dominated by struggle (Burleigh 2000, 195). A key component of the corrupted notion of the 'political solider' was the philosophy of the many over the individual. SS members were encouraged to show a willingness to shed their own blood for the preservation of the larger group and SS ideology reinforced the importance of success over the importance of an individual's life. While the SS certainly valued its members' lives over that of its victims, the organization as a whole universally disregarded the value of any one individual life. Within SS ideology, every life was replaceable; it was the survival of the group rather than the survival of the individual that was important.

It seems reasonable to argue that the SS was aware of the human condition – the fact that each person is mortal. Furthermore, it seems plausible that not only did they understand this fact, they embraced it. As an organization that prided itself on preparing for the ultimate struggle in which the fate of humanity lay, there was no greater purpose in life than dying for the preservation of the larger group. The true meaning of life was the ability to fight for the larger good and defend against any group willing to challenge the superiority of Germany. Furthermore, once the Final Solution was in place, the entire strategy of the Third Reich was based on the annihilation of an entire group of people. It seems implausible that they could send millions of individuals to their deaths without being fully aware of people's mortality.

This certainly does not mean that individual members thought their deaths would occur how and when they did. Following Germany's defeat at the end of World War II, the high levels of suicide continued throughout ex-SS members. It seems unlikely that these individuals believed shedding their own blood would preserve anything and even more unlikely that any of them pictured this end for themselves. It seems more likely that these individuals were unable to accept the defeat of Germany. Within an organization that placed such importance on success, the defeat of Germany and the end of the Third Reich must have been the worst failure of all; the end of the ultimate struggle in which they had failed to preserve the racial purity of the Aryan race. Such a resounding and final defeat must have been too much for many SS members to face and therefore death appeared far better than the world order that would surely follow. Furthermore, the nature of the 'political solider,' as interpreted by the SS, was to fight during the ultimate struggle. With the ultimate struggle over, their purpose in life, their desire to live ceased to exist. Lost and without guidance many SS members felt that life was no longer worth living; without a cause to fight for life simply became meaningless. At first, given my own prejudices, I suspected that suicides among SS members at the end of World War II was simply an act of cowardice. However, it is clear that those individuals did not view their suicide as cowardly; rather, they were so entrenched in SS ideology that they were unable to adjust when the organization disbanded.

This is not to say that all members of the SS committed suicide following Germany's defeat. Many SS members fled Germany, which appears to be a simple act of self-preservation. Realizing that the war was over and Germany defeated, high-ranking SS members fled Europe to avoid capture and possible military trials by Allied forces. On a primitive level, fleeing was a response to the basic fight versus flight instinct that all animals possess. Recognizing that the fight was over, the only option for self-preservation was flight. The high regard for their own lives was in direct opposition to the complete disregard these SS members showed for the lives of their victims. In pursuing racial purity, SS ideology taught that the lives of 'lesser humans' or 'sub-humans' were of no consequence. Furthermore, SS members thought of themselves of elites, which would have made the value of their lives far more important than the lives of their victims.

One of the leading causes behind the Holocaust was the ideology of the SS and the unique view this ideology had on death, the meaning of life, and the moral implications of murder. It cannot be argued that the SS was anything short of evil and there can be no justification for the organization's actions. However, it also cannot be argued that the SS acted randomly, nor did it act without purpose. It presented a concrete and consistent ideology that its members were able to support wholeheartedly. While the SS could be considered one of the more radical portions of the Nazi party, its ideology was not far-fetched for the time. The ideology was not based on the imaginative ramblings of a few unhinged individuals. It merged widely accepted views of the time along with forward-thinking beliefs that offered comfort in a difficult time. As perverted and twisted as this ideology may have been, for its members, it was reality.

Perhaps the scariest part of the SS ideology, is that it makes sense when viewed through the reality it embraces. When viewed in a microcosm, the killing of millions of innocent people seems incomprehensible. However, seen though the eyes of those individuals who believed SS ideology, it seems completely rational. The actions of the SS were not random acts of violence solely for violence sake. Members of the SS did not kill just because they enjoyed the act of taking another humans life. They sent millions of people to their deaths because it was a means to a clearly defined end. The Final Solution was a logical course of action; it was really the only course of action that makes sense given the reality in which they lived.

In considering this more closely, it seems that this only makes the formation of the Final Solution more terrifying. The idea that rational careful individuals could be led to commit such atrocities is far from comforting. This is particularly true when one starts to consider a key similarity between our own ideology and that of the SS. The United States has proven on multiple occasions that it is all too willing to categorize a group of people by one characteristic – their ethnicity, race, or religion. Just as the SS actively rounded up and segregated European Jews in Ghettos and Concentration Camps for no other reason than their religion, the American government interned thousands of Japanese-Americans during World War II for no other reason than their ancestry. While the internment of Japanese-Americans did not end in their murder, it still represents the same prejudices. Categorizing people based on a single qualifier that, in reality, tells us very little about a person leads to the removal of the individual. Individualism is a critical component of American society; the notion that each of us is our own person with our own strengths and our own weaknesses is engrained into us from a young age and helps us find our place in the world. As a culture that places such a large emphasis on individualism it has become a key component to our definition of a human being. If individualism is removed, the process of dehumanization has begun. The American public failed to protect Japanese-Americans during World War II just as the German public failed to protect German-Jews.

Since September 11, our ability to distinguish the individual from the group has been tested once again. The notion that all Muslims are terrorists because those individuals who attacked America are Muslims shows, once again, our readiness to disregard the individual and perpetuate hate based on a single trait. Just as Japanese-Americans' rights were squashed during World War II for the comfort of the majority, Muslim-Americans are facing the same persecution today. In a time when debates between civil liberties and national security occur on a weekly basis it is imperative that we, as the American people, remember that security cannot be bought at any cost. As a nation we must consider carefully what we are willing to do in the name of national security; what rights are we willing to give up, what morals are we willing to compromise in the name of national security.

Finally, we must remember that human life is valuable. It is easy to get caught up in the battle between 'us' and 'them' but we must always remember that even the lives of our enemies have value. We must rise above the temptation to become engulfed by prejudices and hatreds and remember that human life is something that should always be cherished, even in times of war. The line between morally acceptable and morally repugnant is thin – we must constantly assess what side of that line we are on and what side we should be on.

The political and social ideology of the SS fostered a unique view of death, dying, and the importance of life throughout its membership, which inevitably led SS members to bring about the extermination of roughly ten million people. The ideology of the SS was the result of tremendous social and political changes that occurred throughout Europe following the end of World War I and the economic troubles of the 1920s. It contained ideas from traditional German philosophies as well as new concepts proposed by a radicalized middle class. It called for a world order dominated by the Aryan race, corrupted the notion of the 'political solider,' and emphasized 'hardness.' In general, SS ideology led to the devaluing of the individual and a blatant disregard for human life. Those individuals who embraced such an ideology certainly deviated from acceptable behavior and as such could be considered 'monsters' according to Webster's dictionary. However, in labeling these individuals as simply 'monsters' the carefully considered actions of rational individuals bent on fulfilling their political and social goals becomes lost.

Work Cited

Astor, Gerald, 1985. *The "Last" Nazi: The Life and Times of Dr.Joseph Mengele*. New York: Donald I Fine, Inc.

Breitman, Richard, 1991. *The Architect of Genocide: Himmler and The Final Solution*. New York: Alfred A. Kompf

Buchheim, Hans, 1965. Command and Compliance. In *Anatomy of The SS State*, Trans. Richard Barry, 305-396. New York: Walker and Company.

Burleigh, Michael, 2000. *The Third Reich: A New History*, New York: Hill and Wang.

Shirer, William, 1960. *The Rise and fall of the Third Reich*, New York: Simon and Schuster.

CHAPTER ELEVEN

Mussolini on Death

Eli Roth

This chapter explores fascist ideology as it relates to death and the nature of mortality. The author analyzes Mussolini's philosophy of fascism and martyrdom as it pertains to preservation and immortality of the state rather than the individual. This paper examines and analyzes the political theory and ideology of Mussolini in conjunction with the concept of mortality and death by providing a framework for Mussolini's evolution as a fascist and the development of his beliefs.

In the United States, we often wonder what the founding fathers would say about our philosophical musings and moral dilemmas. And while one topic in particular, death, is tragically under-addressed in these discussions, we would do well to consider how all of history's great leaders and thinkers coped with their own mortality. Some authors already have. Liberal democratic capitalism and the many theorists behind it have been criticized for not addressing death. Many argue that the American way of life promotes narcissism by advocating for a culture of acquisition. Some say that limitless materialism and greed lead to an unhealthy attitude about mortality. Perhaps fascism, the political movement that arose in the early twentieth century as a rejection of liberalism, has more to offer man in his constant battle with mortality. Benito Mussolini, the archetypal fascist leader and spokesperson, mentioned death many times in his speeches. He argued that yielding individuality to the state renders a population better prepared to die, and this was one of fascism's chief advantages over liberal democracy. Practically from birth, Il Duce's views on death were evident through his writings and political actions. Did this dynamic leader possess a valuable and pragmatic answer to the mortality question, or was it all insincere propaganda? In unpacking this query, one must delve deep into Mussolini's life, beginning when he was very young.

Benito Mussolini was born in Romagna, a region of Italy known, according to biographer Gaudens Megaro, for violent tendencies. "Nowhere in Italy is the sectarian political spirit more intense than in the Romagna, and many writers from Dante to Byron have spoken of the combative nature of its people," wrote Megaro. "Among the Romagnuoles, the feeling of solidarity binding the members of a political party is almost as strong as the family tie and, if need be, they do not hesitate to resort to the knife in defense of a political faith" (1938, p. 21). His father, Allesandro, was a poor blacksmith, and one of the few socialists in Romagna. Due to the locals' attitudes regarding dissent, Allesandro and his comrades had to cling vehemently to one another. Young Benito absorbed not only his father's Marxist ideas, but his intellectualism and fierceness. When he was eleven years old, he was expelled from school for stabbing another student who insulted him (Megaro, 1938, p. 43). Although often in trouble at the schools he attended, Mussolini stood out from his peers as a very competent student with big ideas and a big ego. Anthony Gregor, the author of Young Mussolini and the Intellectual Origins of Fascism, noted that Mussolini was deeply moved by the writings of Giuseppe Mazzini (1979, p. 35). As was customary in turn of the century schools, teachers often rewarded Mussolini's eagerness with opportunities to publicly address his peers. Speaking at a 1901 memorial service for Giuseppe Verdi, a popular Italian composer, Mussolini seized the opportunity to preach socialist ideas to his classmates (Gregor, 1979, p. 36). It would not be the last time Mussolini used someone's death as a springboard for politics; throughout his career, Il Duce was always sure to irreverently capitalize on speaking opportunities that followed the end of a life.

After a brief stint as an elementary school teacher, Mussolini traveled to Switzerland, seeking work. At 19 years old, Mussolini was arrested for vagrancy after begging for food (Megaro, 1938, p. 55). If the seeds of political leadership were planted at school, his time in Switzerland was when they took root.

Those who knew Mussolini in Switzerland described him as an "active revolutionist" (Megaro, 1938, p. 55). He organized other socialists and wrote politically charged articles in Marxist journals. It was his panache for public speaking, however, that helped Mussolini rapidly gain prominence in socialist circles. On June 18, 1903, Mussolini was arrested for encouraging protests and strikes among laborers. He would be arrested twice while in Switzerland. Many historians skate over the shift in ideas Mussolini went through when he exchanged socialism for fascism, but the massive extent to which his beliefs changed is worth noting. After spending years inciting labor riots, Mussolini explicitly made the labor strike "forbidden" in Article 18 of the Fundamental Laws of Fascism (Mussolini, Fascism: Doctrine and Institutions, 1935, p. 87). Even more shocking, Mussolini was an anti-war draft-dodger (Megaro, 1938, p. 81), and an atheist. The greatest contradiction, however, can be found in a 1902 speech, wherein Mussolini advocated for the "abolish[ment of] private property, the first cause of economic inequality, and **the state**- the instruments of class oppression" (Megaro, 1938, p. 66). This could not be in greater opposition to his later well-known rallying cry; "all within the state, nothing outside the state, nothing against the state." Such a discrepancy would suggest, perhaps, that Mussolini was less concerned with the ideas themselves, and more concerned with his leadership role in promoting them. Indeed, near the conclusion of his text, Megaro notes Mussolini's desire for recognition: "Yes, I am possessed by this mania. It inflames, gnaws and consumes me, like a physical malady. I want to make a mark on history with my will, like a lion with his claws" (Megaro, 1938, p. 327). It is impossible to determine Il Duce's true intentions, but whatever they were, they did not stop fascism's rise. If Mussolini was just an egotistical opportunist, the only lasting impact on Fascist thought and doctrine may be the acknowledgment of man's need for a legacy, which will be discussed in an examination of "Immortality through the State."

When his father died in 1910, Mussolini wrote a biography for him. Being an experienced journalist, this fact alone is not surprising. What is interesting, however, is the callous and impersonal tone with which it was written, utterly unfitting of a son commemorating a father:

> I pen these lines... simply to pay the last homage of my filial devotion on the grave of my father and to add some documents relating to the history of the International in the Romagna... His end was premature. Of worldly goods he has left us nothing; of spiritual goods he has left us a treasure: the Idea. And now, the period of mourning over, Life must go on its way with all its rights" (Megaro, 1938, pp. 22-26).

Much like in his speech commemorating Verdi, Mussolini focused his comments not on the deceased, but on Socialism and its advancement. Would Allesandro be happy with his legacy as a socialist, or would he have liked to be remembered for more? While martyrdom is admirable and frequently necessary, few might chose that fate if the world- and, worse, their own son- would only remember them in the context of that cause. Furthermore, by glossing over the rest of the martyr's life, it diminishes the gesture by making it seem the deceased was not sacrificing anything of great importance. This treatment of life minimizes the implications of mortality.[1] One who does not consider his entire life, and what comes to an end upon death, has not really made an enlightened decision about dying. This could cause him to rush towards death prematurely, or have a deeply disturbing death-bed reorganization of priorities. If the death of his father had an emotional impact on Il Duce, it was not evident in his writings. One thing that did have a significant impact on Mussolini, however, was his eventual military service, and it was perhaps this that began the shift in thinking from socialism to fascism.

---

1   This is true for all martyrs, but Allesandro, in fact, did not even die for socialism, nor did he live exclusively for it. The cause was important for him, but not all-encompassing as Benito suggested. Allesandro lived and worked as a blacksmith to support his wife and send his children to school. Mussolini's focus on a cause "larger" than Allesandro's life greatly diminishes the true accomplishments of his father.

In the years leading up to World War One, Mussolini was very active in the Italian Socialist Party. He edited *Avanti!* a socialist newspaper, and continued to speak publicly when given the opportunity. Mussolini was constantly trying to stir up rebellion in the hearts of his countrymen. In the outbreak of war, the revolutionary leader saw an opportunity to mobilize and excite Italians with the winds of change. Unfortunately for Il Duce, the Socialist Party was staunchly against intervention. Mussolini's fervent nationalism won out over socialism, however, in October of 1914, Mussolini officially broke from the party line. Georgio Pini, author of <u>The Official Life of Benito Mussolini</u> captured the speech given from Bologna: "Do we wish to remain, as men and as Socialists, idle spectators of this grandiose drama? Or do we not wish to become, in some way, and in some sense, protagonists of it?" (1939, p. 71). Mussolini established a new paper to promote the interventionist cause. When Italy declared war later that year, young Benito praised the decision, saying "from today onwards there are only Italians... And we, oh Mother Italy, offer you our life and our death" (Pini, 1939, p. 75). He enlisted immediately, eager to serve on the front lines. Before his first taste of combat, Mussolini showed the beginning signs of fascist ideas growing:

> To those who exhorted him not to expose himself to too serious risks on account of his children, he replied sharply: "What does it matter? It is just because I have children that I can die. This is the thought which gives me the greatest peace of mind; I shall be continued... As far as concerns myself I have no personal anxieties. I am ready to accept all the slings and arrows of fortune." (Pini, 1939, p. 75)

In these comments, Mussolini's attitude towards death is on display. Although clearly very concerned with leaving a legacy, the indifferent tone is surprising. It raises the question, has Benito even considered what a blessing life is, to be so careless? Even more interesting is the obvious narcissism. Mussolini has no desire to survive to be a father for his children; they are only relevant as a continuation of him.

Combat had a profound impact on the young Mussolini. He was touched by the sense of community among soldiers, the camaraderie, and perhaps most of all by the willingness to sacrifice for one another. Men who fought alongside him described the future dictator as practically cheerful, reveling in the masculinity of war, and charging head first into risky situations. It is perhaps this recklessness that led to the end of his service- he was severely injured in 1917 when an Italian grenade in his company malfunctioned (Pini, 1939, p. 82). Despite a premature exit from service, Mussolini's ideological shift was set in stone. Perhaps the most significant impact was the articulation of the warrior ethic. The warrior ethic, as described by Gregor, referred to the phenomenon through which "under peer-group pressure and in mimetic response to the behavior of strong leadership, ordinary men bore the afflictions of wounds and the prospect of death with stoic calm" (1979, p. 211).

The warrior ethic may seem to hold some legitimacy in the quest to come to terms with death. In combat situations, soldiers are forced to acknowledge their own mortality without the crippling anxiety that often strikes those living in denial. The mere acknowledgment of death can help to alleviate intolerance in a society. Many writers, such as Alfred Killilea, author of The Politics of Being Mortal, maintain that our common mortality binds humanity together, "bring[ing] home to us the common concerns and the common destiny of all men everywhere. It draws us together in the deep-felt emotions of the heart and dramatically accents the ultimate equality involved in our ultimate fate" (1988, p. 13). On the field of battle, soldiers, too, are made equal through their common risk of dying. Later, Mussolini would argue that a nationwide willingness to face death does the same for Italians. The problem, however, is that war inherently has an opponent, and the warrior ethic only binds together the soldiers on one side of a conflict, while deeming the other side inhuman. This inherent inequality in fascism, however, prevents Mussolini from "piggy-backing" onto Killilea's logic. Death can only be treated as a great equalizer if one believes that it proves us to be equal. Mussolini did not adopt this necessary stance. Fascism incited racism and other forms of bigotry. Most importantly, Mussolini dehumanized opponents of fascism and non-Italians. The death of an enemy soldier was no tragedy. Loss of life was only significant when the life lost was Italian, and even then it hardly registered. Death, Killilea would argue, only binds humanity together as a people because all lives are of high and equal value. In fascist terms, the logic does not apply.

Despite this, Mussolini still attempted to instill the warrior ethic in the minds of his populace. Like his ideological mentor, Giuseppe Mazzini, who said "without country you have neither name, token, voice, nor rights, no admission as brothers into the fellowship of the Peoples. You are the bastards of Humanity. Soldiers without a banner" (1981, p. 239) Mussolini saw it an honor and a duty to die for the country-to which citizens owed their life in the first place- and this would be the cornerstone of his new political movement:

> Fascism carries this anti-pacifistic attitude into the life of the individual. "I don't care a damn"- the proud motto of the fighting squads scrawled by a wounded man on his bandages, is not only an act of philosophic stoicism, it sums up a doctrine which is not merely political: it is evidence of a fighting spirit which accepts all risks. It signifies a new style of Italian life. The Fascist accepts life and loves life; he rejects and despises suicide as cowardly. Life as he understands it means duty, elevation, conquest; life must be lofty and full, it must be lived for oneself but above all for others, both nearby and far off, present and future. (Mussolini, Fascism: Doctrine and Institutions, 1935, p. 19)

After serving as a soldier, Benito never reconciled with the Socialist Party. He continued his work as a journalist, heavily influenced by his experience on the battlefield and also by the writings of Mazzini and others. His talent for rallying people behind a cause aided him in the formation of the Fascist Party. Eventually, he wrote The Political and Social Doctrine of Fascism and marched on the capital in Rome in order to gain control of Italy. The first Fascist state was officially born in October of 1922. Chip Berlet's 1992 article, *Fascism!*, succinctly and accurately summarizes the ideology as having the following tenets:

- Nationalism and super-patriotism with a sense of historic mission.
- Aggressive militarism even to the extent of glorifying war as good for the national or individual spirit.
- Use of violence or threats of violence to impose views on

others (fascism and Nazism both employed street violence and state violence at different moments in their development).

- Authoritarian reliance on a leader or elite not constitutionally responsible to an electorate.
- Cult of personality around a charismatic leader.
- Reaction against the values of Modernism, usually with emotional attacks against both liberalism and communism.
- Exhortations for the homogeneous masses of common folk (Volkish in German, Populist in the U.S.) to join voluntarily in a heroic mission--often metaphysical and romanticized in character.
- Dehumanization and scapegoating of the enemy--seeing the enemy as an inferior or subhuman force, perhaps involved in a conspiracy that justifies eradicating them.
- The self image of being a superior form of social organization beyond socialism, capitalism and democracy.
- Elements of national socialist ideological roots, for example, ostensible support for the industrial working class or farmers; but ultimately, the forging of an alliance with an elite sector of society.
- Abandonment of any consistent ideology in a drive for state power. (Berlet, 1992)

To ensure all Italians were sold on fascism and the Warrior Ethic, Mussolini, like Hitler, relied heavily on propaganda. Already an experienced propagandist from his socialist days, Il Duce had an easy time swaying his populace from the helm in Rome. In Tracy Koon's text, Believe, Obey, Fight, the "Mussolinian model" is explained:

Hyperbole, imagery, metaphor, and alliterative and onomatopoeic expressions chosen for their sound and evocative power. Official Fascist style emphasized conciseness and vigor of expression, as contrasted with democratic and liberal prolixity. Myths were conveyed in aphorisms, lapidary phrases, and punchy slogans that became a continuing and hammering presence on the walls of offices, factories barracks, party headquarters, and railroad stations; on the radio; and in textbooks, cartoon strips, and newspaper headlines (1985, p. 11).

As is true with most propaganda, thoughts and ideas are repeated quite often. One, in particular, is of special note. Mussolini's speeches frequently used the word "martyr." The word is more than a convenient way to reference heroes and fallen soldiers. Martyrdom has obvious religious implications, and, in religious doctrine, martyrs are rewarded with a place in the afterlife. In this sense, martyrs are immortal. Belief in martyrdom is a way to sidestep the question of mortality. For those who embody every word of Mussolini's speeches, martyrdom can be seen as a way to conquer death.

Italian children were the biggest targets of fascist propaganda. Mussolini, who worked as a teacher and was thus familiar with the influencing of young minds, always had his hand in the running of Italian schools. These schools were less places of learning and more warrior factories. The methods employed were designed to turn war into a game, encourage group-think, and breed hyper-nationalism. Carl Schmidt, author of The Corporate State in Action, writes:

> Under fascism the schools are a powerful instrument of nationalistic, warlike propaganda. It is not easy for children to resist the attractions of wearing uniforms, playing at soldiers, participating in mass athletics, and taking part in imaginary official duties. Those who turn away from these blandishments are exposed to merciless pressures of social ostracism by their comrades (Schmidt, 1939, p. 89).

The mind-control did not end outside of school, however. Mussolini's totalitarian regime permeated its way through all aspects of fascist life, especially in those of children. Youth groups like the Partito Nazionale Fascista, the Italian equivalent of the Hitler Youth, influenced the lives of millions of children. Fascist thought was even evident in the songs they sang:

To arms! To arms! To arms, we are the Fascists
Terror of the communists

We are the components of fascism
We will uphold its cause until death
And we will always fight strongly
As long as we have blood in our hearts.

Always singing the praises of our Patria
Which all united we will defend
Against adversaries and traitors,
Who one by one we will exterminate.

To arms! To arms! To arms, we are Fascists...
(Pugliese, 2004, p. 132)

When bombarded by this rhetoric from birth, it is impossible for a child to think coherently about anyone's death, let alone his own. These effective methods are still, tragically, in use today all over the world for the creation of child soldiers.

Embrace of the Warrior Ethic is perhaps, then, the strongest argument for fascism's utility, if not its moral righteousness. When a liberal society goes to war, the inherent contradiction in liberal thought is made clear. Thomas Hobbes, the father of modern Political Science "could not escape the contradiction of having to ask in an emergency that the citizen be prepared to lay down his life for the defense of a commonwealth he had joined solely for his self-preservation" (Killilea, 1988, p. 71). Mussolini used the same arguments in his challenges to the democracies, insisting this shortcoming would spell their defeat. Should Italian fascism be considered legitimate simply because it is an effective way to let man forget his fear of death? When employing tools like propaganda, this is dangerous thinking. Similar and well-documented methods just North in Germany were enough to lead Germans through the Holocaust. In the hands of experts like Mussolini, Nahimana, and Goebbels, propaganda is the most destructive weapon known to history. When citizens allow it to take hold, they are deprived of their ability to think normally. This has important implications on the fascist treatment of death. When Mussolini spoke about the famous March on Rome, he reminded critics that "there was much discussion but- what was more important and more sacred- men died. They knew how to die" (Killilea, 1988, p. 116).[2] This sounds reasonable. Propaganda and other forms of conscription, however,

---

2   Ironically, this very famous quote is a false claim. In Making of the Fascist Self, Mabel Berezin revealed that no one actually died when Mussolini marched on Rome. The coup was bloodless. A story of "3,000 fascist martyrs," however, was much more compelling in Mussolini's opinion (77).

can also just as easily be used to make men kill as to make them die. Does susceptibility to brainwashing make a man a murderer for all time? Generations of Rwandans and Germans would hope not. If these brainwashed killers are not really murderers at their cores, are those who died for fascism really martyrs? In order to be legitimate, the choice to accept and face individual death must be made with an individual and clear mind. The influence of propaganda removes all gravity from the decision. Fascism, however, is deeper than the propaganda used for its promotion. The institutions Mussolini designed have their own implications on whether or not the system is a sufficient response to mortality. Perhaps the fascist economic system is an answer to Democratic Capitalism's narcissistic tendencies.

In his chapter "From the 'Homo Economicus' to the 'Homo Corporativus'," Fascist critic Gaetano Salvemini, author of Under the Axe of Fascism, explains how fascism appears to offer an alternative to democratic capitalism's narcissism. Mussolini, who had no problem calling his movement "illiberal and anti-liberal" (Berlet, 1992), does not reject the writings of Smith or Hobbes. In a fascist society, man is still expected to act in his own best interest. The difference, however, is that fascists realize that state preservation is the most pressing concern to their own well-being. Mussolini calls a man of this mindset a corporative man, or "Homo Coporativus." "The corporative man is free to pursue his own interests, but his interests are not purely selfish, because he is guided by the 'corporative conscience'... and unlike the 'Homo Economicus' is endowed with a feeling for the higher interests of the national collectivity," Salvemini writes. While the presentation is marred by typically fascist implications of genetic superiority, it is an otherwise interesting idea- made even more solvent by the caveat, "where his corporative conscience falls short, the laws of the Corporative State intervene to keep him on the straight path" (1936, p. 156). Mussolini acknowledges the possibility that even a genetically superior "corporative man" might be compelled to stray from selflessness into the realm of narcissism. The enforced line that separates reasonable acquisition from excess will inevitably be arbitrary, but even the most liberal societies have arbitrary lines written into law books. Speed limits, ages of consent, and minimum wages are all compromises between individual freedom and general welfare. Is it so unreasonable to draw one more line halting greedy narcissists?

In fact, in "The Clash with Capitalism," Killilea notes that "it was the restraint encouraged by noncapitalist values in Tocqueville's day that moderated the effects of an appeal to self-interest" (1988, p. 85). Perhaps Mussolini's economic system, which "as far as production is concerned, aims at retaining individual initiative without allowing it to lead to excesses" (Salvemini, 1936, p. 157), is a fair answer to critics citing capitalism's narcissism.

If Mussolini's answer to capitalism is fine in a hypothetical, communitarian nation of millionaires content with not being billionaires, however, it fails in the real world, and it failed in Italy. In 1939, Carl T. Schmidt wrote The Corporate State in Action: Italy Under Fascism. The text, interestingly dedicated to Gaetano Salvemini, detailed the inner workings of Italy's financial system:

> A widely circulated story contrasts Communism, Socialism, and Fascism: 'The Communists tell the peasant, "We will take all your cows from you"; the Socialists say, "We will take only half your cows; you may keep the others"; the Fascists, however, announce to the poor peasant, "You may keep your cows. But every day we will come and get all the milk".' (Schmidt, 1939, p. 153)

Schmidt explains how "medium-sized and small business men, especially those... unable to get political privileges, fare badly" (1939, p. 150). Mussolini's error has multiple dimensions. Firstly, the line between reasonable acquisition and excess is drawn somewhat haphazardly. No further indication is needed than one speech given to the Chamber of Deputies, where Mussolini said "fortunately the Italian people is not yet accustomed to eating several times a day, and, having a modest level of living, feels scarcity and suffering less" (Schmidt, 1939, p. 91). Surely Italians should have been allowed to expect multiple meals in a day without bordering on excess. Secondly, he neglects the poor, perhaps by naively assuming Italy will be so prosperous none will starve. Whatever the reason, farmers and factory workers got an unfair deal. Fascists made big picture arguments, such as "destiny is rarely just in the distribution of goods among men," but when putting food on the table becomes a daily struggle, what man would still believe "wealth of the few in whose hands capital is concentrated is also the wealth of the proletariat" (Salvemini, 1936, p. 163)? Mussolini also failed to account for the immense possibility of corruption. In Fascist Italy, friends of government officials were routinely given more tax breaks and subsidies than those without connections. This not only drew from state finances, but bred jealousy and competition among the populace. Finally, Mussolini proposes a top-down solution for something that must be addressed at the grass-roots level. All idealistic rhetoric aside, it is more or less understood that even in the corporative state, government would play the big role in limiting greed. Imposing strict regulations on acquisition is not the answer for the fundamental pervasiveness of greed and narcissism in Western culture. If a man wants to acquire beyond his needs, taxing him into poverty will hardly dissuade him. This man is just as selfish and narcissistic as ever, except now he is also angry. The necessary change can only be made internally through personal revelations. The rejection of narcissism- and subsequent acceptance of death- will surely only be the result of a slow cultural awakening, not strict and rapidly imposed government regulations. While Mussolini's propaganda did push for changes in the heart of his citizenry, he devoted far too little effort on selflessness and philanthropy, instead focusing on turning Italy into a savage nation of warriors. Moreover, if fascism was really an alternative to democratic narcissism, Mussolini himself would not have been quite so narcissistic.

In the later years of his rule, Il Duce's ego became increasingly evident. The propaganda in Italian schools shifted from praising fascism to Mussolini himself. According to Koon, "the Fascist press referred to him (or rather Him) as the 'magnificent' Duce, the 'sublime' Duce, and even the 'divine' Duce. Debates over what adjectives to use to describe his animal magnetism were legion, and hundreds of books and pamphlets were published analyzing the deep religious and philosophical significance of his thought or the historical imprint of his personality" (1985, p. 17). The man who once boasted about his abject poverty while in Switzerland lived a lavish lifestyle from his Rome villa, which included several affairs. When one also considers Mussolini's numerous changes of policy and ideology over the course of his life, Il Duce seems much more like someone who simply enjoyed the spotlight. Towards the end of the war, however, rather than lead Italians in a fight to the death with the allies, Mussolini timidly yielded power to Hitler, in order to save his place in power. Self-preservation, not state, was apparently the guiding principle all along.

Perhaps fascism's ineffectiveness as a political and ideological doctrine can be sufficiently evidenced by its failure. When the war effort sputtered, the warrior ethic died out in Italians. Italy's poor- alienated and starving- likely never put the survival of the state ahead of that of their own families. Mussolini's own egoism is proof that, in his mind, the individual would always trump the state. This stance is in absolute contradiction to the ideological foundations of the movement. Was Mussolini truly that lacking of self-awareness? Was he oblivious to his own feelings of self-optimization? If not, one must ask why Il Duce devoted his life to a doctrine destined to fail (for he represented its foil). It is the opinion of this author that Mussolini's promotion of fascism was his own unsuccessful struggle to accept death. There is much evidence for this:

> No mention of any illness was ever permitted in the Italian press, and papers were forbidden to mention his age or his grandchildren... His closest associates were well aware of Mussolini's obsession with youth, which they saw as the explanation for his relationship with the much younger Claretta Petacci (Koon, 1985, p. 16).

> All Mussolini's doctrinal and moral somersaults and divagations, all his outward allegiance to varied and contradictory political theories become intelligible only if it is borne in mind that he cannot pay even lip-service to ideas unless he can utilize them as instruments of his ambition for power, unless he can convince himself of the identity between an idea and his will for power. With him, as with so many men of action, the utterance of an idea and the conviction that he alone can be its standard-bearer are inseparable (Megaro, 1938, p. 327)

> No! Italy will not die, because Italy is immortal! (Mussolini, Mussolini as Revealed in his Political Speeches (November 1914-August 1923), 1923, p. 36)

For Mussolini, fascism represented immortality. Il Duce, eager for recognition, was simply searching for a way to live on through the state. It is not surprising that so many were swept up in the movement. If man could yield his life to the state, he would never really die as long as the nation survived. Death, however, is an individual phenomenon. It is something every single person on Earth must encounter alone. A pack mentality may temporarily side-step this challenge, but it is not a true answer. The fascist solution to our struggle with death is not to prepare the individual, but, as Killilea wrote, to "obliterate" it (1988, p. 117). Nowhere is this more evident, perhaps, than in a reference to fallen soldiers of WWI during a 1919 political rally: "We do not wish to classify the dead... We include in one single loving thought all the fallen, from the General to the humblest soldier, from the most intelligent to the most ignorant and uncultured" (Mussolini, Mussolini as Revealed in his Political Speeches (November 1914-August 1923), 1923, p. 88). Framed as a sentimental idea, it might slip under the radar, but upon careful examination the implications are quite alarming. Mussolini has no desire to recognize those who died beyond the fact that they fought for Italy. Like Allesandro, the lives and deaths of these soldiers were hijacked for a one-dimensional political agenda. If their decision to face death was as simple as doing what was best for the state, then they were not in full appreciation of the gift of life to begin with. Mussolini's suggestion otherwise only works with this overly simplistic view of life, and his answer to mortality thus fails.

Did Mussolini ever truly conquer death? His pride achievement, fascism, is long gone, hurled back and forth as an insult by the likes of Michael Moore. He is not even the most well-known fascist; that ignominious title being held by Adolph Hitler. His last years in power were merely ceremonial, with most major decisions coming from Germany. History will remember Mussolini for his relevance, but not, as he would have hoped, his greatness. If Mussolini ever truly came to grips with death, it would have been through realizing fascism's futility. He never did recant any fascist doctrine or express regret at the lives he destroyed. Were Il Duce's alleged last words, spoken to assassins: "Shoot me in the chest!" the last frantic attempts of a weak egomaniac to live on in the pages of history? Or are they evidence that Mussolini was, truly, unafraid to die? Perhaps. Then again, some sources say Mussolini was shot trying to flee. This would be more consistent with the former theory. As is true with every man, Mussolini's struggle to come to grips with mortality was internal by its very nature. It seems the world will never know.

Works Cited

Anker, C. a. (1999). *The Lost Explorer.* New York: Simon and Schuster.

BBC News. (1999 йил November). Mount Everest Reaches New Heights. London, UK: BBC News.

Beah, I. (2007). *A Long Way Gone.* New York: Sarah Crichton Books.

Berezin, M. (1997). *Making the Fascist Self: The Political Culture of Interwar Italy.* Ithaca: Cornell University Press.

Berlet, C. (1992 йил September). *Fascism!* Retrieved 2010 йил March from http://www.hartford-hwp.com/archives/45/051.html

Coalition to Stop the Use of Child Soldiers. (2006). *Child soldiers and Disarmament, Demobilization, Rehabilitation and Reintegration in West Africa.*

Dawkins, R. (2011, October 8). Texas Free Thought Convention. Texas.

Dawkins, R. (2006). *The God Delusion.* New York: Bantam Press.

Faulkner, F. (2001). Kindergarten Killers: Morality, Murder and the Child Soldier Problem. *Third World Quarterly, Vol. 22, No. 4 .*

Federal Aviation Administration. (2003). *Operations of Aircraft at Altitudes above 25,000 Feet.* Washington D.C.: Department of Transportation.

Firth, P. (2008). Mortality on Mount Everest, 1921-2006. *British Medical Journal .*

Gray, M. (2010, September 20). *Hitchens Won't Be Attending Hitchens Prayer Day.* Retrieved October 2011, from http://newsfeed.time.com/2010/09/20/hitchens-wont-be-attending-hitchens-prayer-day/

Gregor, A. J. (1979). *Young Mussolini and the Intellectual Origins of Fascism.* Berkeley: University of California Press.

Heil, N. (2008). *Dark Summit.* New York: Henry Holt and Co.

Hitchens, C. (2007). *God is not Great.* New York: Twelve.

Hitchens, C. (2010). *Hitch-22: A Memoir.* New York: Twelve.

Hitchens, C. (2010, December). Miss Manners and the Big C. *Vanity Fair .*

Hitchens, C. (2011, January 14). Q & A with Christopher Hitchens. (B. Lamb, Interviewer)

Hitchens, C. (1982, July). The Lord and the Intellectuals. *Harper's .*

Hitchens, C. (2011). *The Quotable Hitchens: From Alcohol to Zionism.* Philadelphia: De Capo Press.

Hitchens, C. (2010, September). Topic of Cancer. *Vanity Fair .*

Hitchens, C. (2010, November). Tumortown. *Vanity Fair .*

Hitchens, C. (2010, October). Unanswerable Prayers. *Vanity Fair .*

Hitchens, C. (2011, June). Unspoken Truths. *Vanity Fair .*

Jaffre, F. (n.d.). *The Use of Children as Soldiers in Africa: A country analysis of child recruitment and participation in armed conflict.* Retrieved 2010 йил 29-4 from

Relief Web International: http://www.reliefweb.int/library/documents/ chilsold.htm

JFK Presidential Library. (n.d.). *JFK Presidential Library.* Retrieved 2011 йил 02-10 from www.jfklibrary.org

Jugalski, E. (2011 йил 24-September). *Ascents-Everest.* Retrieved 2011 йил 10-October from 8000ers.com: www.8000ers.com/everest-general-info-185. html

Killilea, A. G. (1988). *The Politics of Being Mortal.* Lexington, Kentucky: The University Press of Kentucky.

Koon, T. H. (1985). *Believe, Obey, Fight.* Chapel Hill: University of North Carolina Press.

Krakauer, J. (1997). *Into Thin Air.* New York: Anchor Books.

LaGambina, G. (2007, December). Christmas with Christopher Hitchens. *A.V. Club* .

Mallory, G. (1923 йил 18-March). Climbing Mount Everest is Work for Supermen. (N. Y. Times, Interviewer)

May, T. (2009). *Death.* Durham: Acumen.

Mazzini, G. (1981). The Duties of Man. In M. Curtis, *The Great Political Theories* (Vol. 2, pp. 234-242). New York: Avon Books.

McGrath, C. (2011, October 9). A Voice, Still Vibrant, Reflects on Mortality. *The New York Times* .

Megaro, G. (1938). *Mussolini in the Making.* Boston: Houghton Mifflin Company.

Mount Washington Observatory. (2011). *Mount Washington Observatory.org.* Retrieved 2011 йил 15-October from www.mountwashingtonobservatory.org

Mussolini, B. (1935). *Fascism: Doctrine and Institutions.* Rome: Ardita Publishers.

Mussolini, B. (1923). *Mussolini as Revealed in his Political Speeches (November 1914-August 1923).* London: Dent.

National Center for PTSD. (2011). Health Services Use in the Department of Veterans Affairs among Returning Iraq War and Afghan War Veterans with PTSD. *PTSD Research Quarterly* , 1.

National Transportation Safety Administration. (2011). *Traffic Safety Fats.* US Census Bureau.

New York Times. (1941 йил 23-February). Speech Delivered by Premier Benito Mussolini. *The New York Times* .

Pini, G. (1939). *The Official Life of Benito Mussolini.* (L. Villari, Trans.) London: Hutchinson & Co.

Pugliese, S. G. (2004). *Fascism, Anti-Fascism, and the Resistance in Italy.* Lanham: Rowman & Littlefield Publishers, Inc.

Richards, K. P. (1998). Jeunes combattants parlant de la guerre et de la paix en Sierra Leone ("When They Say Soldiers Are Rebels, It's a Lie": Young Fighters Talk about War and Peace in Sierra Leone). *Cahiers d'Études Africaines, Vol. 38, Cahier 150/152, Disciplines et déchirures. Les formes de la violence* .

Salvemini, G. (1936). *Under the Axe of Fascism.* London: Camelot Press Ltd.

Schmidt, C. T. (1939). *The Corporate State in Action: Italy Under Fascism*. New York City: Russell & Russell.

Schoene, B. (2000 йил November). Alive on Everest. (PBS/Nova, Interviewer)

Thompson, C. B. (1999). Beyond Civil Society: Child Soldier as Citizens in Mozambique. *Review of African Political Economy, Vol. 26, No. 80* .

University of Alberta. (2006). *Children and War*. Social Sciences and Research Center of Canada.

War Child. (n.d.). *Child Soldiers*. From War Child web site.

Weathers, B. (2000). *Left For Dead: My Journey Home from Everest*. New York: Random House.

West, J. (1999). Barometric Pressures on Mt. Everst; New Daya and Physiological Significance. *Journal of Applied Physiology* , 6.

Woods, R. (2006 йил 28-May). Has the Once Heroic Sport of Climbing Been Corrupted by Big Money? *The Sunday Times* .

VI. SUICIDE: WHEN LIFE IS MORE FEARSOME THAN DEATH

CHAPTER TWELVE

Suicide in Japan

Anastasia O'Keefe

This chapter is based on field research that I conducted
while studying abroad for four months in Fukuoka,
Japan. My research covers Japanese attitudes toward
life and death, focusing mainly on suicide because,
due to societal pressures, Japan has the highest suicide
rate in the world. The data is drawn from interviews,
historical research, and visits to memorial sites.

Aokigahara Forest, at the base of Mount Fuji is the most popular
suicide destination in Japan, and the second most popular suicide
destination in the world, following only the Golden Gate Bridge in
San Francisco, California. [1]

After the novel Kuroi Jukai ("The Sea of Black Trees") was published
in 1960, in which a young lover commits suicide in Aokigahara Forest,
people started taking their own lives there at a rate of 50 to 100 deaths
per year. In 2002, 78 bodies were found within the forest, replacing
the previous record of 73 in 1998.[2] The authorities sweep for bodies
only on an annual basis, as the forest is too dense to patrol.more
frequently.

There is little doubt that the novel's publication contributed to
the increase in annual suicides at Aokigahara, however, the woods
have long been associated with death. The reasons for its infamy

vary depending on who you ask, but in grade school many Japanese students were taught that the forest's reputation was based on *ubasute,* a routine allegedly practiced in the late 18th and 19th centuries. Ubasute is the custom whereby an elderly relative was carried to a mountain and left to die, usually during times of drought or famine. Japanese legend has it that the forest is still haunted by the ghosts of those who were abandoned.

My brother and I were in Tokyo, approximately 2 hours from the renowned forest when we learned that it was open to the public. Among the 15 square miles of trees so densely packed that a visitor had little sunlight and no cell phone reception were a variety of unofficial trails that are used semi-regularly for the annual body hunt.

Against the advice of my Japanese friends who grew up forbidden to talk about the forest and gasped at its mention, John and I headed to the northwestern base of Mount Fuji.

After spending a week narrowly escaping being hit by a car or trampled in the streets in downtown Tokyo, you can imagine our surprise at boarding an empty bus. I could only recall a few times in the past two months of traveling around Japan that there was even sitting room aboard the public transportation. We boarded the bus and spent the first hour assessing whether or not it was appropriate to ask the driver, Keisuke, about Aokigahara and his experience commuting people back and fourth.

I feel obligated to preface his response and what I made of it by stating that at the time I had only lived in Japan for 2 months and was in my second semester studying the language.

He explained that if Japanese people visited Mount Fuji they avoided the forest, and many failed to even acknowledge its existence. The only people seeking out the forest were foreigners or people with thoughts of suicide. Mount Fuji, known as "Fuji-san" (the only non-human to earn the respect of "san") was sacred to the people of Japan. Unfortunately, he added, its sacredness is what attracted people contemplating suicide. People, most commonly women in their 20's with failed relationships, or men in their 30's and 40's facing financial hardship would come equipped to the forest with miles of rope or string. They would come at night, and in their own cars. Keisuke speculated this was because the drivers didn't change shifts throughout the day, and they would notice if someone didn't return on the bus.

During his last trip, at 10:00 p.m., Keisuke would sometimes notice cars in the parking lot that weren't there during his 6:00 trip, and that would still be there in the morning, and then for days following.

We asked what the string was for, and he told us we would see. People tied string to a tree in the entrance and would let it unravel as they lost themselves in the dark woods. They would then ask the holy Mount Fuji if they should live or if they should take their own lives. Depending on the answer, they would either follow their string back to the entrance, or commit suicide, leaving the forest littered with multi-colored strings and rope crossing each other in web-like patterns.

We pulled into an unnecessarily large parking lot and saw the entrance to the forest, marked with a new (2004) sign that translates "You are a precious gift from your parents, please think about your parents, siblings, and children; don't keep it to yourself, talk about your troubles". Officials were forced to place the signs in the forest due to the high rates of suicide and the amount of international attention it was drawing. Additionally, in 2007, suicide prevention organizations took it upon themselves to nail signs along the way that read "please reconsider" and have the phone number of a 24-hour helpline.

The forest, which has been growing on top of hardened lava since Mount Fuji's eruption in 1707, lacks wildlife and is eerily quiet. I feared stumbling upon the strings knowing John's eagerness to follow them to the site of a suicide or to a decomposing body that had yet to be discovered by the patrol. However, we didn't stray far from the main trail, so most of the strings that we saw had already been cut. Occasionally we came across an abandoned umbrella, a pair of shoes, a backpack, or blankets.

A short documentary, made in October 2010 titled "Aokigahara" follows a "nature guard" whose primary job is to patrol the forest for people who might be debating suicide. He ignores the signs to stay on the trail and goes deep into the woods with his camera crew. He points out multiple nooses, most of which have been cut down, and stumbles upon a year-old skeleton, which he leaves.

Hardly hidden in the woods is a bright yellow tent, which the unnamed nature guard investigates and finds a living person in. The two men have a shocking conversation:

Nature guard:	Are you okay?
Young man:	Yes.
Nature guard:	Camping here is prohibited.
Young man:	I'm sorry.
Nature guard:	I am on suicide patrol. I hope you are okay. Do you have food?
Young man:	Yes, thank you, I have food.
Nature guard:	Do you know your way out?
Young man:	yes.
Nature guard:	Okay. Please follow this path when you leave. I hope you are okay. Think carefully before making decisions and try your best to stay positive.
Young man:	I will. Sorry to have caused you trouble.

The nature guard leaves the man alone, then turns to the camera and says, "It was hard to tell what his motive was. I hope he decides not to take his life." For someone whose specific mission was suicide prevention, his effort hardly seemed like enough. The nature guard acknowledges this sentiment might be a popular reaction and continues "If you are determined to take your life, no one can stop you. In Japan, many people think that suicide is an honorable way to die. I disagree, but there is not much I can do to combat that societal norm that has existed for hundreds of years. I can only give words of encouragement and hope that they listen."

John and I left the forest with similar questions: Are the high suicidal rates in Japan a reflection of society's depreciation for the preciousness of life? Is suicide viewed as honorable in actuality? Does the act of suicide have the ability to give the life of the deceased more meaning? And most importantly, is there a way to change society's views?

Suicide in Japan has become a significant problem nationally, and its consistently increasing statistics have drawn both nation-wide and international attention. The most popular motives, based on information gathered from those close to the deceased, suicide notes, and those who have attempted suicide, are social pressures and financial hardship.

In 2007, the National Police Agency revised the categorization of motives for suicide into a division of 50 reasons with up to three reasons listed for each suicide. Suicides traced to losing jobs surged 65.3 percent while those attributed to hardships in life increased 34.3 percent. Depression remained at the top of the list for the third year in a row, rising 7.1 percent from 2006.

The rapid increase in suicides in the past two decades have drawn specific attention and raised concerns regarding intervention for the first time in Japan's history. In 1998 there was a (huge!) 34.7% increase in the number of suicides over the previous year. Today, Japan has one of the world's highest suicide rates, and the highest amongst industrialized nations.

In 2009, the number of suicides rose 2 percent to 32,845 people annually exceeding 30,000 suicides for the twelfth straight year and equating to nearly 26 suicides per 100,000 people. This amounts to approximately one suicide every 15 minutes. [3]

This figure is somewhat disputed since it is arguably capped by the conservative definition of "suicide" that has been adopted by the Japanese authorities, which differs from the definition provided by the World Health Organization. In 2010, The World Health Organization defines suicide as simply "the act of deliberately killing oneself." Currently, the Japanese definition is "under investigation", based on the critiques that it is too narrow and masks the actual, rather large figure of 60,000 to 80,000 suicides a year.[4]

Despite these allegations, the United Nations figures show that 25 in 100,000 people kill themselves in Japan, which is more than double the rate in the United States.

Currently, the conservative per year estimate is still significantly higher than for any other OECD (Organization for Economic Co-operation and Development) country. In comparison, the UK rate is about 9 per 100,000, and the US rate around 11 per 100,000.[5]

The difference between Japan and the United Kingdom and the United States and the reason for its significantly higher number of fatalities is, no doubt, it's cultural attitude toward suicide.

Suicide has never been criminalized in Japan. Japanese society's attitude toward suicide has been termed "tolerant," and on many occasions a suicide is seen as a morally responsible action. If one brings shame to their family, whether this means unemployment, bankruptcy, divorce, adultery, or inability to find an acceptable mate, it is almost assumed that the individual will restore the honor to their family by taking his or her own life.

This ideology seems outdated (it is traced back to the bravery of the Kamikaze pilots in World War II and before that in Japan's imperial years when a samurai would kill themselves after a lost battle rather than return to their families and admit their defeat). However, the cultural heritage of suicide as a noble tradition still has some resonance. While being investigated for an expenses scandal, Cabinet minister Toshikatsu Matsuoka took his life in 2007. The governor of Tokyo, Shintaro Ishihara, described him as a "true samurai" for preserving his honor. [6]

If one fails to meet the societal pressures –for men it's to provide for their families financially, for women it's to be a wife and mother— suicide is often seen as the only option.

My last month in Japan, my friend Yuki, who was graduating from the local University in March, was growing increasingly anxious about her lack of job prospects and her nonexistent boyfriend. One day I heard everyone screaming in the hallway of our dormitory. I rushed to the commotion and saw everyone congratulating Yuki, who was sitting on the hallway floor hysterically crying. Her friend explained to me that Yuki had gotten a job. By her reaction, I assumed that she must have gotten her dream job. I later found out that, with a B.A. equivalent in both English and Math, Yuki had landed a job as an office assistant in a dental office. Though I didn't admit it, I was confused by her happiness at getting a job that didn't require either of her advanced degrees. The next day I congratulated the glowing Yuki again, and asked her if that job was her first choice. She explained to me that she didn't care what kind of job she had, as long as she had one. For a Japanese woman her age, she is expected to have at least a steady job, or a boyfriend (if not husband) and if not both. If she hadn't gotten a job, she would have been forced to have a boyfriend (regardless of her feelings toward him) to keep her family proud of her. Yuki liked no one in particular, and the thought of being forced into a relationship gave her anxiety and kept her awake at night. Because of her job offer, Yuki, a smart, independent woman, could, by society's standards, acceptably remain single.

Picturing Yuki in a forced, unhappy relationship made me sick to my stomach and I understood her desperation and relief to be hired at any job. If Yuki hadn't gotten the job, and refused a relationship, she would have embarrassed her family and would be left likely facing disownment. It is no wonder that the leading cause of death for Japanese women ages 15-34 is suicide.

A failed relationship, or temporary economic hardship hardly seems worth a human life. By simply looking at the high rates of suicides and the reasons for them, it would be easy to conclude that the Japanese people don't value life or its preciousness as greatly as the majority of nations in the world.

However, its homicide rate would suggest otherwise. Among the lowest in the world, and the lowest of the industrialized nations, Japan takes pride in its crime rate and even lower murder rate. The Japanese people's conscious decision to avoid violence suggests that they do value and appreciate human life. If they didn't, they would resort to murder over small differences and petty arguments. In Japan, the only crimes for which the death penalty is legal is homicide and treason—though the death penalty is ordinarily imposed in the rare cases involving murder or multiple murders, and has taken 776 lives since 1946.

Why is it that people that have an understanding of life's worth would so easily and obediently take their own lives? For example, the spouse of someone committing adultery wouldn't consider the crime worth a human life, if they did they would consider murder just, take the life of their spouse, and Japan would have a much higher homicide rate. However, the guilty party would consider their own crime worth their own human life and turn to suicide as the only possible solution. This self-sacrifice would rid both families of embarrassment and keep the life of the deceased meaningful.

In Japan, the disconnect between the worth of someone else's life versus the worth of your own life is puzzling. Aren't all human lives of the same value in theory? According to Ruth Benedict's Shame Culture/Guilt Culture Analysis, an important factor keeping crime low is the "traditional emphasis on the individual as a member of groups to which he or she must not bring shame. Within these groups—family, friends, and associates at work or school—a Japanese citizen has social rights and obligations, may derive emotional support, and meets powerful expectations to conform. These informal social sanctions display potency despite competing values in a changing society".

To the Japanese people, remaining a member of this "group" is an individual's first priority. Avoiding shame means 1. Not taking someone else's life and 2. Keeping the honor within the group by sacrificing your own life if your have jeopardized its shameless reputation. If you bring shame to the group, and opt not to cancel it out by means of suicide, you are no longer allowed to be a member of the group. Because the group mentality is so important, an individual's life outside of the group is not worth living, which is why suicide is so common.

It is not taking human life lightly that drives so many Japanese people to Aokigahara forest every year. Suicide is seen not only as the last option to save the family, but to save oneself. If a person kills themselves for the sake of protecting their families and groups from shame, they are guaranteed an "after life". According to Shinto, the indigenous Japanese religion, spirits exist in everything—the mountains, the rivers, the streets. It is believed that if an individual commits suicide for the sake of honor, his or her spirit (along with the spirits of those who die of natural causes) moves from their body and contributes to the success and prosperity of those they left behind. In this way, they do not die. If they choose not to take their own life, they are not only guaranteed years of life as a shamed outsider, but they are promised no afterlife. This brings up interesting questions of whether one who creates shame commits suicide for the purpose of honor restoration, or in quest of immortality. If there is nothing worse than the absence of an afterlife (mortality), the promise of a continuum (immortality) could be enough to drive people to suicide.

Despite the Japanese government's efforts in the last decade to prevent suicide, the practice is still increasing. Recently, Japan implemented a fine to the families of those who committed suicide by jumping in front of a train. The fine varied depending on the amount of train delay and chaos the person caused. This system was implemented after the sensitive "Please do not jump in front of the tracks during rush hour" signs failed to decrease the number of people utilizing this method to take their lives. Interestingly, once hefty fines were applied to the families, jumping in front of a train was no longer an honorable way of suicide because it further punished the people that were shamed.[7]

I suppose if the Japanese people were serious about decreasing the number of suicides, they would mimic this system that proved successful and apply a fine to all families of those who committed suicide, no matter what the method was. This would rid the honor attached to suicide and decrease the numbers drastically; but when said out loud this idea sounds admittedly insensitive. But doesn't there have to be another way? Life is far too precious to stand by idly while killing customs carry on.

Works Cited

Strom, Stephanie (15 July 1999). "In Japan, Mired in Recession, Suicides Soar". *Health* (The New York Times). Retrieved 2011-02-20.

"Asia:Japan: Guidelines to Reduce Suicide Rate". *World* (The New York Times). 9 June 2007. Retrieved 2011-03-15.

'Suicide forest' yields 78 corpses". The Japan Times. 7 February 2007. Retrieved 2011-3-24.

"Japan suicides rise to 33,000 in 2009". Associated Press Worldstream. 13 May 2010.

Chambers, Andrew (3 August 2010). "Japan: ending the culture of the 'honourable' suicide". The Guardian (London). Retrieved 2011-03-28.

Interview with Kesuke (Last name unknown) (26 October 2010).

Interview with Yuki Yamamoto, 5 December 2010 and 22 March 2011.

"Mortality and Burden of Disease Estimates for WHO Member States in 2004" (xls). *World Health Organization*. 2009. Retrieved 2011-3-24.

"Suicide definition and statistics, world wide" (xls). *World Health Organization*. 2009. Retrieved 2011-3-24.

Endnotes

[1] "Suicide definition and statistics, world wide" (xls). *World Health Organization*. 2009. Retrieved 2011-3-24.

[2] 'Suicide forest' yields 78 corpses". The Japan Times. 7 February 2003. Retrieved 2011-3-24.

[3] "Suicide definition and statistics, world wide" (xls). *World Health Organization*. 2009. Retrieved 2011-3-24.

[4] 'Suicide forest' yields 78 corpses". The Japan Times. 7 February 2003. Retrieved 2011-3-24.

[5] "Mortality and Burden of Disease Estimates for WHO Member States in 2004" (xls). *World Health*

[6] "Suicide definition and statistics, world wide" (xls). *World Health Organization*. 2009. Retrieved 2011-3-24.

[7] "Asia:Japan: Guidelines to Reduce Suicide Rate". *World* (The New York Times). 9 June 2007. Retrieved 2011-03-15.

CHAPTER THIRTEEN

Suicidology - A Philosophy

Shelby Sullivan-Bennis

Suicidology – A Philosophy is a brief look into how our culture lives and treats suicide today. Mixing current statistics to help understand and focus the topic with philosophical themes that have led people's opinions for hundreds of years, this paper seeks to examine the logical and proper treatment of the topic: Who commits suicide? Why do people commit suicide? How do we treat those who attempt suicide? How do we treat the idea of suicide, in general, and why? Who does this phenomenon effect? Guiding this search to answer some of these basic questions is a quiet moral fiber of the sort that has supported arguments of great philosophers – a general understanding that we, as people, should not be hypocritical or cruel. *Suicidology – A Philosophy* asks and attempts to posit answers (often multiple) to the main issues surrounding suicide in today's society.

How should we understand suicide? The 11th greatest killer of Americans today, suicide is a culturally taboo, widely misunderstood phenomenon. Natural human inclination shies away from topics surrounding death, and outright sprints from the subject of suicide. My paper seeks to understand, and to theorize about our current feelings regarding suicide, and specifically brings under the microscope the negativity that our culture in particular fosters as its connotations.

There are several questions that will serve as segmented prompts for factual data as well as philosophical opinions from giants like Hume and Plato. The first, and arguably the most pressing question among them is, why do people commit suicide? While the majority of suicides can be linked to a form of mental illness, factors such as age, culture, situation, and religion greatly affect suicidal tendencies (Leach, 17).

Suicide is the 3rd leading cause of death amongst 10-24 year-olds and is 50% more prevalent among the elderly (Leach, 8; Suicide Prevention, Awareness and Support). The rates spike in youth and return to a constant and spike again around 65. And although rates vary between nations, and between cultures, these are constant trends. Psychotherapists largely agree that suicide is often an issue of control, or rather, lack thereof. This facet relates specifically to adolescent suicides, as in dealing with life-changes and hormonal angst, young teens often come to grips and often blows over power-play (be it at school in a social setting or at home with parents). Within the 10-24 year-old range, as age increases, fatality does as well, and that is specifically explained by the increasing accessibility and (as well as alluring novelty) of narcotics; about half of adolescent suicide completers have drugs (most popularly alcohol and cocaine) in their systems (Leach, 17). Drugs obviously influence impulsivity and polarize emotional responses, but in addition to that, they often times have the horrifying effect of "cognitive constriction" which is most commonly a symptom of mood disorders, such as depression, but can be induced by drugs. This cognitive constriction can be explained as a limitation in reasoning where it becomes more linear and dichotomous, narrowing life-options and resulting in extreme conclusions (which feeds into the polarizing of emotions) resulting in increased probability of suicidal behavior (Leach, 36). Elderly suicides, although clearly caused by varied major influences, as well as varied fractional ones, are largely explained by age-related depression (/ loneliness), decreased physical functionality and its resultant increased dependency (power), and myriad illnesses (and the interplay between these factors). Making up the highest proportion of completed suicides in the US (25%), the elderly are also the largest growing age-group – an estimated 20% of all Americans will be over 65 (Leach, 60).

Culture and religion largely go hand in hand, and while there's no qualitative way to account for cultural influences, a prime example as I found it posed the case of African Americans and their general tendencies with regard to suicide. Being, on the whole, more religious than the rest of the American community (with eight out of ten claiming religion to be very important in their lives as compared to an average of 56% in the general population), they are more likely to believe in an after-life, and therefore in the concepts of heaven and hell and their associated rules and regulations for entry (specifically, that suicide would put a person in the auto-reject pile for heaven), and are thusly influenced by their religion against suicide (African Americans). In addition to religiosity playing a role with this ethnic group, also their history in America as slaves is proposed to negatively influence the inclination toward suicide – the idea that ancestral struggle yields the concept of a disrespect that would befall the ancestors who endured so much for their progeny, that to end one's life now would be ungrateful. Additionally, the idea that enslaved ancestors withstood so much more than people do in current day, the impetus to struggle on – a "we shall overcome" attitude - pushes African Americans further from suicidal tendencies (Leach, 12). Now, admittedly, these influences are complete generalizations and have been found to widely affect a particular cultural group, but do not claim to hold true on any absolute level, which goes for most theories regarding suicide. Cultural factors are merely tools that therapists use to increase their information base, and therefore understanding of patients, in an effort to best guide them toward safety and happiness.

Going back to the influence that religion has on people's ideas of suicide, another case study highlights in my mind a prime example for a point: this anecdote involves a Baptist minister who's severely depressed and in talking to a therapist mentions that although he desires to end his life, he will not because of his deep religious beliefs – specifically, that he believes he'll spend eternity in hell if he does end his own life. So my question is, is this good that religion has prevented him from committing suicide? Given, to answer this we must already have an answer to whether or not prevention of suicide is always good.

Are we (as his therapist, as society, as an objective onlooker) supposed to be glad that his religion has scared him away from doing what he wants? It seems somehow cruel that religion be used as an instrument of fear, and clearly, it has been used exactly for that purpose explicitly throughout history, but is this a positive effect? Or, more specifically, is it a positive effect of a negative influence? Can it be a negative effect of a negative influence? In order to answer these questions, one must first discuss whether or not suicide can ever be a.) for the better, and b.) a rational decision. The rest of my paper seeks to answer (or at the very least, to discuss) philosophical questions such as these and the various stances that can be taken, and have been taken by several prolific theorists and the resultant cultural attitudes.

Can suicide ever be a rational decision? We associate suicide mostly with chemical imbalances and personality/mood disorders. And justifiably so, but consider this: can suicide ever be the correct decision? Clearly Oregon and Washington State think so. Voluntary euthanasia in particular cases is culturally (and now legally) acceptable in select states in the US and select countries (such as Sweden). In the states, a patient must be diagnosed terminally ill and given only 6 months to live, while also being determined to be of sound mind before said euthanasia can be assisted by medical physicians. This suggests that Americans, on a level, culturally approve of self-administered euthanasia – or plainly, suicide. Legally, the only issue with suicide is in the assisting and no longer with the attempting or committing. (N.B. Many suicidologists actually prefer to use the terms "attempt" and "complete" to refer to the stages of suicide behavior as they tend to avoid the criminal implications of the word "commit" (Leach, 9)). So culturally, we're at least on our way to accepting the desires and rights of people to end their lives when subject to the conditions of habitual physical pain or impending death (or both together), but what about emotional and mental pain? We can give legitimacy to physical pain and the desire to end it, but what about those who experience the latter two? Do we treat it differently because we consider emotional and mental more mutable than physical? Or because we blame the sufferer more for their trials than we would someone suffering from a physical ailment? It certainly isn't fair to do either. Imagine a case where someone suffers from severe clinical, chemical depression. They cannot be blamed for the ailment and it is actually just as much a physical ailment as having ALS or cancer, except it's less blatant to the casual observer and less culturally respectable to have. Now imagine the case of someone who is, because of a situation, causally depressed. Consider that that situation isn't new or striking to them, but that the situation comprises the details of that person's life. This person is alone, hopeless, nothing brings them joy, and it hasn't for a long time. Perhaps they have reason to be depressed and aren't responding to a lack of serotonin or something, but rather, are responding to true factors: poverty, lack of loved ones, lack of ambition, desires. If such a case is possible, absent of the chemical deficiency, and that person does want to commit suicide, is it then a rational decision? Are we right to try to convince them to stay alive in either the case of chemical inducement or the case of brutal reality? Now given, I'm not trying to advocate for suicide, or suggest therapists let their patients exercise their "right" to commit suicide to such an extreme that they don't try to provide them with options, different paths that their "cognitive constriction" may be clouding from their conceivable options. I am, however, considering two things beyond the pure philosophy of the rationality of suicide: 1. cultural treatment of suicide attempters – the shame and blame we connote with the idea and whether it's fair, or correct at all and 2. the idea that a sane person, who isn't a martyr or dying of an illness, can rationally decide to end their life, and that that decision, however sad, should be respected (as well as the maker of the decision).

This leads me to the ever-controversial question of the wrongness of suicide. It is this particular facet that philosophers chose to write on and has largely shaped the cultural treatment of the topic; although "wrongness" is an entirely subjective enterprise, there are certainly points to be made and common ground to be forged. Much of what I asked in the above paragraph either directly or indirectly relates to the wrongness of suicide. If suicide is intrinsically wrong, then my questions about whether it can be rational have an answer, as well as those regarding how society should try to influence attempters. Additionally, my prompt about the Baptist minister being too scared to take his own life would also be given a different lens (although being scared into the right decision is still arguably bad). Much of the moral arguments surrounding suicide obviously center on a God, and in those arguments, for the sake of having them, I'm going to assume that one exists.

There are a few staple stances that philosophers have taken with regard to why suicide is wrong:

a.) it disrespects and interferes with God's omnipotence
b.) it breaks the social contract that we enter and negatively impacts society
c.) it disrespects the gift we're given, is cowardly, and a sign of weakness (often plays into a.).

Most philosophers who are against suicide subscribe to one or another version of a.). Plato, for instance, thought that suicide represents our releasing ourselves (i.e., our souls) from a "guard-post" (i.e., our bodies) the gods have placed us in as a form of punishment and was "an act of cowardice or laziness undertaken by individuals too delicate to manage life's vicissitudes" (Plato). St. Augustine took a different view of the same general theory. He thought taking one's own life is wrong because it's against god's law: "thou shall not kill." He expressly points out the omission of the phrase "thy neighbor," as the predicate and applies the commandment to one's self (Suicide, Stanford). His saintly counterpart, Thomas Aquinas, defended his stance, and added two other reasons to what is more or less Augustine's primary in other words: "Suicide violates our duty to God because God has given us life as a gift and in taking our lives we violate His right to determine the duration of our earthly existence." His other two reasons for its wrongness include its going against "natural self-love, whose aim is to preserve us" and that it "injures the community of which an individual is a part." As far as Augustine goes, there isn't really much of an argument to be had over a God that I've succumbed to accepting for argument's sake and his law (which I must accept as an addendum to that), but for the following two:

1. that a God who gives us the power to end our lives, as well as the desire (for some) to end it, has enabled us to do so, and therefore, the creation of the suicide is no less his than the creation of anything else on earth. Hume gives a kind of satirical commentary on just that:

... tho' death alone can put a full period to his misery, he dares not fly to this refuge, but still prolongs a miserable existence from a vain fear lest he offend his Maker, by using the power, with which that beneficent being has endowed him... all events, in one sense, may be pronounced the action of the Almighty, they all proceed from those powers with which he has endowed his creatures. A house which falls by its own weight, is not brought to ruin by his providence, more than one destroyed by the hands of men; nor are the human faculties less his workmanship, than the laws of motion and gravitation. When the passions play, when the judgment dictates, when the limbs obey; this is all the operation of God, and upon these animate principles, as well as upon the inanimate, has he established the government of the universe. (Hume)

2. Self interest. Augustine, Aquinas, and Plato seem to leave out entirely the interest of the self. Apparently not only are we created by God, but also our sole interests should lie in pleasing him, as is suggested by these philosophies. Where Plato's and Augustine's theories claim a particular disobedience on the part of the suicide completer, and a disrespect to his creator, Aquinas goes on to cite the b to which I referred in my primary breakdown: that of one's responsibility to society. Hume actually does a magnificent job defending one's responsibility to society, so I'll wait to address that aspect and move instead to this "natural self—love" that suicide goes "against." The word "natural" here, suggests God given, considering the speaker, and especially because this nature has an intent – to "preserve us," so it seems as though he's suggesting that a suicide completer would be 1. going against nature, and therefore, god and 2. being ungrateful for what that nature would have otherwise afforded him – protection. With this argument I have the same issue as with the others, which is that it suggests that our only responsibility lies with pleasing and respecting God, and nothing to do with our own desires. What sort of omni-benevolent God puts you on earth to be

miserable and then won't even let you end it? (This goes back to the concept of suicide being God's creation).

One counter-argument to my "God created suicide and our desire for it, so it's just as natural as the oak tree" proposition is that homicide also fits that bill. There is, however, a stark difference that Hume points out most adeptly. Hume says "a man who retires from life does no harm to society: He only ceases to do good; which, if it is an injury, is of the lowest kind" (Hume). The biggest distinction between homicide and suicide is the harm incurred. So if one can make the argument that no real harm is done, if that which is harmed chooses to be harmed, (and does not consider itself harmed, but in fact, bettered) then the argument is nullified (of course the person's sanity would need to be proven, as a person who isn't mentally capable could very well do harm to themselves that they don't consider harm). This whole "not harming society" theory poses a good counter argument to those addressing societal concerns, such as Aristotle in Nicomachaen Ethics:

> The law does not expressly permit suicide, and what it does not expressly permit it forbids. Again, when a man in violation of the law harms another (otherwise than in retaliation) voluntarily, he acts unjustly, and a voluntary agent is one who knows both the person he is affecting by his action and the instrument he is using; and he who through anger voluntarily stabs himself does this contrary to the right rule of life, and this the law does not allow; therefore he is acting unjustly. But towards whom? Surely towards the state, not towards himself. For he suffers voluntarily, but no one is voluntarily treated unjustly. This is also the reason why the state punishes; a certain loss of civil rights attaches to the man who destroys himself, on the ground that he is treating the state unjustly. (Aristotle)

As well as Kant:

> He who contemplates suicide should ask himself whether his action can be consistent with the idea of

humanity as an end in itself. If he destroys himself in order to escape from painful circumstances, he uses a person merely as a means to maintain a tolerable condition up until the end of life. But a man is not a thing, that is to say, something that can be used merely as a means, but must in all his actions be always considered an end in himself. I cannot, therefore, dispose of a man in any way in my own person so as to mutilate, damage or kill him. (Kant)

Aristotle seems to decide that suicide is "contrary to the rule of life." What rule of life? The natural inclination to survive? Can't one's natural inclination change due to circumstances? Isn't it actually natural to want to end pain and suffering? Hume supports me here as well, "none but a fool, however, will voluntarily endure evils which he can avoid without a crime; and it is very often a great crime to suffer pain unnecessarily. He who has not resolution to deliver himself from a miserable being by a speedy death, is like one who would rather suffer a wound to mortify, than trust to a surgeon's knife for his cure" (Hume). Aristotle admits that suicide doesn't harm the completer, but concludes that it must, by omission, be harming the state. But what obligation have we to endure continued suffering for some obscure "sake" of the state to whose social contract we're bound. If we die, don't we just cease to do good in society? Do we owe it to humanity to go on experiencing, simply because we were gifted with the opportunity? Is there harm done if someone were to just go off into seclusion, which is much like suicide as far as society is concerned. Some people don't have quite the same opportunity for happiness, and what sort of thanks or respect would it show to continue on in misery? The issue of self-interest again arises. Should we then remain alive, even if it's at great harm to ourselves?

The issue of social responsibility is certainly a vague and interpretable one, but the particular example which it brings to mind for me is that of dependents. Does this responsibility heighten when the suicidal person has children? And if so, and they owe it to the children to remain alive, how do they decide if this is even good for the children. Although logically, in most cases, a responder would probably think, "well they owe it to their children to struggle through the effort of trying" or "everyone who's suicidal probably does not think it 'good' for anyone, children included, that they remain alive." But consider the possibility that they're right. On a broader note, do we owe it to our friends and family to stay alive because they'll be hurt if we commit suicide? I would think that more than a social contract, a convincing argument could be made of these sentiments.

> Kant's opinion revolves around some vague idea of humanity being "an end in itself," and therefore, cannot force changes made by its members, but doesn't actually address why. He then attacks suicide as using a "person" to "maintain a tolerable condition" and suggests that a person is not a "means" but must be "an end in himself," like humanity, I assume. Kant thinks a person cannot be his own means to satisfy himself, that it's unethical, but fails to really argue why. If a person cannot "be used" to satisfy themselves, that calls into question everything humans do. The argument seems fundamentally fallacious, on the grounds that if we cannot be a means to satisfy ourselves, wouldn't that nullify living as well, if that, in fact, satisfies us? There are so many examples one could use to argue that a person is being used "as a means" to their own happiness, that to outlaw it arbitrarily not only lacks precedence but also rules out any other sort of existence as I see it.

All of the philosophers have merit to their points, especially if God does exist, but I tend to side with Hume. My primary concerns and opinions regarding suicide center on personal rights and happiness. If there were a liberal stance on suicide, I'd embody it. I think people who attempt and complete suicide are unfairly judged as weak, incapable, or downright insane. It's because of these age-old philosophies suggesting an inherent disrespect of God and ungratefulness for the opportunity given by him to experience beauty that we have such negative responses to suicide. Because of the fatalism that accompanies religion, people consider that whatever misery they experience, it was

God's plan for them to experience it; and in considering it an ultimate test like this, it forces the conclusion that those who fail the test, who stop running with everyone else and start heaving on the sidewalk of life's marathon, that they are necessarily weaker. And in keeping with the idea that God preordains all suffering, any other conclusion is hard to come by. It's sad that religion, of all things, with its intent to do good would necessarily lead people to such a callous view of their fellow humans. I think the only remedy to this is for people to consider suicide attempters and completers as just that – fellow humans. They're not weak links that spit in the face of God; they deal with the same struggles as everyone else and it should be pitied not shamed that they no longer want to endure.

On the topic of what emotion should surround suicide, the idea of one's entitlement to it is also relevant. I consider taking your own life as much your right as anything which strictly concerns you. You break the social contract when you refuse to pay taxes but insist on driving on public roads and being carted away in ambulances – not when you make a decision regarding the one thing that is entirely yours. I think suicide is one of the saddest conceivable things and the fact that people disrespect it makes it even sadder. Culture teaches us several entirely arbitrary and unproven things about suicide and my paper was designed as a reminder to keep an open mind. Although there are generalizations and stereotypes for a reason, the conclusions they lead us to aren't always applicable. More common than homicide and more close to each of us than any of us is willing to admit, suicide is a human issue, a global issue that shouldn't be shunned and ignored. People who commit suicide shouldn't have their lives go into the realm of silent shame-treatment (shame either of the completer or of those around them who failed to prevent it), but be celebrated like the lives of everyone else. I read somewhere in the masses of philosophers and clinicians a quote to the effect of: the same reasons people have for living life can be those used for wanting to end it. We should acknowledge our common struggle and view suicide with compassion instead of relegation.

Works Cited

African Americans Top US religious measures – Pew. Reuters.com 30 January 2009. Web. 4 April 2010 < http://blogs.reuters.com/faithworld/2009/01/30/african-americans-top-us-religious-measures-pew/>

Aristotle. Nichomachean Ethics. MIT Classics. 1994. 4 April 2010 <http://classics.mit.edu/Aristotle/nicomachaen.5.v.html>

Hume, David. Essays on Suicide and Immortality of the Soul. St. Anselm College. 1996. 4 April 2010 <http://www.anselm.edu/homepage/dbanach/suicide.htm>

Kant, Immanuel. Foundation of the Metaphysics of Morals. Iowa State University. 10 April 2010 <http://www.public.iastate.edu/~jwcwolf/Papers/KantExcerpt.htm>

Leach, Mark M. Cultural Diversity and Suicide. Binghamton, NY: The Haworth Press, 2006. Print.

Plato. Laws. MIT Classics. 4 April 2010 <http://classics.mit.edu/Plato/laws.9.ix.html>

Suicide. New World Encyclopedia. 15 April, 2008. 4 April 2010 <http://www.newworldencyclopedia.org/entry/Suicide>

Suicide Prevention, Awareness and Support. Suicide.org. 12 April 2010 <http://www.suicide.org/suicide-statistics.html>

Suicide. Stanford Encyclopedia of Philosophy. 18 May 2004. 10 April 2010 <http://plato.stanford.edu/entries/suicide/>

VII. DEATH FLEXING ITS MUSCLES

CHAPTER FOURTEEN

Understanding The Black Death and Mortality

Max Cantor

The terror of the Bubonic Plague struck 14th century
Western Europe with incredible fury and swiftness,
killing an estimated 20 million people in the three-
year period spanning 1347-1350. When the dust finally
settled, the Black Death had claimed more than 25%
of Western Europe's population, indiscriminately
decimating all segments of society. Fueled by a
fundamental misunderstanding of the origins and
transmission methods of the disease, the fabric of
society quickly eroded, leaving only irrational fears
of human contact in its stead. The Bubonic Plague
marked a fundamental shift in the human conception
of mortality, in which unfounded fears of contagion
and the pervasive influence of death combined to
dissolve the social bonds connecting families, friends,
and neighbors. This paper takes an in-depth look at
14th century European civilization, examining the
societal backdrop for the onslaught of the plague as
well as the physical and psychological effects of the
Plague's devastation.

> *Time rushes onward for the perishing world*
> *And round about I see the hosts of dying,*
> *The young and the old; nor is there anywhere*
> *In all the world a refuge, or a harbor*
> *Where there is hope or safety. Funerals*
> *Where'er I turn my frightened eyes, appall;*
> *The temples groan with coffins, and the proud*
> *And the humble alike in lack of honor.*
> *The end of life presses upon my mind,*
> *And I recall the dear ones I have lost...*
> *The Consecrated ground is all too small*
> *To hold the instant multitude of graves*
> Francesco Petrach, 1348

Historical Background:

Our story, that of "the pestilence" (the term "Black Death" was not coined until the 19th century), is set in 14th century Europe; a tumultuous time and place, and what some more cynical individuals might consider to be an excellent stage for our narrative (Cantor, pg. 7). It must be said (and explained) before we embark on this journey, that the sweeping blow of death that manifested itself in the form of the bubonic plague did not fall solely upon any one country or region of the world. However, for the purposes of our account, for reasons of surviving documentation and the intensity of the outbreak, the focus of this tale shall be on the Kingdom of England and its Western European neighbors.

In the year 1300, approximately 40 years prior to the outbreak of the plague, the population of England and Wales stood at almost six million (this number would not be reached again until the mid 18th Century) (Cantor, pg. 8). English Society was overwhelmingly rural and agrarian, with the country's largest city (London) containing only 75,000 people. In the north, livestock outnumbered humans five to one, and sharp population growth due to good weather had recently forced farmers to seed and plow almost every available inch of arable land in the isles (Cantor, pg. 63). The longstanding tradition of feudal serfdom was slowly eroding, paving the way for more capitalistic, cash-for-hire system of peasant labor; a trend that led directly to a growing sense of individualism and freedom among peasants (as well as an increased tax base for the monarchy) (Cantor, pg. 70). English society had begun the inevitable transition from that of a status, class-based society towards a more Lockeian monetary economy in which the capital land market dominated the economic landscape.

It is important to note however, that 14th century England remained a country of extreme economic division. In fact, at the onset of the plague, 60 percent of the wealth of Western Europe lay in the hands of only 300 families, around 50 of which resided in England (Cantor, pg. 59). Political power was no less concentrated, and in England the royal families of the House of Plantagenet held nearly all the political and military faculty.

The War:

On February 1, 1327, England was witness to the crowning of Edward III as ruler of the Kingdom of England and patriarch of the House of Plantagenet (a royal family best known for King Richard the Lionhearted, made famous by the tale of Robin Hood) (Ormrod, Ch. 1). Succeeding his father Edward II, who had been deposed by his wife Queen Isabella of France and her lover Roger Mortimer, Edward III's early reign truly began at 18, when the savvy and resourceful young king exacted revenge in the name of his father, capturing Mortimer in the dead of night and executing him for crimes against England (Ormrod, Ch. 1). This act of brutal vengeance served to foreshadow the power-hungry and authoritative rule of King Edward III, who would rule England for the next 50 years, through the most devastating years of the Black Death.

But let us not forget why we are here. This paper is not intended as a historical record of the royal houses of England, Edward III himself, or any other specific historical characters. For our purposes, it is only necessary to understand Edward III in terms of his actions as the leader of England during the time of the Black Death, for it is some of these actions that helped to shape and mold the cultural and societal backdrop for the epic tragedy that lay just around the corner.

As noted above, Edward III was the son of Edward II a member of House Plantagenet and Isabella the daughter of Phillip IV, the King of France. After the untimely deaths of Isabella's only three brothers (Edward III's uncles), the throne of the Kingdom of France stood without a direct heir for the first time since the 10th century (Hundred, pg. 1). Being the young and ambitious king that he was, Edward III proclaimed himself the legitimate heir to the throne of France. As is not difficult to imagine, the French nobility were not terribly thrilled to see an English king attempt to assert dominion over their homeland. So on April 1st, 1328 the French responded by crowning another of King Phillip IV's nephews (Phillip Valois) as ruler of France (Hundred, pg. 1). It was this dispute over the rights of succession that led to what we know call The Hundred Years' War, which ultimately served as the bloody backdrop for the onset of the Black Death.

The Hundred Years' War is significant and relevant to our study of the Black Death for a number of reasons. First, in order to understand medieval society at the time of the plague, it is vital to be conscious of the effect the war had on English and greater European society. This seemingly endless war and the political strife that accompanied it brought with it a cultural understanding of the fragility of death that both enhanced and diminished the effects of the Black Death on European society. The Hundred Years' War helps to illuminate, for modern historians and philosophers, just how unexceptional death was in 14th Century England. In a society where most men died of natural causes before age 45 and war ravaged the population at every turn, it is not difficult to envision the difference in the perception of death between 14th century society and contemporary populations. Secondly, The Hundred Years' War was witness to a military revolution in terms of the style of warfare in Europe, a revolution that would have resounding affects on the both the nature of war in Western Europe and the role of the commons in the political process.

The Infantry Revolution:

Prior to the Hundred Years War, medieval European armies were composed primarily of feudal warrior-aristocrats, who served not as volunteers, but instead as involuntary servants who owed military service in exchange for lands held in fief (Rogers, pg. 2). These aristocratic, knightly warriors, as we often picture them from medieval folklore, fought mainly as heavily armored cavalry, utilizing the lance and broadsword as their weapon of choice. The brute force of muscle and steel dominated the battlefield, and the doctrines of chivalry and socio-economic classism weighed heavily on the strategies of war (Rogers, pg. 2). In comparison to modern war, military death tolls were quite low in those days, with the vast majority of battles ending in surrender rather than slaughter (Rogers, pg. 2).

With the Hundred Years War came the invention of the English longbow, and what Clifford Rogers refers to as the "Infantry Revolution." The longbow allowed archers to fire arrows from far greater distances, leading to a missile-fire dominated battle strategy rather than one of domination through sheer numbers (Rogers, pg. 3). The military mission transitioned from one of surprise and capture to fire and slaughter, creating an era of military casualties the likes of which had never been seen in Western Europe. The longbow and the corresponding changes in battle stratey created a growing need for foot soldiers and longbow archers, and vastly diminished the usefulness of armored cavalry. This in turn led to a substantial increase in the number of for-pay, common peasants serving in the military (Rogers, pg. 3). Peasants fought and died in huge numbers alongside feudal aristocrats, and war began to shift from a political chess game to a nationalistic fight to the death.

These shifts in military tactics had rippling effects that extended far beyond the battlefield. The so called "infantry revolution" brought with it a number of significant social and political changes. The growing usefulness of the peasant infantry coupled with the gradual transition towards a modern capital-based economy gave rise to the increasing political influence of the commons; a shift that would have intriguing effects on the cultural reaction to the Black Death (Rogers, pg. 3).

The Church:

The morality and cultural consciousness of Europe in the 1300's was dominated by the teachings of the Catholic Church. Christianity and the age of faith still reigned supreme, and the church had a hand in nearly every aspect of politics, war, and society. However, the power and domination of the church would soon begin to decline, based in large part on societal reactions to the bubonic plague.

There is little disagreement among historians that the 14th century was one of the most tumultuous and straining historical periods for the papacy and Christianity as a whole. Beginning in 1300, a number of strategic blunders on the part of the Church hierarchy led to a serious decline in the commanding power of the Church in Western Europe.

In the year 1300, in a move intended to expand papal influence over the European monarchies, Pope Boniface VII attempted to enforce papal authority over France's King Phillip IV (Edward III's maternal grandfather) (Classzone, pg. 1). In response, Phillip asserted his own royal authority over all French bishops, severely damaging the relationship between the French throne and the papacy (Classzone, pg. 1).

In 1305, two years after Pope Boniface's death, King Phillip IV was able to convince the College of Cardinals to select a French archbishop as the new pope, and additionally, to move the Holy See of the Catholic Church from Rome to a new home in Avignon, France (Classzone, pg. 1). To the north, the English saw the move as an attempt by the French to gain control over the political power of the Church, and they viewed the new pope, Clement V, as a puppet of the French throne. In the south, the Italians were deeply wounded by the move, and continued to demand that papal rule return to the Vatican (Classzone, pg. 1). In 1378, confusion and political strife among the Church hierarchy led the College of Cardinals to select two new popes, one residing in Avignon and the other in Rome, effectively dividing the followers and influence of the Church (Classzone, pg. 2). This great papal divide later became known as the "Western Schism", a bisection of religious influence and leadership that served as the backdrop for the Black Plague.

At this point we find ourselves on the eve of the Black Death. England's King Edward III and France's Phillip Valois were fighting an immensely bloody battle over the right of French royal succession, the Church was in disarray and losing more credibility and power with each passing day, peasant society was undergoing vast changes in terms of both military service and economic systems, and unseasonably warm weather and crop success had led to unprecedented population growth in the British Isles. The stage was set, the characters were in place, and the greatest biomedical disaster in human history loomed just off stage.

> *So nature killed many through corruptions,*
> *Death came driving after her and dashed all to dust,*
> *Kings and knights, emperors and popes;*
> *He left no man standing, whether learned or ignorant;*
> *Whatever he hit stirred never afterwards.*

Many a lovely lady and their lover-knights
Swooned and died in sorrow of Death's blows...
For God is deaf nowadays and will not hear us,
And for our guilt he grinds good men to dust.
-William Langland, late 14th Cent.

The Pestilence:

A popular children's rhyme is often heard wafting from circles of contemporary youth standing hand in hand at playgrounds all over the Western World.

Ring around the rosies
A pocketful of posies
Ashes, ashes
We all fall down
-15th century, author unknown

The lyrics and tune of this popular rhyme seem all too familiar and innocent, but in fact, their origin is far more sinister. This well-known poem is in reality a reference to an attempt by those not yet afflicted by the gruesome symptoms of the Black Death to mask the smell of ever-present death and decay with a "pocketful of posies" (Medieval slang for bunches of potpourri) (Cantor, pg. 5). This popular English rhyme is best understood as an attempt to humanize and grasp psychologically the incredible and overwhelming levels of death that engulfed European society during the time of the plague.

The Spread:

Infectious diseases and pandemics are not an unfamiliar occurrence in the history of the human drama. The Spanish Influenza ravaged American and European populations in the aftermath of World War 1, outbreaks of Bird Flu, Swine Flu, and anthrax have etched their way into the modern American psyche, and HIV continues to spread like wildfire through much of the world's population. However, at no time in history has a single disease had a more drastic influence on the societal consciousness of the world's population than the devastation that we now refer to as the Black Death.

The pestilence killed at least 25 percent of Western Europe's population, 20 million of whom died in the three-year period from 1347-1350 (Cantor, pg. 7). However, much is still unknown about the virus that leveled much of the world, and only recently have scientific developments allowed us to look deeper into one of death's greatest historical weapons.

At this point, contemporary researchers have been able to fully agree on at least one thing, that the Black Death was primarily the result of the bubonic plague (some medical historians argue that it was in fact a combination of bubonic plague and some form of anthrax) (Cantor, pg. 14). Bubonic plague is a bacillus known scientifically as Yersinia Pestis, carried on the backs of rodents (most notably, the Black Rat) and transmitted from host to host through the bite of infected fleas (Black Death, pg. 1). How the infected rodents made their way to Western Europe is still a matter of debate, but many historians believe that it was the result of international trade from the Asian Mongols traveling the Silk Road and the Arab Muslims trading spices around the Mediterranean (Classzone, pg. 3). Unlike modern animal based pandemics, like Mad-Cow and Hoof and Mouth Disease, the scientists and doctors of the Middle Ages were unable to identify the source of the pandemic as an animal based disease or furthermore the manner in which the disease was communicated.

Without any knowledge of the disease's origin or its method of transmission, medieval doctors assumed that the disease was an airborne epidemic, transmitted from person to person through inhalation of infected respiratory droplets (similar to smallpox) (Cantor, pg. 22). The mass dissemination of this misdiagnosis had a monumental affect on European lifestyle and society. A wave of fear swept the continent, leading many of the unafflicted, especially those of the aristocratic classes, to flee the cities for the safety of rural, isolated retreats (Cantor, pg. 22). Many windows were covered with large, thick tapestries in order to protect homes from what the vast majority of people thought to be contaminated air, a practice referenced by the Italian author Villani just before his death in 1348: "the air was so infested that death overtook men everywhere, wherever they might flee" (Knox, pg. 1).

While some of these exodus-esque preventative tactics were mildly effective due to the higher prevalence of rats in urban population centers, attempting to escape the plague proved far more difficult than many assumed. Rodents, especially rats, were exceedingly common in the Middle Ages. The lack of adequate sewage disposal (upon which rats feed) and the generally unsavory hygienic condition of cities and their inhabitants created a rat haven, in which rodent populations spread like a diseased, scurrying conflagration (Cantor, pg. 21).

Medieval medical practices only worsened the situation. Bathing was considered dangerous due to the opening of pores, supposedly making one more susceptible to the disease. This led many commoners to forego bathing altogether and nobles to resort to daily cologne massages instead of risking the dangers of a proper bath (Cantor, pg. 23). As hygiene worsened, people grew weaker, making them easier prey for the rodent transported disease contributing significantly to the 40 percent mortality rate in the substantially fouler urban centers (Cantor, pg. 22). Limitations on the number of available clergy coupled with the lacking availability of cemetery space, led to the creation of mass graves in which the sick were buried without honor or dignity, left to rot in steaming pits of death and disease (Renius, pg. 1). Giovanni Boccaccio wrote of the phenomenon is his book the *Decameron*, noting that,

> *Although the cemeteries were full they were forced to dig huge trenches, where they buried the bodies by hundreds. Here they stowed them away like bales in the hold of a ship and covered them with a little earth, until the whole trench was full.*
> -Giovanni Boccaccio, *Decameron*

Death:

Burials were not the only undignified aspect of a bubonic death; the symptoms and resulting death were excruciatingly painful and unsavory. Four out of five people who contracted the disease were dead within two weeks, the symptoms beginning with a simple headache and chills, and perhaps some nausea and fever to boot. The disease quickly escalated its onslaught, and within a few days swellings appeared on the neck, under the arms, and on the inner thighs. These growths (known as buboes) quickly turned black, splitting open, seeping pus and blood. At this point recovery became a pipedream, and internal bleeding quickly followed suit. Blood would appear in the urine, stool, and in an increasing amount of black boils all over the body. Death came swiftly for the afflicted, and the vast majority of sufferers died within a few days of the appearance of the boils (Snell, pg. 1). While a simple dose of antibiotics could have treated the disease, the invention of penicillin was many centuries away, so nearly every person who contracted the disease suffered a vile and undignified end to life (Cantor, pg. 12).

The pestilence, like death itself, was a democratic menace. The bubonic plague carried no inherent internal prejudice, killing peasants, nobility, and clergy alike. Though urban peasant populations suffered from slightly higher rates of mortality due to their particularly unsavory lifestyles, the bubonic plague also claimed the lives of millions of aristocrats and Church hierarchy, including Edward III's own daughter Princess Joan (Cantor, pg. 47). Entire villages and cities were wiped out, leaving only the unmistakably foul stench of bubonic puss as a clue to what had occurred. In the end, the Black Death claimed untold tens of millions of lives around the world, decimating the English and greater European populations to the point of near non-recovery, and shaking medieval civilization to its core.

The Reaction of the Leadership:

As noted above, the great forces of political and cultural power in England at the time of the plague were the Church and the Monarchy, and it was to these pillars of Medieval society that the commons turned for answers, explanations, and hope. They received nothing of the sort.

The Church hierarchy, along with the ignorant medical professionals of the day, attributed the plague to God's punishment for the sins of a decreasingly pious society, a judgment that did not sit well with the peasant populations (Cantor, pg. 23). Ever-confident in the ways of God, the Church promised cures and treatment for the plague (most of which were in the form of prayer), promises upon which they were unable to deliver (Renius, pg. 2). However, these issues were only a few of the Church's growing list of problems. High levels of contact with poor, urban populations led to a relatively high mortality rate among practicing clergy. As the plague wore on, there were fewer and fewer clergy available to oversee proper burials and even fewer available for confession and other everyday services

(Renius, pg. 1). Inevitably, the Church began **to** decline in power and influence. The newly empowered peasant class was unhappy with the lack of respect shown by the Church in regard to improper burials and mass graves, and a newfound desire for a closer relationship with the God who continued to punish their friends and family drove many commoners to question the need for the clergy altogether (Renius, pg. 1). Many scholars believe that these reactions to the Black Death led directly to the Protestant Reformation of the 16th century.

The ruling Monarchy, unsure of what or who to blame, turned to a combination of divine punishment and the astrological placement of Saturn in the house of Jupiter as the best possible explanation for the epic devastation (Cantor, pg. 22). Concerned more with the economic impacts of population decline than with any genuine consideration for the lives of commoners, the rulers and aristocracy turned to Parliament in order to stymie the growing bargaining power of the dwindling labor force. Parliament in turn enacted the "Statute Of Labourers", which served to peg newly higher wages to pre-plague levels. This action led directly to the Peasants Revolt of 1381, in which an army of angry peasants nearly toppled the English government in an attempt to establish a Christian socialist regime (Cantor, pg. 24).

When the dust finally settled in the 15th century, both the Church and the various monarchies of Europe found themselves far weaker than when the plague had begun. The Western European population had been reduced by 25%, and the social, political, and economic systems were badly strained. It would take more than 150 years for the population to recover, and the effect of such overwhelming levels of death on the greater cultural psyche of Europe remains open to interpretation. The world had experienced the greatest biomedical holocaust seen before or since, affecting the surviving populations' view of death in ways unmatched by any other event in human history.

> They said that the only medicine against the plague-stricken was to go right away from them. Men and women, convinced of this and caring about nothing but themselves, abandoned their own city, their own houses, their dwellings, their relatives, their property, and went

> abroad or at least to the country round Florence, as if God's
> wrath in punishing men's wickedness with this plague would
> not follow them but strike only those who remained within
> the walls of the city, or as if they thought nobody in the city
> would remain alive and that its last hour had come.
> -Giovanni Boccaccio

Cultural Reactions and Thoughts on Death:

Like all great disasters in history, especially those that involve instances of sudden and severe population decline, the Black Death left deep scars in the cultural identity of the affected population. However, what the Black Death appears to have lacked that other comparably large disasters seem to have had in common, was the ability to bring together and unite a population. Instead, the bubonic plague tore society apart, deeply affecting the consciousness and behavior of individuals, families, and communities (Classzone, pg. 2). The inhumane devastation of the plague affected English and European society not only in terms of its physical manifestation as an agent of population decline, but also in terms of its determined eroding of the humanistic bonds that held together and stabilized society (Cantor, pg. 25). People turned against each other, knowingly and intentionally severing the ties of interpersonal relationships. Self-interest became the name of the game, and it would take many years for society to recover.

Giovanni Boccaccio, a writer residing in Florence at the time of the plague, wrote of the drastic, self-interest driven changes he saw manifested in Italian society during the time of the plague.

> One citizen avoided another, hardly any neighbour
> troubled about others, relatives never or hardly ever
> visited each other. Moreover, such terror was struck into
> the hearts of men and women by this calamity, that brother
> abandoned brother, and the uncle his nephew, and the
> sister her brother, and very often the wife her husband.
> What is even worse and nearly incredible is that fathers
> and mothers refused to see and tend their children, as if
> they had not been theirs.
> -Giovanni Boccaccio, *Decameron*

Unlike modern disasters like that of the September 11th, 2001 terrorist attacks, the Black Death failed to unite a nation or community behind any common cause or purpose. In fact, it seems to me that the Black Death did quite the opposite, and in some unique way managed to revert European populations back to some obscure version of Hobbes' state of nature.

Thomas Hobbes wrote of three forces that drive men to self-interested conflict in the state of nature, "The first maketh men invade for gain; the second, for safety; and the third, for reputation" (Hobbes, Ch. 14). In the case of the Black Death, an instinctive desire for safety and self-preservation acted to erode the social contract between citizens, effectively deposing the centuries old patchwork of communities, replacing it with an individualistic, self-centered, post-apocalyptic state of fear. The life of Western Europeans during the Black Death, especially the peasant class, truly was: "solitary, poor, nasty, brutish, and short."

However, it was not as if the entire European population had somehow fallen into a theoretical pit of individualism; it was far more animalistic than that. Hobbes would later write that the first law of nature is that each man ought to endeavor for peace (Hobbes, Ch. 14). The actions of the citizenry at the time of plague were just that, an endeavor for peace. However, it was not threats from invading armies and greedy neighbors that threatened society; instead it was a battle for self-preservation against the inevitable spread of a mysterious and unseen terror, a terror that claimed far more victims than any longbow ever dreamed of.

As I noted earlier in this paper, death was not an unknown foe to the citizens of 14th century England and France. The drama of the Black Death was played out on a stage in which disease was common and a devastatingly bloody war raged in the background. The infantry revolution and the advent of the longbow were rapidly transforming the battlefield into a more sanguinary place, and even those who managed to live long enough to enjoy a natural death rarely survived for more than a half-century. Few populations understood the fragility of death better than pre-plague Europeans. So for a society so used to direct confrontation with mortality, it seems strange that cultural reactions to the plague were so strong and woeful. So the question begs asking: what was it about the Black Death of the 14th century that struck such fear and individualism into medieval society?

The answer is based not in the sheer scale of death that occurred or in the horrid way in which the plague took its victims, though both these attributes of the plague played a contributing role. Instead, it was the failures of 14th century European science and medicine to understand the source of the bubonic plague and how it was communicated from host to host that were the origin of the terror and hysteria that invaded society. The misdiagnosis of the pestilence as an airborne miasma created scientifically unfounded and irrational fears of human contact, and in turn led to the degradation of medieval society. Misunderstanding of the way in which the disease was communicated struck mass panic into the hearts of the unaffected, allowing the Black Death to erode the foundations of culture and society, leading directly to the intense self-interested and individualistic actions so evident in the texts of the period.

It is for this reason that the Black Death is such a distinctly unique event. It was the Black Death's ability to inspire such mass hysteria that differentiates it from all other similar instances of mass catastrophe and death. Because the disease could not be explained by science, the death associated with the bubonic plague could not be rationally grasped by society. Unlike the Hundred Years War, the Nazi Holocaust, the bombings of Hiroshima and Nagasaki, the tsunamis in Indonesia and Japan, or even the great wars of the early 20th century, the Black Death's victims lacked the scientific understanding to comprehend what was happening to them.

It is due to this misdiagnosis of the bubonic plague as an airborne pathogen that I believe it unlikely that a similar event will ever occur again. Contemporary science and medicine, seems to me at least, to be far too advanced to allow for such a prolonged misinterpretation of an epidemic. The misappropriation of HIV as the "Gay Disease" in the 1980s is a contemporary example of the effects of a misdiagnosis of an infectious disease, but this error was corrected. Medieval science and medicine were not equipped with the tools or knowledge necessary to handle such a large-scale epidemic, and their shortcomings and ill advice acted as the catalyst for the crumbling of society.

The Black Death helps reveal to us the importance of cognitive understanding in the face of our own mortality. Even in modern

American culture we see a distinct obsession with understanding the exact cause and source of our individual mortality. Science and medicine were as helpless as the Church in defending against the newfound menace, and I believe that this lack of understanding contributed heavily to the decay of medieval society at the time of plague. The bubonic plague struck without warning or reason, taking children and priests alike. The fear of death from contact with unnamed friends and neighbors drove people to irrational, inhuman acts.

What I also find intriguing, and what seems to be a bit at odds with the terror and confusion created by the misdiagnosis, was the pervasiveness of the denial of death in plague society that seems rather evident in the writings of Giovanni Boccaccio. It appears that the plague drove many to force the thought of death from their minds, replacing it instead with hedonistic pleasures and meaningless actions. Boccaccio wrote of the varying reactions of individuals to plague induced death in the following passage:

> *Some thought that moderate living and the avoidance of all superfluity would preserve them from the epidemic. They formed small communities, living entirely separate from everybody else. They shut themselves up in houses where there were no sick, eating the finest food and drinking the best wine very temperately, avoiding all excess, allowing no news or discussion of death and sickness, and passing the time in music and suchlike pleasures. Others thought just the opposite. They thought the sure cure for the plague was to drink and be merry, to go about singing and amusing themselves, satisfying every appetite they could, laughing and jesting at what happened. They put their words into practice, spent day and night going from tavern to tavern, drinking immoderately, or went into other people's houses, doing only those things which pleased them.*
> -Giovanni Boccaccio, *Decameron*

Boccaccio seems to present two distinct ways in which individuals dealt with the spread of the plague. Boccaccio notes that while many attempted to live without a conscious recognition of the spreading pestilence by locking themselves away from their communities and allowing "no news or discussion of death", others took to the streets and found comfort in denial through distraction and amusement. What seems common to both descriptions is that both groups seem to have taken the route of self-indulgence, placing their own self-interest and pleasure atop of the ladder of importance.

In the classic work of contemporary American non-fiction entitled *Tuesdays With Morrie*, the central character (Morrie) claims that, "Everyone knows they're going to die, but nobody believes it... If we did, we would do things differently" (Albom, pg. 81). Perhaps Boccaccio's account of the varying reactions of individuals to the plague is in line with Morrie's thought. The bubonic plague forced individuals to confront their own mortality, creating a situation in which the fragility of life took center stage. Yet the denial of death seemed to remain the only acceptable route, and the quest for hedonistic pleasure and self-preservation displaced all other purposes.

Conclusion:

There is perhaps no other event in recorded history that has so deeply affected the human conception of death than the biomedical disaster known as the Black Death. The unflinching epidemic wiped out entire towns, cities, and communities, claiming untold millions of lives and reducing Western Europe's population by 25 percent. Occurring in a time and place not unfamiliar with death, the plague's devastating affect on the European psyche is all the more remarkable. Due in large part to widespread fear sparked by the misdiagnosis of the plague as an airborne pathogen, European society deteriorated into an individualistic and self-centered pit of hedonism; the social, political, and religious ramifications of which would be felt for years to come. The lessons of the Black Death remain relevant to contemporary society, and its ultimate affects on various parts of history stand as testament to the power of death. Only in reflecting on the devastation and the resulting shifts in consciousness can we truly see how misunderstanding and fear can drive society into disarray.

Works Cited

1. Albom, M. (1997). *Tuesdays with Morrie: an old man, a young man, and life's greatest lesson*. New York: Doubleday.

2. Black Death. (2011). In *Encyclopædia Britannica*. Retrieved from http://www. britannica.com/EBchecked/topic/67758/Black-Death

3. Boccaccio, G., Musa, M., & Bondanella, P. E. (1977). *The decameron: a new translation : 21 novelle, contemporary reactions, modern criticism*. new york: W. W. Norton.

4. Cantor, N. F. (2001). *In the wake of the plague: the Black Death and the world it made*. New York: Free Press.

5. Hobbes, T., & Gaskin, J. C. (1998). *Leviathan* . Oxford : Oxford University Press.

6. Hundred Years' War. (2011). In *Encyclopædia Britannica*. Retrieved from http://www.britannica.com/EBchecked/topic/276526/Hundred-Years-War

7. Knox, E. (n.d.). The Black Death. *Boise State University*. Retrieved March 30, 2011, from http://boisestate.edu/courses/westciv/plague/18.shtml

8. Ormrod, W. M. (2000). *The reign of Edward III* (Updated ed.). Stroud: Tempus.

9. Renius, A. (n.d.). The Black Death and the Decline of the Influence of the Catholic Church | Socyberty. *Socyberty | Society on the Web*. Retrieved March 30, 2011, from http://socyberty.com/history/the-black-death-and-the-decline-of-the-influence-of-the-catholic-church/

10. Rogers, C. J. (n.d.). The Military Revoutions of the Hundred Years. *De Re Militari: The Society for Medieval Military History*. Retrieved March 30, 2011, from http://www.deremilitari.org/resources/articles/rogers.htm

11. Snell, M. (n.d.). Death Defined - Black Death Causes and Symptoms. *Medieval History - Life in the Middle Ages and Renaissance*. Retrieved March 30, 2011, from http://historymedren.about.com/od/theblackdeath/a/death_defined.htm

12. The Hundred Years' War and the Plague. (n.d.). *Classzone*. Retrieved March 30, 2011, from www.ihs.issaquah.wednet.edu/.../ Hundred%20Years%20 War% 2014%204 .pdf

CHAPTER FIFTEEN

The Evolution of the Reaper

Daniel Magill

This paper explores the concept of death and human mortality through the lens of Western culture's popular figure "The Grim Reaper." The author analyzes the role of the Reaper throughout its existence as a mechanism human beings utilize to come to grips with their own mortality and eventual death. Through this analysis of the forms and roles of the Reaper throughout its history, this paper examines how having a fictional character to represent or personify death makes mortality a more palatable reality.

Fiction is first and foremost a source of entertainment. It serves as an escape from reality, allowing for fantastic scenarios that are simply unattainable elsewhere. In the right hands, however, it is also an elegant tool, one that reflects the state of public consciousness at the time it is produced. The themes and morals of a story can show us the feelings of the author and, in aggregate, those of society as a whole. It stands to reason, therefore, that to examine the representation of death in fiction gives insight to the evolving perception of death in society. To get the most distilled and straightforward insight into the very concept, then, we must cast aside the distractions of drama and circumstance that surround death as an event, and examine death itself. In fiction, this means examining the very personification of death. Today, this means examining the Grim Reaper.

Before going any further in this examination, there is a distinction that must be made. The actual personification of death is itself something of an evolution, stemming from the earlier mythological concept of the psychopomp. A psychopomp, the Greek word for "conveyor of souls," was simply a supernatural being charged with moving spirits between the realms of the living and the dead. Examples of this include figures such as Charon, Hermes, Saint Peter, Azrael, Michael, Anubis, the Valkyries of Old Norse mythology, among countless others. Though they appear in nearly every known mythology, and their precise duties may vary, the essential concern is that they serve as a guide, escorting a soul to the afterlife.

From the psychopomp, however, evolved the far more familiar figure in modern folklore, that of the Grim Reaper. This is the version of death seen far more often today, as psychopomps are often a strictly mythological figure, whereas the Grim Reaper has become wildly prevalent in countless works of fiction. The concept of an individual charged with death itself rather than simply travel between worlds is not terribly new, of course. Among others, the Greeks had Thanatos, the Bretons Ankou, and the Hindus Yama. The common thread, however, is that all these figures were gods. Historically speaking, the lords of death occupied a role in a pantheon, presiding over departed souls as Demeter did the harvest. It is crucial to realize that these entities were gods first, and death second. It wasn't until the emergence of the Reaper that we saw Death truly walk the earth.

The Grim Reaper, as we know him today, first came to prominence sometime around the 15th century, after first appearing in the 14th with the Black Plague. He is the figure that is instantly associated with death in modern society, a foreboding and mysterious individual in a black cloak, carrying a large scythe. Sometimes he is skeletal, other times simply pale. The Grim Reaper is the first instance we see of a figure who not only fulfills the duty of death, but truly personifies it, performing its functions and embodying its traits in humanoid form. The Reaper is as mysterious, menacing, and inevitable as death itself.

In the face of this inevitability, however, human beings naturally began trying to find methods to make it more evitable. Thus began the notion and trend of trying to outsmart the Reaper, and with it, death. Again, this is an idea that goes back to ancient times. In the classic tale of

Sisyphus, the titular figure angered the gods by betraying Zeus' secrets. When Zeus ordered Thanatos to chain Sisyphus to Tartarus, the man cleverly tricked the death god into chaining himself in his stead. With the god of death trapped, no human could die, and Ares, bored that no one died in war, freed him. Sisyphus tricked the gods once more, however, having his wife throw his body into a public square, instead of burying him properly. Once in the Underworld, Sisyphus obtained permission to return to the living world in order to chastise his wife, and refused to return. The gods finally grew tired of his deceptions, and he was dragged back to the Underworld, where his punishment awaited him.

In the modern era, however, this idea was most famously immortalized in *The Seventh Seal*, an immensely classic film by directorial virtuoso Ingmar Bergman.The film told the tale of medieval knight Antonius Block returning to his home country of Sweden after ten years fighting in the Crusades, only to find his country ravaged by the Black Death, and Death itself awaiting him. Block challenges Death to a game of chess, explaining that he has seen Death play in paintings. The painting Block refers to is presumably the mural in the Täby Church in Sweden, painted by Albertus Prictor in the 1480s. As long as he plays, the knight stipulates, Death lets him live, and should he win, he is set free. The two play their game throughout the film as Block travels, coming across Death time and time again throughout the land. Eventually, Block resorts to cheating, knocking over the board and upsetting the pieces. Death, however, is implacable, and simply places the pieces back where they were, winning the game on the next turn. He departs one final time before returning at the end of the film to take the lives of Block and his companions.

It is apparent that the concept of chess with death goes back to at least the time of Prictor's mural, in the 15th century. Even before that, though, Geoffrey Chaucer wrote the *Book of the Duchess* in the 14th century, which featured a knight playing chess with Fortuna, Greek goddess of luck, for his wife's life. Before chess even entered the equation, we see the attempt to outwit death in a game or with trickery as early as Sisyphus. So why does this occur? Why do human beings feel it is necessary to combat death in such a way?

In my experience, human beings have distinct difficulty addressing the concept of inevitability. We seek to bargain, we hope against all odds that there is some action we can take, at the very least in an attempt to change the outcome of a situation. Thusly when faced with death, the ultimate inevitable scenario, we seek to find a way to "beat" death. The simplest way to envision that is to face death in a simple game, or to outwit it, to be placed in a situation in which there is a clear winner and loser. In most serious works, however it is to no avail. That same inevitability comes through in the end, and death always wins.

With the possibility of victory available, however, not everyone has been able to resist the temptation of having their characters succeed, and actually defeat death. As with nearly all characters of folklore, Death has suffered a certain loss of dignity and mystique in modern fiction. In the extreme cases of this loss of dignity, Death slips from the ineffable adversary to an outright fool, the character often played for laughs at its expense. Though older examples of this particular concept are decidedly scarcer, there is no greater example of this shift in modern times than the comedy classic of the early 1990s, *Bill and Ted's Bogus Journey.*

In the movie, when the titular protagonists Bill and Ted are killed by evil robot versions of themselves, they are sent to Hell and meet with the Grim Reaper himself. Being surprisingly genre savvy, however, the pair invoke the legend established in *The Seventh Seal,* and challenge Death to a game with their lives at stake. Relenting, Death allows them to choose the game, and the two friends manage to beat him at Battleship, Clue, electric football, and Twister in turn. With each loss, a frustrated Death pettily demands more games, necessitating best of three, five, seven games before finally giving in on his fourth loss. Thoroughly beaten, the Reaper not only returns them to life, but spends the rest of the story as a good natured and bumbling sidekick for the duo, going as far as joining them in the rock concert climax of the film, where he dances, raps, and plays upright bass.

Though handled with quite a bit more dignity, it is also worth noting the fallibility of another incarnation of Death, the Shinigami. After the concept of the Grim Reaper reached Japan in the 19th century, the idea was gradually changed and adapted, and the name translated as "Shinigami," or God of Death. Originally a single figure, the Shinigami have evolved to represent an entire race of psychopomps, although their specific attributes vary nearly as much as those of the western vampire. One common trait, however, is that despite or perhaps because of their deific label, the Shinigami are often considerably less powerful than the western incarnation of death.

Whereas the western Grim Reaper represents the inevitability of death, the Shinigami, under the Reaper's guise, reverse the trend and are once again simply psychopomps. This leads to considerable disconnect as the large amounts of media exported from Japan often feature Death as a character or plot device, but one vulnerable to defeat, or in some cases, funnily enough, death.

This aspect is simply the other approach to resolving inevitability. Beyond the scope of a simple challenge, Death is made to be vulnerable, so that by rightful contest, trickery, or sheer brute force, there is hope for victory. In the case of a foolish portrayal, this is taken a step further. Whereas the aforementioned "serious" works eventually bow to the inevitability of death, these simply cast it aside. Death, the ultimate adversary of all living things, is made to be not only vulnerable but a complete pushover, turning our ultimate fate into nothing more than an lighthearted amusement.

Eventually, with the addition of vulnerability to the character, there comes a loss of distance and mystery between death and humanity. This change allows a new facet of the character to surface, and we begin to see Death with a personality. As such, Death becomes more human, it is much easier to get around automatically seeing it as an adversary. The simplest and most gradual incarnation of this change simply shifts Death back from the Grim Reaper to somewhat of a psychopomp. In more extreme cases, Death is even seen as a friend.

It is important to note that while the Reaper is altered to once again perform the function of a psychopomp, it remains distinctly the embodiment of death. Similarly to the case of the Shinigami, these characters retain the characteristics of the Grim Reaper, but now more accurately represent bureaucrats than the traditional adversarial nature of Death. The Reaper now fulfills its duty because it must be done, rather than for itself. This is a concept often utilized in comedies, showing death in a comparatively mundane daily grind. Unlike the role of the fool, however, there is often a note of sincerity in this role. Death remains powerful and inexorable, but no longer works explicitly against human beings. Many of these stories opt to illustrate the utter necessity of death by removing that same bureaucrat from his post, often with disastrous consequences.

In Terry Pratchett's wildly successful *Discworld* novels, Death is a prominent character, and one of the more benevolent supernatural beings in the universe. Whereas most of the deities follow the old-world tradition of self-interest and negligence, Death is responsible, and to some extent kind. In particular, the novels *Mort* and *Reaper Man* examine the character in depth, with the former exploring the concept of Death's accepting an apprentice, and the latter having him fired, and sent to go live among humans. These books both stress the importance and magnitude of Death's service to humanity, not his menace.

The concept of the Shinigami and Pratchett's not-so-Grim Reaper, however, are both lesser incarnations of a newer trend and greater reversal than any of the other manifestations to date. The buffoonish Reaper present in *Bill and Ted* did much to dispel the aura of inapproachability present for much of the character's history. Beyond that, the stress upon the necessity of Death's function further weakens Death's menace, while still maintaining his dignity. In some cases, though, the extra step is taken to portray death as not only necessary, but kind. We see some of it in *Bill and Ted*, as the Reaper becomes an ally of the protagonists, but this is largely out of compulsion and adherence to his word. It is hinted at further with Pratchett's portrayal, but the character straddles such a dichotomy between comedy and menace, his kindness can be difficult to grasp.

In classic literature, a kindly Death appears in Emily Dickinson's poem *Because I Could Not Stop for Death*. The poem details an incident where Death "kindly stops" for the narrator, and the two take a decidedly pleasant drive together. Critically acclaimed adventure game *Grim Fandango* placed the player in the role of Manny Calavera, giving the fairly unique experience of featuring a Grim Reaper as the protagonist. Manny works as a Reaper for the "Department of Death," effectively a travel agency for deceased souls. It is Manny's job to bring souls to the Land of the Dead, and depending on the virtue of their lives, ease their journey to some extent. Over the course of the game, the player finds Manny to be a very humorous and compassionate individual, as he strives to uncover corruption in the Department of Death, and help the unlucky souls falling victim to it.

Perhaps the most unusual Reaper to date, however, appeared in Neil Gaiman's landmark graphic novel *Sandman*. The series follows Dream of the Endless, a family of seven anthropomorphic personifications including Dream, Desire, Destiny, and the second eldest of the siblings, Death. Over the course of the series' 75 issues, we encounter Death time and time again, both through encounters with Dream and in her own solo side stories. The extremely unique interpretation of the character has led to lasting popularity amongst fans of the series. In complete defiance of any tradition, Death is portrayed as a perky, attractive young goth woman, and is quite easily the kindest and most relatable of the siblings. Suggested to be one of the most powerful forces in the universe, she acts as a nurturing older sister to the protagonist, and is shown to be exceptionally compassionate towards the souls she collects. According to the mythology of the series, Death spends a single day every century living and then dying as a mortal, leading her to be possibly the only being in existence who truly understands the value of life.

These myths, together with those of the Shinigami, suggest something of a return to form with Death. In ancient times, the god of death was not always an inherently frightening figure. As with any member of a pantheon, they featured a wide spectrum of personalities, and death was simply a function they performed. It is something of a western tradition to portray gods of death or darkness as inherently evil, but this was not always how it was. Now, it seems, writers are coming full circle on the opinion, and deciding that if these gods can be decent people, why can't Death itself?

The original incarnation of the psychopomps was established for the same reason as any other god: an attempt to understand and explain that which cannot be understood. The Grim Reaper first emerged in a time of unimaginable grief and anguish. With the advent of a newly horrific death, a new face was needed. So human beings made the Reaper, a horrific, inexorable figure that captured the reality of the horror that surrounded them. As time passes, however, society as a whole is coming to terms with death. I would propose that the portrayal of the Grim Reaper shows something of a macrocosm of the Kübler-Ross model of grief.

The horrors of the plague saw the creation of the Reaper. Humanity was in denial that something so terrible could occur without reason. So we gave it a face. A ghastly skeletal figure that could be understood, that could bear motivation. Now, however, it was no longer an anonymous act. We grew angry with the monster that victimized us, so we made it a fool. We mocked death to lessen its power, and take our revenge. As the anger faded, we sought to bargain. We faced death in games, attempting to create a scenario in which the inevitable could be foiled. When this too fails, we slip into a depression as death becomes the boogeyman once again. Finally, however, we have begun to accept death. We recognize not only the inevitability but the necessity of death, and we accept the possibility that perhaps death could be a friend.

Though this comparison does not fit the progression of the steps perfectly, it bears witnessing all the same. Chronology aside, we can see a basic reaction with which to grieve the great calamity of the human race: mortality. The unwavering and universal threat that all human beings must face manifests itself in the mask of the Reaper, and through the Reaper, humanity begins to cope. Though originally nothing more than a villain, in recent years we have seen the inevitable decay native to all villainous or mythological figures, of which the Reaper is both. Distance is lost, and we see new sides of the character. Whether this manifests in methods through which we defeat or befriend the character, the result is the same. We consider avenues of thought beyond simple fear.

I, for once, heartily condone this evolution. Not only does the narrative variety allow for far more interesting storytelling, but the recent "acceptance" movement seems to indicate a much healthier perspective of death in society. Popular fiction plays a significant role in public opinion, and for far too long western civilization has automatically associated any kind of darker topic with malevolence. Instead, we're beginning to come to terms with death, and consider other possibilities for its role in our lives. If, in the process, we acquire more diverse and engaging fiction, I certainly won't complain.

Works Cited

Camus, Albert. "The Myth of Sisyphus." Web. 14 Mar. 2011. <http://www.nyu.edu/classes/keefer/hell/camus.html>.

The Seventh Seal. Dir. Ingmar Bergman. Perf. Max Von Sydow, Gunnar Björnstrand, and Bengt Ekerot. Svensk Filmindustri, 1956. DVD.

Bill & Ted's Bogus Journey. Dir. Peter Hewitt. Perf. Keanu Reeves and Alex Winter. MGM, 1991. DVD.

Pratchett, Terry. *Mort.* New York, NY: New American Library, 1987. Print.

Pratchett, Terry. *Reaper Man.* London: Victor Gollancz, 1991. Print.

Dickinson, Emily, and Helen Vendler. *Dickinson: Selected Poems and Commentaries.* Cambridge, MA: Belknap of Harvard UP, 2010. Print.

CHAPTER SIXTEEN

Chaplains on Death Row

Liana Goff

A long-time hot button topic, execution in the United States is a polarizing debate in which supporters and protesters alike draw upon biblical text to support their respective viewpoints. In the midst of the debate are the thousands of prison chaplains on America's death row, who distribute bibles, conduct worship services and provide counseling to the criminals awaiting execution. While the job description of a death row chaplain requires the individual bear witness to the execution of the prisoners, it does not necessarily follow that all chaplains support capital punishment. Fascinated with the morality and belief in an afterlife that religion preaches, and on a quest to more clearly understand religion's relationship with death, I set out to find chaplains on death row who were willing to speak on the subject and share their personal beliefs and issues surrounding life on death row. I wanted to discover how the chaplains' experiences affected their beliefs on life, religion and death. What I found bore greater insight into how

one measures a life well lived, and a deserving death,
than I could have ever imagined.

In the United States, there are an estimated 3,260 inmates on Death
Row awaiting execution. Religious clergy and average citizens alike
all hold differing opinions as to what the correct method of dealing with
these dangerous prisoners should be. Some death penalty advocates
cite biblical verses, such as "an eye for an eye", as support for capital
punishment. Opponents of the death penalty can also find support
from religious texts through Jesus' message in the New Testament to
"turn the other cheek."

Chaplains in America's death row distribute bibles, conduct
worship services and provide counseling to the criminals awaiting
execution. Face to face with our mortality and seeing it come to
actualization more frequently than most of us would like - or will
be - in a lifetime, prison chaplains stand in the unique position of
developing a relationship with an individual and proceeding to walk
with them towards a clearly defined date, time and means of death.
Two death row chaplains were able to offer insight on the subject:
Reverend Barbara Sadtler, a retired death row chaplain in Virginia, and
Chaplain Julie Perry, current chaplain at the Fluvanna Correctional
Center for Women. Because Ms. Perry still holds her position, she was
unable to provide as much insight or opinion on the matter as Ms.
Sadtler. Regardless, detailed and explored below are what I found to
be the most resounding and revealing perspectives on life, and death
from our exchanges... Raised a Unitarian Universalist, I learned
in Sunday school the basic teachings of the most widely practiced
religions. However, coming from a family who did not encourage or
speak about faith or religion, it was first important to understand which
church the chaplains affiliated themselves with and the resulting view
on death their religious texts held. As a Christian, Perry explained
her belief that death is "actually the gateway into another realm of
being, another life..." When questioned if she thought perhaps her
belief in an after-life was a means of avoiding the fact that the life we
live now will eventually end, Perry did not respond. Also Christian,
Sadtler too explained to me her belief in an after-life. Interestingly
enough, her belief in the after-life seemed to emphasize heavily the
importance of our time on earth now, rather than looking to life

after death as that which has the most meaning. She told me that the God she sees seems very concerned with community in this life: "... families, clans, nations, Israel, church. It seems incomprehensible to me that God would suddenly switch us to nothing, so I choose to believe. However...for me faith would indeed be worth it even if it were only for this life." Sadtler learned on death row that even if it were not for an after-life, our lives still can and do have significant meaning and impact through community ties and relationships. I t is these very relationships that drew both Sadtler and Perry to the prison chaplaincy to begin with. Both shared goals of helping the prisoners through the experience and walking through it with them; to help them be honest about "the reality of what they faced." Most emphasized was the importance of helping prisoners find the spiritual significance and meaning of their life experiences, rather than looking toward their future. Through this increased understanding of their life experiences, Perry hopes "they can be transformed spiritually...at this most critical point in their lives." It seems both Sadtler and Perry's most important role as a chaplain on death row is to help guide the prisoners towards a realization of Tolsoy's "real thing," in order to meet death with open arms, satisfied with how they've lived. What troubles me most about helping prisoners to this realization, or bringing anyone to this realization for that matter, is the content of an individual's life. The guilty prisoners on death row, should they be happy with what they have done? At ease with the lives they lived? This strikes me as the biggest challenge to the chaplains on death row. To ignore the acts of those they are helping, which are in direct conflict with the laws of our nation, the teachings of the Bible, and help lead them to a peaceful and accepting death all the while aware of the treacherous crimes they have committed. But again, this is exactly what both Sadtler and Perry's missions consist of: developing meaningful relationships and community ties in order to bring meaning to their own lives and the lives of others.

Undoubtedly the relationships both chaplains developed with their prisoners impacted their views on the meaning of life in the face of death. The death of a prisoner on death row is especially unique because it is an on going process that is actively progressing throughout the formation of the relationship. Though I suppose the same could be said of all relationships, in prison all parties involved are painfully aware that death is lurking in the shadows of each prison cell. Both chaplains seemed in their responses to be opposed to the death penalty, though only Ms. Perry came out and said it. As a former hospital employee, Perry was accustomed to being close to death prior to becoming a chaplain. However, she described her experience of being a witness to an execution as very different from any other death: "...it felt morally wrong and shameful to me. The power dynamics felt very strange, with so many people there to see the execution of one individual, who at that particular time was totally powerless." Sadtler described a similar feeling towards the situation, noting that it makes a "parody of what we usually imagine as a death scene surrounded by loving family members...the man is lying on a gurney, surrounded by people who worked to kill him." Both felt they were in the midst of a moral crisis by watching a human being killed and making no effort to stop it. Perry casually remarked on the process of execution, a comment which I find to bear great implications about the overall subject of death in our culture; "I find it significant that state executions are always done at night, under cover of darkness. This says something, I think, about how we view them..."

Because both chaplains had prior experience dealing with death in close proximity to their lives, it seemed that execution did not bring to reality the finality of death. What it did seem to highlight, however, was both women's preference for avoiding death. Even though most if not all of those executed committed unspeakable crimes, and even though we are all actively traveling towards the end of our lives, both would have rather spared the lives of the prisoners and pushed death to the side until another day. Unfortunately, this is not possible. Prisoners are given a set year, month, day and time of death and most live out the rest of their days with this fact looming in the distance. Both prisoner and chaplain must acknowledge this and work towards accepting the life they have lived so far and continue to try and develop meaning in the days left.

Sadtler explained her belief that prisoners are able to continuously find meaning in their lives throughout their stay. She had prisoners pen sermons for the juvenile chapel, and others who reached out to teens in trouble with the law. Not only were the prisoners serving the community, they were "find[ing] their own voice and using it... They knew from their own experience that there would be no instant conversions from their messages and were content to do what they could do...They were having meaningful lives; the purpose they found was reflected in their behavior in the prison as well." As author Yeager Hudson concludes in *Death and the Meaning of Life*; "it is death which introduces into human existence the possibility of meaning." The same can certainly be said based on Sadtler's statements about her prisoners. Perhaps their lives had been void of any significant relationships or positive impact. However, knowing that death was upon them, and through their relationship and growth with the prison chaplains, they were able to introduce into their lives the possibility of meaning.

Through her work on death row, Sadtler told me her hope was "that the work [she is] doing in [her] own life will leave [her] to face death without regret and with only the physical suffering (which medication can dull) to endure...that [her] children will suffer less as well, mourning only [her] future absence, not any unfinished business..." Professor Shelly Kagan of Yale discusses this idea in his lecture about dying alone and questions whether the primary badness of death lies in the effect(s) on those who are left behind rather than that of the deceased. Whereas Kagan's central thesis throughout the discussion is that the badness of separation lies in the emotions of those surrounding the victim, Sadtler attempts to live her life and "keep it clean", in order to cherish her relationships so as not to leave her loved ones suffering when she passes. While it seems Sadtler conducts her life in a manner that presumably acknowledges that it will not always exist, her statement about facing her own death proved to be quite contrary.

Not only has Sadtler been a source of guidance and a witness to 17 prisoner executions on death row, she also witnessed a close childhood friend's death at the age of 11. Given these experiences, one would assume Sadtler has been given ample opportunity to understand the reality of her own immortality. However, Sadtler explains:

> I have struggled with the reality of my own death...
> When I really think about it, the stark reality
> of nothingness or horror are ghastly. So I prefer
> escapism into hoping for a really big hug and bigger
> smile from Jesus and a reunion with those I have
> loved. And mostly I focus on this life as a form of

escape from thinking about that soon-approaching day. Knowledge of death is a curse. I can't wait to talk to God about why we, unlike the animals (as far as we know), are so aware. Is it the true punishment for our knowledge of good and evil?

Here within Sadtler's statement lies a challenging intellectual dilemma. It seems she fits all the criteria set forth by countless authors and great minds for someone who realizes their mortality and lives their life accordingly. What, then, do we do with a person who has gone through all the motions yet still views an awareness of the limits of mortality a punishment? Is it so clear that if we develop meaningful relationships, take joy in life's simple pleasures, engage in our community, understand that we cannot live forever, witness the death of another first hand or seize a rare opportunity, that we have accepted that we will one day not be alive? Is there really a direct connection between living in the moment versus living for the moment and embracing our mortality? And furthermore, in the case of Chaplain Perry and myself, if we oppose the death penalty, does that mean we wish to keep death at bay? And by wanting to keep death at bay, does it directly follow that we therefore do not comprehend the preciousness and fleeting characteristic of our lives on earth? On the other hand, if we purchase life insurance, does it automatically mean we understand we will one day cease to exist? Or in Chaplain Sadtler's case, if we have discussed our death with our loved ones, and seek to live a "clean" life so as to not leave any loose ends, have we therefore accepted death is waiting for us? Or is it something else? Perhaps we choose to live our lives in appreciation of rare opportunities, as a member of a community, as a caring mother, father, girlfriend, boyfriend, sister, husband, brother, or wife, simply because we want to. Because the joy that comes with such activities is enough for us. To help a prisoner understand their life's meaning and the significance of their actions, to impact another's life, just feels good. Some may label this as self-motivated or selfish, but I don't think so. On top of the service we provide or impact we have on others, why else do we do these things? I have a boyfriend, who I care very much about. I value my relationship with my parents and my sister. I have a handful of great friends who are irreplaceable. Like Sadtler, I too fit the description of someone who values their life and my "precious power to share life with others". Yet, also like Sadtler, I am uneasy with the idea of my mortality. I flew to Florida recently, and even with the slightest bit of turbulence I feared for my life. I am easily upset when hearing others talk about their imminent death, or at the idea of leaving my loved ones behind. But I don't regret anything I have done. I know I have made mistakes, plenty of them. But I also know that some of those mistakes have improved my moral fiber today. And some of those mistakes lead to the most meaningful relationships I have. So, is it possible to live a meaningful life sans the knowledge that it will not one day exist? It is difficult to answer. It is even more difficult to pinpoint what exactly constitutes knowing that we will die. I understand I am not immortal. I know one day I will die. But I don't want that day to be any time soon. I think if I were to fall ill today and have but a few hours to live, I would feel wronged. I would want more time on earth, to be with those I love. Yet, at the same time, I feel as if I understand the "real thing", that I take advantage of every opportunity presented to me, and spend as much time with those I love as I possibly can. This brings me to a major roadblock on the journey to accepting my mortality. There is a great need for a clarification between accepting mortality and wanting to be mortal. Yeager Hudson tells us that we should not want to be immortal, because things would lose their significance. Every moment could be replaced by an infinite amount of identical moments to come in the ever-lasting future. But even if I accept that I will one day not rest easy in the comfort of a lover's arms, is it wrong to wish that I could lay there forever? Where my philosophy on death lies is somewhere between living with the knowledge that I will one day die and cherishing those around me as if we would live together until the end of time.

Approaching the topic of death with the Chaplains, I felt unsure that I would be able to derive much meaningful insight from their responses. I have always been skeptical of religious people. I found their reliance upon an almighty power to "take care of things" to be an excuse to not create change through their own means. It also has been often labeled as a way to avoid thinking about death. With religion, one can easily say that they do not have to deal with death because they will have an after life. No need to worry about loved ones passing or leaving unresolved issues behind, they can be dealt with in the next life. Yet at the same time, I've always had a deep respect for an individual to be able to trust in a higher power to make sure things turn out the way they should. I was envious that religious people didn't need to worry about saying goodbye to their cherished friends and family, because they would be reunited again some day. After speaking with Ms. Sadtler and Ms. Perry, I understand that religion serves a much deeper and greater purpose. Religion is not a crutch, it is a means for those who have made mistakes or live with regret to rectify their lives. What impacted my ideology more so than my revelations on religion were those on death. Specifically after speaking with Ms. Sadtler, I came to realize that I personally believe that one can live a good, meaningful life without embracing our imminent death. Undoubtedly, Sadtler understands the reality of death after having seen executions carried out 17 times. Furthermore, after our lengthy exchange, I also believe Sadtler to be living a life in recognition of the "real thing" through various ties within her community, the numerous relationships she has formed throughout her lifetime, and her empathy for and understanding of mankind and our ability to falter. I was shocked when Sadtler told me she found death to be ghastly, and a bit troubled when she wondered if our knowledge of death was a punishment. Her statement that God forces us to realize our mortality as a result of our recognition of good and evil is in direct disagreement with the manner in which she conducts her life. After reviewing Sadtler's statements and contemplating her line of work and the way in which she represented herself, I understand where she is coming from. I personally do not think the realization we must die is a punishment. Nor do I think the realization we must die automatically brings meaning to our lives. I think death is undoubtedly an alarming end point, especially for those who already believe themselves to be leading meaningful lives. I also think realizing death can force us to reevaluate our life choices and live a more meaningful existence from the point of recognition forward. Understanding death is to be awakened to the infinite value of life. Even if we cannot embrace the idea of leaving our lives behind, we must embrace the idea of living our lives right now. The most important thing about our lives is not that we die, but that we have limited time to live.

Reference

"Statistics." <u>Anti-Death Penalty Information</u>. 11 Mar. 2011. Anti Death Penalty Organization. 15 Mar. 2011 <http://www.antideathpenalty.org/statistics. html>.

Tolstoy, Leo. *The Death of Ivan Ilyich*. Toronto: Bantam, 1981. Print.

Hudson, Yeager. "Death and the Meaning of Life." Print. Yale University 2010. Web.

Killilea, Alfred G. *The Politics of Being Mortal*. Lexington, KY: University of Kentucky, 1988. Print.

"Statistics." *Anti-Death Penalty Information*. Anti Death Penalty Organization, 11 Mar. 2011. Web. 15 Mar. 2011. <http://www.antideathpenalty.org/statistics. html>.

IBID

Tolstoy, Leo. *The Death of Ivan Ilyich*. Toronto: Bantam, 1981. Print.

IDIM

Hudson, Yeager. "Death and the Meaning of Life." Print. "Yale University 2010." Web.

Killilea, Alfred G. *The Politics of Being Mortal*. Lexington, KY: University of Kentucky, 1988. Print.

Hudson, Yeager. "Death and the Meaning of Life." Print.

Tolstoy, Leo. *The Death of Ivan Ilyich*. Toronto: Bantam, 1981. Print.

VIII. THE EXCITEMENT OF LIVING NEAR DEATH

CHAPTER SEVENTEEN

Facing Death at the Top of the World

Peter Zubof

Often, athletes and adventurers who pursue endeavors that carry significant risks are described as having a "death wish". Climbers that attempt to summit Mount Everest are often included under this moniker. This paper will attempt to contradict this assessment. It will argue that climbing Mount Everest is life-affirming rather than death defying. The adventurers that tackle this enormous feat certainly understand the dangers that they face on the mountain, but do not gain any joy by flirting with disaster. Rather, they use their athletic prowess and their wits to challenge themselves and push their bodies and minds to the test, hoping to better their lives through the experience. Statistical evidence, as well as narratives from the climbers themselves, will paint a picture not of capricious adrenaline junkies, but rather some of the last great adventurers and explorers on earth.

George Leigh Mallory made three attempts to conquer the tallest mountain in the world, Mount Everest, from 1921-1924. His first two attempts met with disaster, resulting in the deaths of seven of his Sherpa guides in an avalanche but leaving Mallory to continue to dream of reaching his goal. During an interview with the New York Times on March 18, 1923, Mallory was asked why he wanted to climb the mountain, to which he responded famously, "because it is there" (Mallory, 1923). Just over a year later, on June 8th, 1924, Mallory disappeared on Everest, having last been spotted within 1000 feet of its summit (Anker, 1999). There is still some debate on whether or not Mallory and his climbing partner, Andrew Irvine, ever reached the summit of Everest. What is certain, however, is they became the most famous, but certainly not the last, victims of the great mountain. Death will always be an integral part of such a dangerous endeavor. For mountaineers, however, it serves as a reminder of the limits of our lives, not the limits of our dreams.

Since Mallory's first expedition up Mount Everest in 1921, 213 climbers have been killed in an attempt to reach the summit (Jugalski, 2011). Many of their bodies still litter the slopes, some nearly frozen in place since the moment they died. It has been argued by many that those who attempt these climbs are thrill seekers, laughing in the face of death. In fact, Todd May argues in his book, <u>Death</u>, that mountain climbers are examples of individuals who, "court death" in an attempt to get a rush from the experience (May, 2009, p. 34). I will argue that climbers do not at all tread lightly in the face of their own mortality, but rather use the knowledge of that mortality to allow them to push their physical and mental limits.

Extreme climbers, like those who attempt Mount Everest, have no desire to dance with death. Their joys at attempting ascents such as Everest stem more from a desire to achieve the difficult and test their bodies and minds. As George Mallory went on to explain in his famous interview, he wanted to climb Everest because, "Its existence is a challenge. The answer [to why I want to climb Everest] is instinctive, a part, I suppose, of man's desire to conquer the universe" (Mallory, 1923). Men and women climb Mount Everest because there exists within each one of us a desire to pursue the limits of our existence and challenge our preconceptions of what can or cannot be accomplished.

The Myth of the Mountain

To the Nepalese, it is called Sagarmatha, Goddess of the Sky. The Tibetans know it as Chomolungma, the Goddess of the Universe. Most of the remainder of the world knows it as Everest, named for British surveyor-general of India in 1865 (Krakauer, 1997, p. 16). Everest has captured people's imaginations for thousands of years. During the height of British colonialism, her mystic embrace travelled west to Europe and lured adventurers to try to carve their names into the history books by climbing to heights considered unreachable for millennia.

After George Mallory's ill-fated attempt, 32 years would pass before the summit of Everest would finally be conquered. On the 29th of May, 1953, Edmund Hillary, an adventurer from New Zealand, and Tenzing Norgay, his Sherpa companion, became the first men to successfully summit Mount Everest and return to tell the tale (Krakauer, 1997, p. 20). Since then, thousands of would be adventurers have followed, very literally, in their footsteps.

As a testament to globalism, George Mallory's dream has become more accessible than ever. Everest has become an ultimate adventure tourist destination, with client-climbers paying expedition-guide companies upwards of sixty thousand dollars for a chance to climb. These companies take care of every logistical detail of climbing Everest. They arrange for permits, set up base camps, provide cooks, and hire local Sherpa climbers to assist the paying customers. While adventurers of yesteryear hailed from the upper crust of the British Empire, modern adventurers come from dozens of countries and all walks of life, all speaking the language of the climb, hoping to ascend the natural Tower of Babel.

Modern expedition outfitters go to great lengths to try to set up successful, safe climbs. The companies involved use their own experienced guides, as well as Sherpa support staff, to set fixed safety lines all the way to the summit. As we will see, however, these are no guarantees of success, or even survival. In the end, it is up to the individual climbing team, just as it was with Hillary and Norgay, to make their climb a success and to live to tell the tale.

Everest By the Numbers

Using the latest in GPS equipment, the National Geographic Society measured the peak of Mount Everest at 29,035 feet or 8,850 meters (BBC News, 1999). It is a colossal peak, one of only 14 in the world to break the 8,000 meter height mark. Mt. Washington, the highest peak in the American Northeast at 6,280 feet (Mount Washington Observatory, 2011) is as a foothill in comparison. In fact, Everest base camps, the campsites and operations centers for all climbers, sit at just over 19,000 feet, higher than any peak in the 48 contiguous states (Weathers, 2000, p. 14).

The atmospheric pressure at the summit of Everest, about 346 millibars, is only about a third of that at sea level (West, 1999). This reduced pressure results in a corresponding level of oxygen above 8,000 meters that is incompatible with human life. This region is actually referred to by mountaineers at the "death zone." Climbers do everything in their power to minimize their time above this dangerous elevation marker. Physical performance above 8,000 meters, even with supplemental oxygen is drastically reduced. Mental capacity is equally crippled, reaffirming the need for climbers to be experienced; able to rely on their instincts to perform when their higher mental capabilities fail them. In the "death zone," the body literally eats itself, burning 12,000 calories per day, while simultaneously reducing the digestive systems performance to near nothing (Weathers, 2000, p. 25). Despite these intense physical and mental challenges, 5,104 intrepid souls have reached the highest point on earth by the end of the 2010 climbing season (Jugalski, 2011).

So how dangerous is climbing the tallest mountain in the world? A comprehensive study commissioned in 2006 looked at this history of deaths on Everest from a statistical point of view. Since it was initially attempted in 1921, 14,138 climbers have attempted to summit. Of those, there were 192 deaths (219 by 2010), a rate of about 1.3 percent (Firth, 2008). Statistically, that number doesn't elicit much sense of dread at all. In fact, the chance of dying in a motor vehicle accident in our lifetime similarly hovers around 1.5 percent (National Transportation Safety Administration, 2011). By this logic, the act of driving the children to a game should make a soccer mom just as big of a daredevil as these extreme climbers. So why is the Everest ascent viewed as such a death defying feat while the act of driving, which is statistically just as dangerous, falls into the realm of mundane? We will explore this contradiction later.

The Climb

Everest sits on unique property, straddling the border between Nepal and Chinese controlled Tibet. Each side has a main route to the summit and debate abounds as to which climb contains more challenges and dangers. One hundred and one climbers have perished on the Northern Route and ninety-five on the Southern (the remainder of the fatalities having occurred while attempted alternate routes). The southern route, pioneered by Sir Edmund Hillary, has maintained its accessibility throughout the course of Everest mountaineering. The northern, by comparison, has often been caught in the political crossfire of the Tibetan independence movement.

Climbing the southern face of Everest certainly provides both cultural acclimatization, as well as physical. Modern adventurers fly into Kathmandu, Nepal's capital city, and through a combination of vehicular travel, yak caravan, and good old-fashioned footwork, carve their way up to Everest base camp over the course of approximately a week through successively smaller and more spartan patches of civilization. Climbers set up primary residence on the mountain at the southern base camp, at approximately 19,900 feet in elevation. During their acclimatization, they will travel back and forth between base camp and Camp II (also known as advanced base camp) to get their bodies used to the difficult climbing conditions.

Unfortunately, between the two camps lies the Khumbu Ice Fall, a field of monstrous seracs, or ice towers, atop the Khumbu glacier. As the glacier moves beneath it, the ice-fall becomes unstable, often collapsing these seracs, weighing hundreds of tons. Climbers unlucky enough to witness one of these movement events often do so as a final experience in their lives. It is their last living sight, and this area is responsible for many deaths on the southern route. Fifty-six percent of deaths on the southern ascent route occurred below 8000 meters, many as a result of the Ice Fall (Firth, 2008).

The north base camp can be more easily accessed, usually via Land Rover caravan, allowing climbers to be on the mountain within a couple of days of arriving in Tibet. While this allows them to forego a long hike into the mountain, it also robs climbers of a chance to begin to let their lungs acclimate to the thin Himalayan air. As a trade off, however, the climbers do not have any direct dangers to contend with in their acclimatization climbs. The dangers of the north side don't show themselves until much higher on the mountain, historically at the first, second, and third steps. These rock obstacles, not more than 15-20 feet high, would not offer much of a challenge at sea level. At 28,000 feet, however, and with drops of thousands of feet offered as a result of a miss-step, they are dangerous indeed. As climbing has become more and more popular, these have also become locations of "bottle-necks" as climbers move up and down in tight quarters. As a result, 85% of the deaths on the north route occurred in the "death zone" (Firth, 2008).

No matter which side of the mountain is chosen, Everest expeditions usually spend an average of approximately 60 days on the mountain. Less than 21 of those days are spent in actual climbing evolutions. The remainders of the days are spent fending off boredom in base camp, allowing the body to naturally acclimate to living at high altitudes. This process actually allows the body to build a much larger supply of red blood cells, storing more oxygen in the body with each breath (Schoene, 2000). Without acclimatization, climbing the mountain, even with a supplemental oxygen supply, would be impossible. In fact, an average person suddenly transported from sea level to the summit of Everest would lose consciousness in roughly 30 seconds if their body were not acclimated (Federal Aviation Administration, 2003).

Dangers during the climb, no matter which route is attempted, include avalanche threats and often slippery, difficult climbing terrain. Exhaustion and exposure to the elements, often a direct result of becoming lost in one of Everest's infamous sudden changes in weather, have been responsible for approximately 20 percent of climbing deaths. These factors aside, some unlucky climbers are cursed with bodies that resist the acclimatizing process. High altitude pulmonary and cerebral edema (HAPE and HACE respectively), a condition involving swelling of the lungs and brain, often befalls these climbers. Luckily advances in technology and medicine, allowing for such life saving measures as portable pressure chambers, have increased the survivability of such incidents (Firth, 2008).

Icons of the Mountain

George Mallory and Sir Edmund Hillary are two names as synonymous with Everest as John Glenn and Neil Armstrong are to space exploration. They were, in their time, on the cutting edge of mountaineering, literally climbing to heights never attempted by other human beings.

George Leigh Mallory, an Englishman, schoolteacher, and father of three, caught the climbing bug early in life as a member of the British Alpine Club. He was the driving force behind three successive expeditions to first survey, then to conquer Mount Everest.

Mallory's first expedition never made a serious attempt to summit the mountain. The members were, however, the first westerners to even reach the slopes of Everest, having required the blessing of the Dalai Lama to proceed. The expedition did chart the initial ascent, however, climbing as high as the North Col, a saddle of rock at approximately 23,000 feet that connects the mountain with nearby Changtse (Anker, 1999).

Mallory returned the following year with a fresh expedition, this time hoping to make an attempt at the Everest summit in earnest. He and his team made three successive summit pushes, climbing as high as 27,000 feet, an altitude record at the time. On their third attempt, however, tragedy struck. An avalanche swept across the expedition, taking the lives of seven Sherpas, the first recorded deaths during an Everest summit attempt (Anker, 1999).

In 1924, George Mallory once again returned to the North Face of Everest, intent on making the summit. At 37 years old, Mallory believed this would be his last chance to lead an expedition of this sort. On the 4th of June 1924, he and fellow climber, Andrew "Sandy" Irvine, began their assault on the Everest summit. For the next four days, the two advanced slowly but steadily up the mountainside. On The 8th of June, fellow expedition member Noel Odell, himself at 26,000 feet spotted the two climbers approximately two thousand feet above. Shortly thereafter, a cloudbank obstructed his view. It was to be the last time George Mallory was seen for over 75 years. His body was discovered in 1999, at an altitude of 26,760 feet (Anker, 1999). Andrew Irvine's body has yet to be found. As previously mentioned, there is a great deal of debate as to whether or not the pair ever reached the Everest summit. Perhaps Sir Edmund Hillary, the first person to reach the summit and return, summed up the debate most succinctly. He stated, "If you climb a mountain for the first time and die on the descent, is it really a complete first ascent of the mountain? I am rather inclined to think personally that maybe it is quite important, the getting down, and the complete climb of a mountain is reaching the summit and getting safely to the bottom again."

Twenty-three years later, Edmund Hillary, perhaps the most famous man in mountaineering, was the first man to ever set foot on the top of the world. Climbing with an expedition of roughly 400 people, his team was a virtual army of explorers and support staff, driving towards the ultimate goal of an Everest summit.

Hillary, like Mallory, was an Alpine climber, a hobby that drew him towards dreaming of the Himalayas. He first travelled East in 1951 with a surveying team, then later joined a climbing expedition, which would become the first to successfully summit the tallest peak in the world.

The bond that connected George Mallory to Edmund Hillary extended far beyond their climbing careers to what really connected them as adventurers. Both were military men, Mallory being a veteran of the First World War and Hillary the second. Aside from these formative experiences, however, the men led fairly humble lives, using climbing as an escape to adventure. Mallory made his living as an educator and Hillary as a humble beekeeper. They were both also family men, married, with three children apiece.

Mallory and Hillary both certainly craved adventure and, while not intentionally reckless, were willing to take incredible risks in the pursuit of their dreams. They were pioneers in much more than their mountaineering. They were educated men who considered the pursuit of new frontiers to be worth the perils they faced, and in Mallory's case, succumbed to. As I will argue, Mallory, Hillary, and the Everest climbers that would follow were not daredevils. They were careful, methodical explorers, much like the first astronauts. Their pursuits certainly required acceptance of risk. Their goals, however, were knowledge and exploration, not thrill-seeking.

The Deadliest Seasons

The 1996 and 2006 climbing seasons have seen the most fatalities on Everest since climbing began in 1921, having claimed the lives of a total of 26 climbers. This statistic alone makes these two seasons tragic, but the intense media coverage of both seasons allows us access to details about these seasons that may have otherwise been lost to history. Both tragic seasons generated numerous books, some from a journalistic standpoint and a couple written autobiographically, by Beck Weathers (1996) and Lincoln Hall (2006), which describe harrowing tales of a return from near death.

The 1996 season was well covered in Jon Krakauer's book, Into Thin Air, which chronicles his first person account of events as a climber and writer for *Outside* magazine. In his book, he criticizes the commercial aspects of modern Everest expeditions, arguing that climbing outfits put money and success rate above the safety of their clients. A sudden snowstorm on May 10, 1996 took the lives of seven climbers at once. Several of these climbers, lost in the blinding winds, reportedly plunged to oblivion, never to be seen again. At least one, Tsewang Paljor, a policeman from India, became an icon in death on the mountain. Succumbing to exposure during the storm, he sought refuge in a shallow cave, with only his green boots visible from the outside. He died just feet from the main climbing trail, where his body remains, leaving future climbers with a grim reminder of the seriousness of their pursuits. For all those who pass him to this day he is known simply as "green boots."

The 2006 season became embroiled with an even more basic controversy endemic to Everest mountaineering: what to do with a climber who cannot descend from the mountain on his or her own power. Recorded, as it happened, by a Discovery Channel film crew, and later chronicled in Nick Heil's book Dark Summit, the 2006 expedition took the adventure, and seriousness of the Everest climbs, into living rooms everywhere.

Since the beginning of Everest ascents, there has been a general rule amongst climbers that argues that, if a climber became injured or ill in the "death zone" (above 8,000 meters), that the risk involved with bringing him down would put too many other lives at risk to be worth the tradeoff. During the 2006 expedition, David Sharp, a British mountaineer climbing without the usual logistical support offered by most expedition outfitters, fell ill from altitude sickness at 28,000 feet. About 40 climbers passed Sharp both on the ascent and descent, but Sharp still died where he fell. Accounts differed on how much aid was afforded Sharp, as well as how dire his condition was when he first collapsed. Several climbers claimed that he was beyond help from the onset of his symptoms (Heil, 2008).

Russell Brice, owner of Himalayan Experience, a top Everest expedition company was criticized directly for allowing some of his guides and climbers to pass Sharp by without offering assistance. Brice fired back, saying that even though his guides did offer assistance, his primary responsibility, and that of his guides, was to his paying customers, who counted on him to support their own summit attempts. Brice found fault with Sharp's budget climbing plan, which, without a support network, left him even more exposed to the dangers of the mountain. Sir Edmund Hillary later piled on to the criticism of Brice, a crushing blow to a man who worshiped the Everest pioneer, stating that no ascent was worth a life lost (Heil, 2008). The risk associated with the reliance on self, however, may be the thing that best defines the nature of climbing Mt. Everest.

Every man and woman who climbs Everest knows, and accepts that risk. Unlike David Sharp, however, most do their utmost to mitigate the dangers. Beck Weathers (1996) and Lincoln Hall (2006) were two near death survivors who went on to write accounts of their own near disasters. Both men were family men, cautious and calculating, trying to achieve their dreams, not abandon their loved ones for needless dangers. Even David Sharp, a mathematician by trade, was a well prepared, careful climber, who perhaps simply overestimated his own skill level. Sharp's mother, after his death, somewhat vindicated his fellow climbers, by saying her son very clearly knew the risks he faced in pursuit of his dreams (Woods, 2006).

Today May Very Well Be the Last Day of My Life

Why does the prospect of our imminent death seem more terrifying when we have a conscious choice in its acceptance or avoidance? Why does the specter seem more real when we have a clear timeline (or at least potential timeline)? These are key questions that separate the soccer mom from the Everest climber.

When one drives an automobile, one accepts a certain chance that it will be the last excursion ever made. That chance, however, is spread across one's entire (at least adult) lifetime and so, on any given day, one is able to push considerations of any possible disaster out of consciousness. There is also a collective, if irrational, safety involved in dangerous pursuits such as driving. Everyone drives; therefore we are able to rationalize that it must be a safe activity. Moreover, we view driving as a necessity whereas mountain climbing, quite clearly, is not. For this reason we need to expose ourselves to driving dangers, while we choose those of climbing.

Broken down by the number of driving days in our lives, our chance of dying in an automobile accident on any given day is less than one in a million. Although a mountaineer has statistically a similar chance of dying attempting to summit Everest in his lifetime (most climbers only attempt the trip once), his chances are nearly all focused on the day of the summit attempt. In fact, even though most climbers spend two full months on the slopes of Everest, 82 percent of the fatalities occur on the single summit attempt day (Firth, 2008).

This is incredibly important because Everest mountaineers, unlike their mini-van wrangling counterparts, wake up the morning of their potential death with complete realization of the possibilities. They know that if the mountain is going to take their life, it will be today and not any other. Like soldiers going to war, they often make contact with their families one last time. Just in case. Beck Weathers, who was famously left for dead during the 1996 season, only to be found alive the next day, sent a farewell fax to his wife from the mountain just hours before his presumed death (Weathers, 2000, p. 31).

Because It Is There

In *Death*, author Todd May claims that, "the fact that we die is the most important fact about us" (May, 2009, p. 4). I beg to differ on this point. I believe our ability to create, and by extension dream, is what separates humans from animals. Although it can be slanted to the negative in pursuits of power and money, ambition drives all human pursuits.

Largely spurred on by the explorations during the height of the British Colonial Empire, human beings have increasingly been able to pursue their adventures 'because they are there,' as opposed to pursuing them for monetary gain. The space race may have been spawned by an ideological conflict between democracy and communism, but the men who put their lives on the line in its pursuit, did so for the adventure and challenge. These sorts of individuals have pushed humanity forward, and those who climb Everest today strive to grab a taste of that experience.

There are people who live in death's shadow, ignoring it or hiding from it. Mountain climbers are amongst those who step out of that shadow. They are not reckless, nor do they take unnecessary risks with their lives, but they do not let their limitation be defined by their mortality.

In September 1962, President John F. Kennedy gave a speech at Rice University. Memorably, he said, "We choose to go to the moon. We choose to go to the moon in this decade and do the other things, not because they are easy, but because they are hard, because that goal will serve to organize and measure the best of our energies and skills...". This simple quote drove Americans to achieve what had, for all of human history, been a thing of dreams and fantasies. It did, in fact, bring out the best in people. Their sense of adventure, desire to achieve and willingness to accept immeasurable risks, were the driving forces that put men on the moon. There was more to this speech though. Kennedy closed with these remarks, "Many years ago the great British explorer George Mallory, who was to die on Mount Everest, was asked why did he want to climb it. He said, 'Because it is there.' Well, space is there, and we're going to climb it, and the moon and the planets are there, and new hopes for knowledge and peace are there. And, therefore, as we set sail we ask God's blessing on the most hazardous and dangerous and greatest adventure on which man has ever embarked." (JFK Presidential Library)

Everest, Politics, and the Meaning of Life

Climbing a mountain such as Everest may be one of the great equalizing activities still available to modern man. Although the expedition costs may seem high, climbers come from a wide variety of socio-economic backgrounds. Some scrape together every nickel to make their dreams come true while others are more economically comfortable. Everest summiteers represent 85 different countries of nearly every political ideology and religion (Jugalski, 2011). Even the mountain itself straddles, literally, between democracy and communism. Climbers on the mountain experience elements of both philosophies.

Necessarily and fundamentally, part of the Everest experience is, in microcosm, socialistic in nature. Climbers live in a communal environment, eating the same food, in the same living conditions and striving for one common goal. Marx would have been very satisfied with the actual conditions on the mountain, even while he would be appalled by the capitalistic ventures required to fund modern expeditions.

Externally, however, a trip to climb Everest may be one of the truest expressions of freedom, capitalism, and democracy. Climbers are able to face their mortality because they have complete choice and control while on the mountain. Any climber can, at any time, stop their ascent to preserve their own lives, independent of the movement of the collective team.

The blending of socialistic and democratic ideals is possible and indeed necessary for the pursuit of lofty goals. In the space race, as in climbing, there was a huge requirement to make sacrifices for the good of the many. In the end, however, there was an equal portion of democracy and traditional western individualism. Neil Armstrong summed this up in his quote, "this is one small step for man, one giant leap for man-kind."

World renowned climber Ed Viesters is often quoted by Everest climbers as saying, "Getting to the top is optional, but getting down is mandatory. A lot of people get focused on the summit and forget that." Experienced climbers don't forget that. They plan ahead and take stock in their own limitations. They know that climbing Mount Everest is not about defying death, but experiencing life. It is about exploration, both of the mountain, and of our innermost fears, desires, and limitations.

For some who summit Mount Everest, it will be the highlight of their lives, a culmination of a life spent dreaming. For others, it will be just a step in an ongoing adventure. Some may never reach the top of the world, but will still push to their own personal limits, finding that satisfying enough. Finally there will be those who do not leave the mountain. Their deaths, while tragic, do serve a purpose.

You cannot have an adventure to the limits of human endurance, without knowing that it is possible to step over those limits. Those who perished on the slopes of Mount Everest died pursuing their dreams. The dead bodies forever entombed on Mount Everest do not deter future climbers. They serve as a reminder of man's mortality and as a reminder that some dreams really are worth dying for. Every living thing dies, but what really makes us human is our ability to dream.

Confronting Death

Works Cited

Anker, C. a. (1999). *The Lost Explorer.* New York: Simon and Schuster.

BBC News. (1999 йил November). *Mount Everest Reaches New Heights.* London, UK: BBC News.

Beah, I. (2007). *A Long Way Gone.* New York: Sarah Crichton Books.

Berezin, M. (1997). *Making the Fascist Self: The Political Culture of Interwar Italy.* Ithaca: Cornell University Press.

Berlet, C. (1992 йил September). *Fascism!* Retrieved 2010 йил March from http://www.hartford-hwp.com/archives/45/051.html

Coalition to Stop the Use of Child Soldiers. (2006). *Child soldiers and Disarmament, Demobilization, Rehabilitation and Reintegration in West Africa.*

Dawkins, R. (2011, October 8). Texas Free Thought Convention. Texas.

Dawkins, R. (2006). *The God Delusion.* New York: Bantam Press.

Faulkner, F. (2001). Kindergarten Killers: Morality, Murder and the Child Soldier Problem. *Third World Quarterly, Vol. 22, No. 4* .

Federal Aviation Administration. (2003). *Operations of Aircraft at Altitudes above 25,000 Feet.* Washington D.C.: Department of Transportation.

Firth, P. (2008). Mortality on Mount Everest, 1921-2006. *British Medical Journal* .

Gray, M. (2010, September 20). *Hitchens Won't Be Attending Hitchens Prayer Day.* Retrieved October 2011, from http://newsfeed.time.com/2010/09/20/hitchens-wont-be-attending-hitchens-prayer-day/

Gregor, A. J. (1979). *Young Mussolini and the Intellectual Origins of Fascism.* Berkeley: University of California Press.

Heil, N. (2008). *Dark Summit.* New York: Henry Holt and Co.

Hitchens, C. (2007). *God is not Great.* New York: Twelve.

Hitchens, C. (2010). *Hitch-22: A Memoir.* New York: Twelve.

Hitchens, C. (2010, December). Miss Manners and the Big C. *Vanity Fair* .

Hitchens, C. (2011, January 14). Q & A with Christopher Hitchens. (B. Lamb, Interviewer)

Hitchens, C. (1982, July). The Lord and the Intellectuals. *Harper's* .

Hitchens, C. (2011). *The Quotable Hitchens: From Alcohol to Zionism.* Philadelphia: De Capo Press.

Hitchens, C. (2010, September). Topic of Cancer. *Vanity Fair* .

Hitchens, C. (2010, November). Tumortown. *Vanity Fair* .

Hitchens, C. (2010, October). Unanswerable Prayers. *Vanity Fair* .

Hitchens, C. (2011, June). Unspoken Truths. *Vanity Fair* .

Jaffre, F. (n.d.). *The Use of Children as Soldiers in Africa: A country analysis of child recruitment and participation in armed conflict.* Retrieved 2010 йил 29-4 from Relief Web International: http://www.reliefweb.int/library/documents/chilsold.htm

JFK Presidential Library. (n.d.). *JFK Presidential Library.* Retrieved 2011 йил 02-10 from www.jfklibrary.org

Jugalski, E. (2011 йил 24-September). *Ascents-Everest.* Retrieved 2011 йил 10-

October from 8000ers.com: www.8000ers.com/everest-general-info-185. html

Killilea, A. G. (1988). *The Politics of Being Mortal.* Lexington, Kentucky: The University Press of Kentucky.

Koon, T. H. (1985). *Believe, Obey, Fight.* Chapel Hill: University of North Carolina Press.

Krakauer, J. (1997). *Into Thin Air.* New York: Anchor Books.

LaGambina, G. (2007, December). Christmas with Christopher Hitchens. *A.V. Club* .

Mallory, G. (1923 йил 18-March). Climbing Mount Everest is Work for Supermen. (N. Y. Times, Interviewer)

May, T. (2009). *Death.* Durham: Acumen.

Mazzini, G. (1981). The Duties of Man. In M. Curtis, *The Great Political Theories* (Vol. 2, pp. 234-242). New York: Avon Books.

McGrath, C. (2011, October 9). A Voice, Still Vibrant, Reflects on Mortality. *The New York Times* .

Megaro, G. (1938). *Mussolini in the Making.* Boston: Houghton Mifflin Company.

Mount Washington Observatory. (2011). *Mount Washington Observatory.org.* Retrieved 2011 йил 15-October from www.mountwashingtonobservatory.org

Mussolini, B. (1935). *Fascism: Doctrine and Institutions.* Rome: Ardita Publishers.

Mussolini, B. (1923). *Mussolini as Revealed in his Political Speeches (November 1914-August 1923).* London: Dent.

National Center for PTSD. (2011). Health Services Use in the Department of Veterans Affairs among Returning Iraq Warand Afghan War Veterans with PTSD. *PTSD Research Quarterly* , 1.

National Transportation Safety Administration. (2011). *Traffic Safety Fats.* US Census Bureau.

New York Times. (1941 йил 23-February). Speech Delivered by Premier Benito Mussolini. *The New York Times* .

Pini, G. (1939). *The Official Life of Benito Mussolini.* (L. Villari, Trans.) London: Hutchinson & Co.

Pugliese, S. G. (2004). *Fascism, Anti-Fascism, and the Resistance in Italy.* Lanham: Rowman & Littlefield Publishers, Inc.

Richards, K. P. (1998). Jeunes combattants parlant de la guerre et de la paix en Sierra Leone ("When They Say Soldiers Are Rebels, It's a Lie": Young Fighters Talk about War and Peace in Sierra Leone). *Cahiers d'Études Africaines, Vol. 38, Cahier 150/152, Disciplines et déchirures. Les formes de la violence* .

Salvemini, G. (1936). *Under the Axe of Fascism.* London: Camelot Press Ltd.

Schmidt, C. T. (1939). *The Corporate State in Action: Italy Under Fascism.* New York City: Russell & Russell.

Schoene, B. (2000 йил November). Alive on Everest. (PBS/Nova, Interviewer)

Thompson, C. B. (1999). Beyond Civil Society: Child Soldier as Citizens in Mozambique. *Review of African Political Economy, Vol. 26, No. 80* .

University of Alberta. (2006). *Children and War.* Social Sciences and Research Center of Canada.

War Child. (n.d.). *Child Soldiers.* From War Child web site.

Weathers, B. (2000). *Left For Dead: My Journey Home from Everest.* New York: Random House.

West, J. (1999). Barometric Pressures on Mt. Everst; New Daya and Physiological Significance. *Journal of Applied Physiology* , 6.

Woods, R. (2006 йил 28-May). Has the Once Heroic Sport of Climbing Been Corrupted by Big Money? *The Sunday Times* .

CHAPTER EIGHTEEN

Jane Goodall: The Peace of the Forest in a Deforested World

Ashley Stoehr

Jane Goodall forever changed human definitions with her discovery of primate culture. Chimpanzees, like humans, exhibit intelligence, tool making, planning and execution of tasks, prolonged emotional bonds, and mourning behaviors. Such appearances of humanity in non-humans have forever changed perceptions of human specialness. Anthropodenial separated humans from the natural world and permitted the temporary rejection of mortality; yet despite false dichotomies, humans and chimpanzees alike will succumb to death, nature's ultimate equalizer. Further, the resemblance between humans and chimpanzees is genetically, morphologically, and behaviorally undeniable. Accounts of cognition, morality, and social systems, by Goodall and others, have revealed potential evolutionary roots for conscious mortality, morality, and political systems, indicating that supposedly unique human attributes first originated in other animals. Such accounts may have reasserted the human presence in the animal kingdom, but reintegration is slow compared to rates of extinction fueled by flagrant human materialism. Declining chimpanzee numbers coupled with increased observations of sentience has prompted several questions concerning evolutionary trajectories, acceptance of death, chimpanzee conservation, and most importantly, "what does it mean to be a meaningful human in the human and non-human world?"

I.   Introduction: Redefining Humans in a Blurred World

As human beings we often place ourselves above the natural world, but like the dinosaurs before us, the laws of nature retain the right to whimsically destroy *Homo sapiens* as a species. What then permits us to consider humans as special beings with "magical" souls, and to assert anthropomorphism as a falsified conviction; in essence, what defines humanity? Many define this "specialness" based on the supposed, unique cognitive development, moral aptitude, and social systems that interact with human conscious mortality. These characteristics seem anomalous in the animal kingdom, yet such appearances are deceiving and our deep ancestral connections strong:

David Greybeard sits staring into the forest, delicately manipulating the foliage with his dexterous hands. The undergrowth rustles behind him as the figure of a young woman emerges. She is out of breath and out of place, but David accepts her. Together they sit side-by-side, species by species. The woman with her delicate fingers pulls a palm nut from the dirt and presents it to David. He rejects the offering. The woman inches closer, her palm still outstretched. Abruptly, the chimpanzee turns and reaches towards the nut. David's hands are big, but the fingers, lines, and wrinkles could easily pass for human form. He drops the nut to the ground, but his hand lingers on hers with a gentle, reassuring pressure. It is a moment of pre-historical communication; the gift is refused, but the gesture accepted (Goodall, 1971; 1999; 2000). The woman and chimpanzee eventually break touch and continue eating, but the entire world has changed in an instant. This human, Jane Goodall, is no longer alone or above the natural world, but intrinsically connected to the past, present, and endangered future of the Gombe chimpanzees.

Jane Goodall, an influential biologist and politically active conservationist, changed the face of human definitions with her discovery of primate culture. The appearance of humanity in non-human animals has had far-reaching consequences in philosophical and political debates, and forever changed views concerning human souls and specialness. The fear of unquestioned anthropomorphism has cast doubt on animal motivations and suggested that humans are alone in intelligence (de Waal, 1997); yet Frans de Waal, a renowned primatologist at Emory University, believes these conclusions may be products of "anthropodenial," a manufactured blindness to the humanlike characteristics present in other animals (de Waal, 1997; 2009). The resemblance between humans and chimpanzees genetically, morphologically, and behaviorally is undeniable. This manuscript explores human definitions and draws parallels between human and chimpanzee mortal consciousness based on Goodall's first hand accounts of chimpanzee cognition, morality, and social systems. Specifically, anecdotal and experimental evidence concerning the behavior of chimpanzees and other animals is used to describe the potential evolutionary roots of conscious mortality, morality, and their relations to political systems. Unlike past researchers, Goodall has created bonds with her subjects and viewed them in both human and natural contexts. Whether directly or indirectly, she has reasserted the human presence in the animal kingdom. Jane Goodall has witnessed the wonders and horrors of the Gombe chimpanzees, and her experiences in Africa have undoubtedly modified her spiritual journey, as well as questions concerning human-animal definitions. The major question has now become, "what does it mean to be a meaningful human in the human and non-human world?"

II. Jane Goodall: Childhood to Chimpanzees
(Goodall, 1999; 2000; 2001)

In a recent interview, American journalist Bill Moyers posed the simple question, "Is there anyone who doesn't know Jane Goodall?" Valerie Jane Goodall, born April 3, 1934 in London, would grow to live a life far from normal, blurring the lines formally demarcating humans from non-humans. Goodall, whose ambitions were constantly supported by her mother, Vanne, and grandmother, Danny, quickly transgressed from envy of Tarzan's Jane to a real-world jungle. In between, of course, were days littered with wilderness dreams, secretarial school, and countless boyfriends; but at age 23 she was able to befriend Dr. Louis Leakey, visit Africa and become his "Chimp-girl." Subsequently, in 1960, Goodall and Vanne traveled to Tanganyika study the Gombe chimpanzees. These were Goodall's days of peace, watching chimpanzees from a hill as they gradually accepted her presence. In 1964, Goodall married photographer Hugo van Lawick, and in 1967 she gave birth to her only son Hugo Eric Louis, called Grub. She obtained a PhD from Cambridge based on her work in ethology, without ever obtaining the prerequisite bachelor's degree. In the late 1960s Goodall and Lawick divorced. She remarried to Deryk Bryceson, Director of the National Parks in Tanganyika (then Tanzania) in 1975. Sadly, he died of cancer four years later. Goodall returned to Africa a bitter woman, but the peace of the forest and the compassion of the chimpanzees strengthened her spirit and resolve (Goodall, 1971; 1999; 2000; 2001). Over time Goodall's interests have gradually shifted from behavioral research to conservation and public efforts. Today, the Jane Goodall Institute is responsible for research, economic, and conservation programs. Although she misses her time in nature, Goodall feels that her work in conservation and animal rights is more valuable (Goodall, interview with Bill Moyers). Jane Goodall's life has been filled with unbelievable accomplishments and tragic personal losses; despite exposure to disease and death in humans and chimpanzees alike, she has remained a dedicated survivor. Jane Goodall is an inspiration to everyone she meets, but perhaps it is truly the chimpanzees that inspire Goodall.

III. Greybeard's Grace and the Human Connection

Goodall has witnessed the bonds and brutality of the Gombe chimpanzees. She has observed the curves of their human-like hands and ears. These physicalities coupled with human-like behavior changed the human-animal divide and accentuated similarities between man and beast (Goodall, interview with Bill Moyers). Goodall's emotional connection with the animal world and her "Greybeard moment" are not rarities. Others including Frans de Waal, Rick Swope, and myself have experienced the innate primate bond, with its impossibly doubted connection of intelligence, compassion, and understanding.

There is some pre-historical, pre-lingual language common among sentient beings. Goodall first discovered this language in David Greybeard's reassuring motions. I discovered it in the comprehension of a young tamarin christened "Little Man". We were divided by a sheet of glass, but the monkey sat staring. Suddenly, he straightened his posture holding his hands before him. He glanced from his hands, to me, and back again. I mimicked his motions. Squinting his eyes, Little Man examined my hands, wrists, and fingers, followed by his own. Our hands, so often described as a human symbol, were nearly identical from the bony wrists to the delicate fingers. Our hands were one in the same; we were both born into nature and would die in nature. Frans de Waal recounts the tale of the female gorilla, Binti Jua, that cradled a young old boy who had fallen into her exhibit before laying him at the caretaker's doorway (1997; Allchin, 2009). Even more heart-wrenching was the story told to Jane Goodall by Rick Swope, who risked his life to rescue a drowning chimpanzee. Swope, truly a hero to man and beast, ignored the screams of zoo-keepers and chimpanzees to save the poor individual, flailing and gasping in the water (Goodall, 1999). When Rick Swope was asked why he would risk his life for a mere animal, Swope replied ""I looked into his eyes it was like looking into the eyes of a man. And the message was 'Won't anyone help me?'" (Goodall, 1999).

Bill Moyers once asked Goodall "How do humans attach emotionally to animals?" The answer is simple, humans attach emotionally to animals because humans are animals; the connection between man and ape cannot be denied. The notion that humans are separate from animals is a misguided assertion. The wasting away of such naive assumptions can be clearly seen in Goodall's early letters where she quickly moves from describing the chimpanzees as males and females, to gents and ladies, and finally by their human inspired names coupled with the collective "friends" (Goodall, 2000; 2001). Goodall states "we are all part of the animal kingdom" and it is this cohesion that permits emotional attachment between species (interview with Bill Moyers). Many people, however, deny this simple answer. They have not seen what Goodall, Swope, de Waal, and I have seen; they have not been forever changed by the eradication of personal anthropodenial.

IV. Clarifying the Chimpanzee and Deconstructing Death

Ernest Becker, a past professor and cultural anthropologist at Simon-Fraser University, asserted that human civilization is a defense mechanism against the knowledge of human mortality (Becker, 1973). Becker saw the human condition as dually split and under constant turmoil because although humans were the product of nature, their intelligence created illusions of power (Becker, 1973; Killilea, 1988). The development of culture and religion served to separate humans from nature and permitted the denial of death (Becker, 1973; Killilea, 1988). Becker may have been correct in the origin of turmoil, illusions of grandeur, and purpose of religion, but regardless of intent humans remain concretely within the natural world.

Ernest Becker was among numerous scholars including John Locke and Thomas Hobbes, who related human nature to different aspects of human society, as well as the human role in the natural world. Many humans, most notably Americans, view nature through John Locke's lens of capitalism and liberalism: nature is a challenge, not a tutor, meant to be exploited and manipulated (Killilea, 1988). Chimpanzees, the closest extant animals to humans in genes and perhaps cognition, cannot bend nature to every whimsical desire but instead must accept nature's adversity. This acceptance and calmness strengthened Goodall's belief in some greater power (Goodall, 1999; 2000; 2001). Despite Becker's theories not all spiritual beliefs serve to remove man from nature. Goodall's belief system mirrors that of many Native Americans employing natural spirits. Modern Catholicism accepts shared ancestry with divergent evolutionary trajectories in humans and apes. Finally, the atheistic beliefs I myself adhere to concretely mark humans as direct components of nature, from dust to dust. For Goodall, the chimpanzees, and me there is no human-animal divide; the window was opened by the similarities, anatomically and metaphorically, of David Greybeard's and Little Man's fingers. This connection between humans and the humanity of non-humans, however, raises numerous identity-based questions, mainly: what does it truly mean to be human?

Chimpanzees and Cognition

Human beings were originally defined by their ability to create and utilize tools; Goodall shattered this definition with her observations of the high-ranking male Goliath, selecting, preparing, and manipulating a thin vine for termite mound fishing (Goodall, 1971; 1999). Today, the manipulation of tools has been observed in numerous taxa including other primates, cetaceans (whales and dolphins), and birds. (Dugatkin, 2009). Chimpanzees are now known to be intelligent individuals, capable of making tools, planning and executing tasks, maintaining prolonged emotional bonds, and mourning. Goodall witnessed innumerable occasions where chimpanzees executed complex tasks via planning. Figan, a juvenile male, once spotted a pile of bananas unknown to the high-ranking Mike nearby. Rather than immediately retrieving the bananas, which would have led to theft by Mike, Figan ignored their presence. He even moved his position so as to not inadvertently alert Mike with his gaze. After Mike's departure, Figan reaped his rewards (Goodall, 1971). On a separate occasion, Figan manipulated his mother into leaving a termite mound by kidnapping his infant brother and fleeing; his mother quickly followed (Goodall, 1971). Other studies involving the coordinated manipulation of two ropes by two individuals to gain food have also documented planning and cooperation in chimpanzees. In fact, chimpanzees were found to recruit the best of collaborators based on past experimental trials. Recent studies have also revealed similar abilities in elephants. (Melis et al, 2006; Hirata and Fuwa, 2007; Plotnik et al, 2011). Still, people continue to dismiss chimpanzee intelligence as inconsequential compared to human relationships and associated emotions; nevertheless the humanity in this non-human species can be seen in the kissing of hands, greeting embraces, and youthful escapades of tag and tug of war (Goodall, 1971; de Waal, 1997; de Waal, 2008; 2009). Chimpanzees also travel in family units, recognize friends after prolonged periods of time, and perhaps most importantly, mourn their dead.

Olly, a well known female chimpanzee, sauntered cautiously into camp, her ill infant gripping her belly, and her daughter Gilka ambling beside her. The infant belted agonizing screams with each of Olly's movements, sudden or meticulous, causing the simple crossing of 100 hundred yards to take a painful half hour. Finally, the family rested with Olly eating a banana as Gilka groomed her shoulder. Gradually, Gilka moved towards the infant. She took his small hands in hers, tentatively touching and exploring. The infant screamed. It began to rain. The family later left with the peaking of the sun, the infant's limp head and lifeless limbs dangling in Olly's arms. The mother soon began to handle the infant differently as if having recognized the death of her child. No longer delicate, she simply threw the corpse over her shoulder when traveling. Olly and Gilka continued to carry and groom the infant for days, swatting flies from the green, pungent body. Its presence must have provided some comfort, and only days later did Olly and Gilka return without the lifeless corpse (Goodall, 1971).

The mourning behavior of chimpanzees resembles that of humans, exemplifying the sanctity of the body, prolonged sadness, and family connections. Primates, however, are not the only animals capable of mourning. There are documentations of elephant and cetacean mourning. Wild elephants have been observed digging what appears to be shallow graves, covering the deceased in leaves, and standing guard for a periods of hours to days (Moss, 2000). Similarly, following the passage of their mother two male orcas were observed to exhibit potential mourning behavior. They avoided contact with other orcas and continuously visited places their mother had frequented. Researchers have interpreted these motions as sentiments of grief (Simmonds, 2006). Additionally, mother dolphins have been observed pushing at their deceased calves in an effort to bring them to the surface and elicit diving (Bearzi, 2007). Finally, there is the famous story of Koko, the gorilla who knew sign language and was able to not only comprehend, but predict that her beloved cat "Allball" had perished when simply told "Koko, something bad has happened" (Patterson, 1987; Patterson and Gordon, 1993). Koko was also able to discuss "what happens when one dies, but became fidgety or uncomfortable when asked to discuss her own death or the death of her companions" (Patterson and Gordon, 1993). Emotional responses like these provide a way to gauge cognitive ability, as such responses are commonly associated with intelligence. Such mourning behavior reaffirms death as the ultimate equalizer. Everything in nature dies, and perhaps all sentient beings mourn; understanding death may be a key event in intellectual and spiritual evolution.

Koko's story raises a key question: are some animals consciously aware of their own mortality? In spite of Koko and Allball, Goodall does not believe that chimpanzees possess prolonged mortal forsight. Although, she admits that the level of awareness they do attain is thus far unknown (Goodall, interview with Bill Moyers). Should this be true, conscious mortality, may compose a main difference between humans and the remainder of the animal world. According to Becker, mortal consciousness in humans led to the development of broader intellect and multiple philosophies concerning existence and non-existence. There is no evidence to suggest that chimpanzees also possess mortal forsight; however, I disagree with the broad classification of awareness, or lack there of, that Goodall attributes to primates. Alternatively, moral consciousness could vary between primate individuals similar to human individuals. Olly, for example, may have altered her perception of death following her experience with her infant's mortality. Goodall further asserts that there are fundamental differences between the human and chimpanzee perception of death, and it is foolish to compare even the smartest chimpanzee to a human (Goodall, interview with Bill Moyers). In contrast, although the comparisons may not be strong, I believe some are warranted. The chimpanzee intellect bares resemblance to that of Goodall's son, Grub, during his toddler years. It was at this time that the Gombe research group experienced the death of a student, Ruth, who had previously befriended Grub. Goodall recalls that even though no one had informed Grub of Ruth's passing, he intrinsically understood the finality. When asked of Ruth, Grub simply responded, "Ruth all broken now" (Goodall, 1999). Some children are capable of understanding that their ultimate destination is death, and like children not all chimpanzees should be immediately classed at the same level of intelligence, emotion, or spirituality.

It is thus questionable to assume that consciousness of death is unique to the human condition, not only because other animals may or may not be perpetually cornered by their own mortality; but because there is variation in acceptance between humans. Socrates believed consciousness of death was the fundamental difference between humans and animals, while Jacques Choron, past professor of philosophy at the New School for Social Research in New York, believed mortal consciousness pairs with human individuality (Killilea, 1988). Some humans are able to confront, comprehend, and accept death, while others deny mortality until the inevitable. The inability to confront death appears to run counter to the notion of an understood mortality universal to the human conscience. It is this universality that is the flaw. Goodall documented different personalities in her chimpanzees (Goodall, interview with Bill Moyers); is it too much to suppose that this difference was a connection seen in the great equalizer, an understanding of death? Goodall would argue no, and having never met the chimpanzees I can only hazard my guesses. Frans de Waal notes that in the study of animal behavior the target cognitive ability should not be considered independently of its components, meaning there should be a greater appreciation for the quantity and quality of building blocks composing the behavior, conscious mortality, present across species (de Waal, 2008; de Waal and Ferrari, 2010). Goodall has personally witnessed the death and mourning of her beloved chimpanzees. They understand death at the doorstep, but the range remains unidentified. Chimpanzees, Goodall believes, can never have the bonds developed by humans, because they can never deliberately give their life for a fellow friend. This may be a unique human attribute in that chimpanzees cannot understand death in the neighborhood, but then again maybe Koko the gorilla could...

Chimpanzees and Spirituality

The most natural events experienced are birth and death. All modern and ancestral humans have experienced these events; but when did spirituality arise? According to Goodall, spirituality is fundamental to pondering the universe and the meaning of life (Goodall, interview with Bill Moyers). A chimpanzee is not on the same spiritual level as human beings, but is it possible they are undergoing their own spiritual evolution? Rudimentary religious rituals and moral beginnings have been observed in chimpanzee behaviors. Chimpanzees are mystified by water; and frequently during the first rains or when approaching a body of water, individuals erupt into a "rain dance", running, jumping, and swaying in trees. The dance culminates in peace, as the chimpanzees sit, staring at the water, gazing with awe (Goodall, 1974; interview with Bill Moyers). It is this same awe that Goodall once felt upon entering a cathedral: it was too beautiful; it could not be chance (Goodall, interview with Bill Moyers). Goodall believes that with improvements in communication this rain dance could become animistic (Goodall, interview with Bill Moyers). Thus, this dance may relate to the evolution of religion, belief in an afterlife, and the denial of death. Goodall asserts, and I agree, that the chimpanzees have not experienced religious culmination. The spiritual evolution is not complete. It should be noted, however, that such evolution does not possess a singular trajectory. Convergence with human spirituality might not occur, and rather than the creation of mass religious organizations an atheistic course could be taken where "cathedral" beauty in nature is created by chance.

Religious aspects, namely morality, are already present in the every day dealings of chimpanzees. Counter to the beliefs of many religious devouts, morals are not intrinsically related to a religious deity and can also arise by natural processes. Normally, if a low-ranking chimpanzee simply picks a banana, a high-ranking chimpanzee will steal the fruit. This behavior is not prevalent in regards to hunting and meat-eating, probably because the acquisition of meat is a difficult process. During one such occasion a low-ranking male, Rodolph, killed a young baboon. The high-ranking male Mike sat nearby staring, but made none of the typical moves to remove the meat from Rodolph's possession. It was almost as if Mike accepted the meat belonged to Rodolph (Goodall, 1971). Occurrences like this may not only represent the beginning stages of property, but also the beginning stages of morality. In the western world, morals are often related to the Ten Commandments. Interestingly, at least three of these commandments relate directly to property: do not steal, do not covet your neighbor's belongings, and do not covet your neighbor's wife. Perhaps, there is a greater relationship between Locke, morals, and religion than many political theorists suspect, and there is a greater link between chimpanzees and spiritual evolution than typically explored. Recent studies concerning the evolution of morality have used the building block approach described by Frans de Waal and have found different modes of cooperation, similar neurological pathways associated with moral responses, and variability in social system moralities in an array of animals including humans and chimpanzees (Allchin, 2009).

The chimpanzee is aware of its physical surroundings, but beyond this no one can truly surmise its comprehension or spiritual trajectory. Spiritual evolution, however, is not something Goodall wishes to explain, "I don't believe faith can be explained by science, and I don't want to explain it" (interview with Bill Moyers). I, on the contrary, wish to explain everything in scientific terms; it gives my life foundation in understanding. The presence of faith is not necessary for Goodall to determine the chimpanzees' final destination: if humans have a soul, a chimpanzee has a soul; regardless of whether chimpanzees possesses the mental capacity and spirituality necessary to ponder existence. Goodall's spiritual journey and understanding of the ultimate human destination and commitment has been drastically changed through her work with chimpanzees; "humans are moving towards a spiritual evolution where we no longer have to ask why." "But isn't asking why a fundamental human quality?" Moyers asked. "Perhaps, we ask why too much. Perhaps, we should just be content" (interview with Bill Moyers). And thus, Jane Goodall the ever optimist joins others in the notion that maybe life does not need to be explained or have meaning; maybe we are allowed to just be. Sadly, however, human conquest and materialism may have made the notion of simply being more easily said than done.

Chimpanzees and Coins

Death has been, is and always will be a part of complex life forms. Single celled organisms may possess immortality, but they lack the complexity of higher-level organisms; without death the human intellectual evolution could never have occurred (Killilea, 1988). Death may define intelligent life. After all without binary opposites how could we ponder existence and non-existence? Since the dawn of plants and animals, over 98% of species in existence have gone extinct (Goodall, interview with Bill Moyers); extinction is a part of life, so what is different now? According to Jane Goodall, we humans are the difference (interview with Bill Moyers). Binary opposites, extreme poverty and extreme wealth, have created a world in which animal habitats are destroyed as people seek to survive and expand. Death may be the ultimate equalizer, but this time death is different.

Materialism is an unnecessary condition born from the proliferation of property. According to E.O. Wilson, If the global population equally experienced the standard of living common to the developed world an additional 3-4 planets would be necessary to sustain society's materialistic wants (Goodall, interview with Bill Moyers). The Western capitalist system has led to a culture of acquisition and "buy, buy, buy," a mantra that hopes to mask the truth: immortality cannot be purchased (Killilea, 1988). It appears that few Westerners are capable of tolerating non-materialistic lifestyles, but does this deprive life's meaning as some would suggest? Goodall and her chimpanzees find happiness in the simplicity of the Gombe forest. And, although a spontaneous shopping spree may inspire a brief euphoria, my true happiness comes from long walks in the sunny weather and swimming in the sea. Chimpanzees, unlike humans, live in a simplified world of markets and possessions, yet despite the absence of materialism, traces of human society can be observed in chimpanzee interactions. Politics, for example, although often associated with human civilizations, is not unique to human behavior. Social hierarchies can be found in most primate, elephant, and cetacean groups. These groups involve "highly differentiated relationships that include long-term bonds, higher-order alliances, and cooperative networks that rely on learning and memory" (Marino et al, 2007). Individuals commonly switch positions depending on specific social situations (Marino et al., 2007). Politics is thus not a human condition, nor is economics as many species of ape are known to trade goods and services (Dugatkin et al., 2009).

Goodall initially believed that chimpanzees were innocent in comparison to mankind, and although in many respects chimpanzees remain innocent, they exhibit similar brutality and violent politics common to the human species. The social hierarchy of chimpanzees is similar to a Hobbesian structure, with low-ranking individuals seeking protection from high-ranking individuals. Further supporting this notion is the fascination with violence and aggression displayed by juvenile males; conflict is thrilling (Goodall, 1971; 1999). This fascination and imitation of adult aggressive behavior is also common in human children (Dugatkin, 2009), and may help to explain the ready recruitment of young boys into the military (Goodall, 1999). Inter-community chimpanzee warfare also displays striking similarity to primitive human warfare consisting of raids and killing sprees along territorial boundaries (Goodall, 1999). There are certainly notions of prejudice and xenophobia among the chimpanzee communities; not only are nearby communities ostracized and hunted, former friends afflicted with strange diseases are often ignored or threatened (Goodall, 1971; 2000). The in-group, out-group mantra common in war theory literature may have its evolutionary roots in animal communities. Current research has shown that intergroup biases are also present in rhesus macaques (Majajan et al, 2011). Finally, chimpanzees have been witnessed committing needless acts of violence as do some members of human society. Females Passion and Pom readily practiced the murder and cannibalism of chimpanzee infants over several years (Goodall, 1971; 2000). Today, many theorists cite the capitalist system as causing inter-state aggression and violence. Realistically, however, these behaviors may be deeply engrained in our evolutionary history. Materialism has negative consequences, but it is only an extraneous factor contributing to violence.

If violence is deeply engrained in the human conscience, how can it be overcome? If this is the case, changing modern methods and infrastructure may not solve problems of global politics and community values, but this does not mean the solution is lacking. Cultural transmission is often stronger than genetic predispositions and current systems should be reformed to teach people to modify automatic intergroup biases and promote fair treatment (Dugatkin, 2009; Grewal, 2011). Goodall is the first to reveal that chimpanzees have many methods of peace-keeping and defusing tense situations (Goodall, 1999). Even though a dark, evil nature may be rooted in the human past, humans are aware of evil and possess the intelligence to prevent such actions. After all, although aggression may have been inherited from the chimpanzees so were love, compassion, and altruism (Goodall, interview with Bill Moyers; Allchin, 2009). Inheritance is not an excuse for violence.

It appears as though many human institutions are not intrinsically related to being human as forerunning behaviors can be observed in chimpanzee relatives (Allchin, 2009). Yet, the advent of capitalism, money, property, and materialism seem to have reduced the human connection to nature, and have created a "disconnect between the brain and heart" (Goodall, interview with Bill Moyers). The reforming of this connection for Goodall was evident during the rainy season. Most humans run for cover, and in most cases Goodall did as well; yet she felt guilt for her warm bed with her dear chimpanzees sheltered only by fronds (Goodall, 1971; 1999). In the modern world, most people are not aware of this bond, and most people have lost their connection with nature. Many people are consumed with politics, prejudice, and market systems. The happiness Goodall finds in the forest's simplicity should be an inspiration to all those seeking to find happiness in materialistic trends. Instead they should embrace a natural, long-lasting euphoria by turning to the beauty of a tree, flower, or mountain.

We, as humans, have undergone an intellectual evolution giving us the power to shield ourselves from nature, but also the misconception that we are separate from it. Yet, no matter the amount of wealth amassed everyone will die and nature will be victorious. This is what the chimpanzees can teach us. The similarities make us realize that we, as humans are very much a part of the natural world, and the differences make us realize that we have the power and responsibility to be a change for the better (Goodall, interview with Bill Moyers). Humans have a commitment to improve the quality of life not only for other humans, but also other species that are endangered due to thoughtless anthropogenic actions (Goodall, 1999). This planet was not inherited from our parents, it was borrowed from our children and now it is time to begin paying back. If everyone gave up, if everyone stopped, Jane Goodall and I would not like to think of the egotistical, barren world of our great-grandchildren (Goodall, interview with Bill Moyers). Humans are linked to the natural world through birth and death. We find our immortality not in purchases, but in the bloodstream of the chimpanzees.

V. The Gombe of Greybeard's Grandchildren

The Africa of the 20th century was a dark, mysterious continent. In the 1950s there were thousands upon thousands of chimpanzees. Today, the population has been reduced by over two thirds. Communities are fragmented and spread across states, without help the outlook is bleak (Goodall, interview with Bill Moyers). Goodall began her conservation efforts in 1986 following a conference in Chicago. The exposure to hunting horrors, shrinking habitats, and desolate conditions of captive animals forever changed her life. Her conservation rabble-rousing days had begun (Goodall, interview with Bill Moyers). She holds hope for the future based on four tenets: the human brain, the resilience of nature, the energy and enthusiasm found in youth, and the indomitable human spirit (Goodall, 1999).

Chimpanzees need and warrant human help. Many contend that the advent of symbolic thinking in humans occurred after the evolution of modern morphology, and was integral to becoming modern *Homo sapiens* (Tattersall, 2009). Would cognitively basal humans be granted more rights than chimpanzees? Studies of human ancestry focus on tracing relationships between other hominids like the famous Lucy, *Australopithecus aforensis*. As Frans de Waal states, "if we owe Lucy the respect of an ancestor, does this not force a different look on the apes?" After all, as far as we can tell, the most significant difference between Lucy and modern chimpanzees is found in their hips, not their craniums" (de Waal, 1997). Death is fundamental to life, but the extinction currently facing chimpanzees is an entirely different matter. It is the nuclear warfare of the animal world, and only with deterrence, and proper conservation efforts, can complete annihilation be avoided. Although my optimism runs far short of Goodall's graces, I too hope that I shall not see the last chimpanzees. The destruction of nature, and therefore the past and future, even for an atheist is a sin. I have been inspired to join the natural world surrounding me and it can only be hoped that the stories provided by Goodall, the anecdotes of intelligence, can inspire the necessary action in my peers.

What would happen if the last chimpanzee died? According to Goodall, no one can truly know the extent of what would be lost. There would likely be severe ecological consequences, but also the human connection to the animal kingdom, which we try so hard to be removed from, would be gone. The evolutionary window focused on human behavior would be shattered; so many questions would be left unanswered (Goodall, interview with Bill Moyers). Luckily, Goodall is dedicated to the conservation of chimpanzees. Her books, fundraisers, and lectures serve to broadcast the specialness of the human-chimpanzee connection. The "Take Care" and "Roots and Shoots" programs are offshoots of the Jane Goodall Institute that seek to financially improve the lives of villagers and to involve them in conservation projects. The use of micro-credit and other financial aid programs has increased the quality of life for villagers and subsequently decreased deforestation. For the people surrounding the Gombe forest there is a positive correlation between comfort in living and concern for the forest and the chimpanzees (Goodall, interview with Bill Moyers). Now, if only this correlation carried to the Western World...

There are no more excuses; the time for action is now. Chimpanzees are sentient beings maybe even exhibiting some rudimentary spirituality. They have forced the redefinition of what it means to be human countless times. The cognitive abilities of chimpanzees and other creatures cries to the need for conservation reforms. Immediate action should include further studies into the consciousness of non-human animals. Such studies, as in the case of chimpanzees, have led to revelations concerning mortal consciousness based on comparative cognition, morality, and social systems. Integrating the research results into education is vital at intellectual, cultural, and political levels (Allchin, 2009b). Understanding the components of mortal consciousness, such as morality, within an evolutionary framework will provide significant insights into cultural evolution, demythologize biological determinism, and provide better political platforms for combating criticisms of conservation and evolution (Allchin, 2009b). Extinction of the chimpanzees would be a failure of the human race. Look to the ears of the chimpanzee, the hands, the eyes. The eyes cry "why won't you help me?" (Goodall, 1999) There is some prehistoric level of communication, and there is some fundamental understanding of death. Their extinction will not separate us from nature. It is a futile attempt; it is nearly genocide, and we will still cease to be. The extinction of these humanlike non-humans will not be natural, but a product of unnecessary materialism. I fear to see the day when the newest trend, be it a Ferbie or an iPhone, outweighs the natural wonder of a magnificent, intelligent being. If our closest relatives cannot succeed, how can we? They are the beauty and we are the beast.

VI. Conclusions

Someday, human beings will be extinct. Why? Humans are very much a part of the natural world and extinction is an evolutionary course. Unfortunately, in the case of the chimpanzees it is the disconnect between human materialism and nature causing extinction. The demise will not be natural. And the true tear-jerker will be that chimpanzees did not have their own definition of specialness, but rather shared in the meanings of human specialness: tool making, planning, emotions, and spirituality. The wonder of the natural world, including the evolution of intelligence, will soon be lost because humans must fight nature and death; and because of this, everything else must die.

Normally chimpanzees live their lives in the shadow of man, but Jane Goodall has lived her life in the shadow of the chimpanzees. Since the beginning she has witnessed their births, friendships, and deaths. Sometimes these were peaceful, and other times they were horrid. Take for instance the polio inflicted Mr. McGregor. He was sadly shot by Jane and Hugo, after he was found covered in feces and flies, an arm dislocated. They had been feeding, grooming, and cleansing him for days, since the discovery of his paralyzed legs. The chimpanzees isolated him; his only connections were the humans and his one friend Humphrey. That morning, Hugo put the poor old man out his misery. The death was quick and painless, far from the horror of lone starvation. Humphrey was not present, but for weeks later he could be seen wandering, searching for McGregor and later mourning for the loss (Goodall, 1971; 1999; 2000). Goodall and Humphrey mourned together for their brother, the chimpanzee. For that is what humans and chimpanzees are: brothers, connected through a supposedly immortal bloodline. Our assumption that cognitive ability triumphs over nature is simply not true. Death is the great equalizer and we will all die regardless of intellectual ability. This must be accepted if we are to find the meaning in life, and our place in the natural world.

Each one of us matters, has a role to play, and a difference to make (Goodall, interview with Bill Moyers). We can all be saints by living life in the service of humanity and all living things (Goodall, 1999). This is the meaning Jane Goodall has found in her own life and seeks to impart to those surrounding her. She is a righteous and spiritual woman, one with a vision and agenda. She is an inspiration simply because she walks the walk and talks the talk. I may not agree with her spiritual beliefs or scientific conclusions; but I do believe the world is a better place because she existed, filled with greater intelligence and a stronger connection between humans and animal brethren. Jane Goodall once wrote ,"death is such a convenient endpoint, even if we believe in a changing of worlds" (1999). I cannot tell you of Jane Goodall's death because she is still fighting for her chimpanzees, but like Bill Moyers I can simply say "Jane Goodall, thank you for the book, the conversation, and the life."

Acknowledgements

I would like to thank Alfred Killilea and the University of Rhode Island Department of Political Science, as well as Aubrie Pascale, Ron Casey, and Kelsey McKenna among others who have provided comments and/or the inspiration to think differently and critically.

References

Allchin, D. 2009. "The Evolution of Morality." Evolution: Education and Outreach. 2: 590-601.

Allchin, D. 2009b. "Why We Need to Teach the Evolution of Morality." Evolution: Education and Outreach. 2: 622-628.

Bearzi G., Agazzi S., Bonizzoni S., Costa M., Azzellino A. 2007. "Dolphins in a bottle: Abundance, Residency Patterns and Conservation of Bottlenose Dolphins." *Tursiops truncatus* in the semi-closed eutrophic Amvrakikos Gulf, Greece. Aquatic Conservation: Marine and Freshwater Ecosystems 17. doi:10.1002/aqc.843.

Becker, E. 1973. The Denial of Death. Simon & Schuster: New York.

de Waal, F. 1997. "Are We in Anthropodenial?" Discover Magazine, http://discovermagazine.com/1997/jul/areweinanthropod1180

de Waal, F. 2008. "Putting the Altruism Back into Altruism: the Evolution of Empathy." Annual Review of Psychology, 59: 279-300.

de Waal, F. 2009. "Darwin's Last Laugh." Nature, 460: 175.

de Waal, F. and Ferrari, P.F. 2010. "Towards a Bottom-up Perspective on Animal and Human Cognition." Trends in Cognitive Sciences, 14: 201-207.

Dugatkin, L.A. 2009. Principles of Animal Behavior, 2nd edition (ed. Michael Wright). W.W. Norton &Company: New York

Goodall, J. 1971. In the Shadow of Man. Houghton Mifflin Company: Boston.

Goodall, J. 1999. Reason for Hope: a Spiritual Journey. Houghton Mifflin Company: Boston.

Goodall, J. 2000. Africa in my Blood: an Autobiography in Letters, the Early Years. Houghton Mifflin Company: Boston.

Goodall, J. 2001. Beyond Innocence: Autobiography in Letters, the Later Years. Houghton Mifflin Company: Boston.

Goodall, J. Interview with Bill Moyers. Bill Moyers Journal. PBS. 27 November 2009.

Grewal, D. 2011. "The Evolution of Prejudice." Scientific American, http://www.scientificamerican.com/article.cfm?id=evolution-of-prejudice.

Hirata, S. and Fuwa, K. 2007. "Chimpanzess (*Pan troglodytes*) Learn to Act with Other Individuals in a Cooperative Task." Primates, 48: 13-21.

Killilea, A.G. 1988. The Politics of Being Mortal. The University Press of Kentucky.

Mahajan, N., Martinez, M.A., Gutierraz, N.L., Deisendruck, G., Banaji, M.R., and Santos, L.R. 2011. "The Evolution of Intergroup Bias: Perceptions and Attitudes in Rhesus Macaques." Journal of Personality and Social Psychology, 100: 387-405.

Marino, L., Connor, R.C., Fordyce, E., Herman, L.M., Hof, P.R., Lefebvre, L., Lusseau D., McCowan, B., Nimchinskey, E.A., Pack, A.A., Rendell, L., Reidenberg, J.S., Reiss, D., Uhen, M.D., Van der Gucht, E., and Whitehead, H. 2007. "Cetaceans have Complex Brains for Complex Cognition." PlOS Biol, 5: e139.

Melis, A.P., Hare, B., and Tomasello, M. 2006. "Chimpanzees Recruit the Best Collaborators." Science, 311: 1297-3000.

Moss ,C. 2000. Elephant Memories: Thirteen Years in the Life of an Elephant Family. University of Chicago Press: Chicago.

Patterson, Francine. 1987. *Koko's Kitten.* Scholastic, Inc.

Patterson, F. and Gordon, W. 1993. "The Case for Personhood in Gorillas." In: The Great Ape Project (Cavalieri, P. and Singer, P. eds). St. Martin's Griffen: New York. pp. 58-77.

Simmonds, M.P. 2006. "Into the Brains of Whales." Applied Animal Behavior Science, 100: 103-116.

Tattersall, I. 2009. "Becoming Modern *Homo sapiens.*" Evolution: Education and Outreach. 2: 584-589.